Kashful Baghaavat Gorakhpur
Unveiling of the Revolt at Gorakhpur

Eyewitness Account of a Sufi which unmasks the other side of the rebels of 1857.

Kashful Baghaavat Gorakhpur

Unveiling of the Revolt at Gorakhpur

Eyewitness Account of a Sufi which unmasks
the other side of the rebels of 1857.

Authored by

Ahmad Ali Shah Miyan Sahib

Transliteration and Translation from Urdu-Persian by

Farhat Nasreen

Rupa . Co

Copyright © Farhat Nasreen 2010

Published 2010 by
Rupa Publications India Pvt. Ltd.
7/16, Ansari Road, Daryaganj
New Delhi 110 002

Sales Centres:

Allahabad Bengaluru Chandigarh
Chennai Hyderabad Jaipur Kathmandu
Kolkata Mumbai

All rights reserved.
No part of this publication may be reproduced, stored in a retrieval system, or transmitted, in any form or by any means, electronic, mechanical, photocopying, recording or otherwise, without the prior permission of the publishers.

The author asserts the moral right to be identified as the author of this work.

Typeset by
Mindways Design
1410 Chiranjiv Tower,
43 Nehru Place
New Delhi 110 019

Printed in India by
Rekha Printers Pvt. Ltd.
A-102/1 Okhla Industrial Area, Phase-II
New Delhi-110 020

Hal jazaa ul ehsaane illal ehsaan
Fabe aiye aalaaye rabbekuma tukazzebaan

Is the reward of goodness aught save goodness?
Which is it, of the favours of your Lord that ye deny?

To the goodness in Shakeela Wahajuddin

Contents

Acknowledgements

I thank Al-Azeem for everything. I am grateful to Janaab Adnan Farrukh Ali Shah Miyan Sahib for the confidence he placed in me. I have a lot of respect for him, as Sufi who combines modernity with tradition. His mother, Mohtarama Najma Mazhar Ali Shah's affectionate cooperation can never be forgotten.

I am thankful to Janaab Amit Banerji who helped me through the inception and completion of this work. Janaab Rajan Mehra has been extremely kind and generous in agreeing to publish this book and I shall always be profoundly indebted to him. Mohtarama Debasri Bhattacharya has made very valuable inputs as an editor and I thank her. I thank Mohtarama Kadambari Mishra. I am grateful to the Freedom Movement Memorial Committee, Secular House, New Delhi, for allowing me to use pictures from their collection.

I am grateful to Janaab Najeeb Jung. Professor S.M. Azizuddin Husain Sahib's unceasing encouragement stands behind most of my academic endeavours. I thank Professor Iraq Raza Zaidi Sahib and Janaab Jawaid Hassan for their kind help. I thank all those who taught me at Lady Shri Ram College, Delhi University and Aligarh Muslim University. I thank all my friends and colleagues at Jamia Millia Islamia.

My father, Mohammad Wahajuddin was a humble and honest Judge at the Allahabad High Court. My mother, Shakeela was beautiful in every way. They both lived by the ideals of simplicity and selflessness. They loved me unconditionally. I can always feel their doting presence near me, because love loves to defy death.

My sisters and brothers, Mohammad Sirajuddin, Mohammad Riazuddin, Durrey Shahwar Idris, Shaheena Athar, Mohammad Faiyazuddin Farooqui and Nuzhat Iqbal have done much more for me than I can ever thank them for. My nieces, Samreena, Ariba and Nameera have been friends and helpers. I thank my husband, Mohammad Asif Kamal for his unfailingly polite and open-handed attitude. My daughter, Yusuf Rana Kamal is the light of my eyes. She plays kaleidoscopically diverse roles in my life; the only and exceptionally constant part is that, she is a permanent source of inspiration and enthusiasm. For me, she is the very personification of happiness.

I thank all those who prayed for me and wished me luck.

Preface

In October 2000, I visited Gorakhpur to meet my mother (Amma), Shakeela Wahajuddin. Life's worries froze in the luxury of her love and pampering. My daughter Yusuf and I spent hours conversing with her and these long sessions of stories and family gossip carried us, three generations of women, on a journey through the past, holding the hands of the present.

Once, Amma recalled, when my father was posted as the District Judge of Agra, a *faqir* who had come to our bungalow, asked her to tie knots on a thread, the knots being equivalent to the number of problems that she had, and to hold it inside her closed fist. He then recited some chants and blew over her fist and asked her to open it and examine the thread; to her surprise all except one knot in the thread had disappeared. On being asked why only one knot had remained, he said it had lingered on as a symbol of the almighty God.

During our reminiscences, Amma mentioned the name of Roshan Ali Shah, a Sufi of Gorakhpur, said to have possessed extraordinary mystical powers. His descendants are popularly known as 'Miyan Sahib'. Impressed by his miraculous capabilities, Nawab Asaf-ud-Daula of Awadh and many local Rajas and Ranis showered him with land and monetary endowments. Respecting the Nawab's wishes, Roshan Ali built an Imambara and took on the responsibility of doing *Azadaari* in Moharram. The traditions of *Azadaari* established by him were unparalleled and unique and from these evolved the famed Miyan Sahib cult. Gold and silver *tazias* bestowed on the Imambara by the Nawab are still extant there. With the rising popularity of the Imambara, there began a steady flow of grants of various kinds from the local chieftains and businessmen, so much so that the Miyan Sahib once owned a substantial part of the present-day Gorakhpur. It is widely acknowledged that Ahmad Ali Shah, the immediate successor of Roshan Ali, had played an active role in safeguarding women and children during the Revolt of 1857 against the British.

My interest greatly piqued by this peep into a turbulent phase of India's history, I was keen to meet Mazhar Ali Shah, the then Miyan Sahib. Fortunately, my brother, Siraj was able to arrange an audience, and I was invited to his stately white mansion, Al Hilaal. Mazhar Ali Shah reflected the humility of a Sufi and the dignity of a nobleman. During our conversation, he mentioned a book written by one of his ancestors, in which he had described the conditions in Gorakhpur at the time of the Revolt of 1857. Despite my keen interest, I was not able to see the manuscript then and finally when I did call him, I learned that he had been injured in an accident. Unfortunately, he passed away before I could meet him again.

Three years passed before I could speak to his son, Adnan Farrukh Ali Shah Miyan Sahib on this subject. Seeing my desire to sift through the manuscripts of his ancestors and work on them, he very kindly invited me to Gorakhpur to visit their Imambara and other historical buildings attached to it. It was ultimately in February 2003 that I found myself before the *dhooni* of Roshan Ali, where the fire is still kept burning to mark the spot where he sat in meditation, oblivious to his worldly existence. In the three days that I stayed there, Farrukh *bhai* took me over all the places associated with his ancestors, and I also met a number of his relatives who gave me valuable insights into the family's *Azadaari* traditions and the Miyan Sahib cult. Enthralled at this undocumented view into the past, I carried back with me a number of old photographs, books and official records. Among them was a copy of a book, so old and fragile that the pages almost disintegrated in my hands even as I touched them lightly; it was authored by Ahmad Ali Shah during 1857–1860 and was titled *Kashful Baghaavat Gorakhpur*.

Introduction

It was only after visiting Miyan Sahib's Imambara and learning about its origin and practices that I realized I had stumbled upon one of the finest Sufi-*Azadaari* traditions in India. Not only has the tradition survived the passage of time, but has grown. The Miyan Sahib cult is undoubtedly one of the richest Sufi cults in the world. It is believed that Roshan Ali's grandfather, Syed Mir Aqil, and his father, Syed Ghulam Ashraf, had moved to Delhi from Bokhara during the reign of Mohammad Shah (1719–1748). During one of the invasions of Ahmad Shah Abdali (1756–57/1761), Syed Ghulam Ashraf left Delhi and settled at Shahpur. They later shifted to Murshidabad and from there, Roshan Ali came to Gorakhpur. Here he inherited a substantial piece of land from his maternal grandfather, Haji Daud and uncle, Sheikh Amanullah.

Roshan Ali was an eremite mendicant who led an abstemious life; dedicated to prayer and meditation. He lived in a jungle and had hardly any possessions. There are popular beliefs that he had the power of gnosis and was an hierophant. According to legends, he could communicate with animals and could tame wild animals. It is also said that he used to ride lions if he wished to and that he had an animistic relationship with florae and faunae and treated nature on a singular social plane with human beings. His altruism made people look up to him for guidance and blessings. Roshan Ali is held in great reverence to this day.

During my visit, Adnan Farrukh Ali Shah Miyan Sahib narrated an interesting family lore. There were two twin-like massive Sal trees called Sunder and Munder in the jungles of Kusmi and these were the special favorites of the saint. Another popular local belief is that while the Imambara was being built, a log of wood to be used in the ceiling fell short, and Roshan Ali prayed for the growth of the same log; and lo and behold! When the workers arrived at the site the following morning, they found that the dead log had grown overnight. This particular log is still preserved in the Imambara.

Azadaari of Moharram was observed by Roshan Ali with the greatest dedication. Being a Sufi, sectarian divisions would have hardly had any logic for him. He began construction of the Imambara and the adjoining mosque in the year 1780. In those times, the area around these structures was scarcely populated. Even though Roshan Ali was a recluse who was averse to worldly interaction with people, yet his spiritual powers attracted people to him. They came with requests of prayers and blessings and indeed his prayers seemed to be powerful enough to be heard and answered. There are available documentary evidences, some as early as AD 1773–74, which prove that he was approached by people to dispense justice in cases of civil disputes and minor offences. He was patronized by the local Rajas and Zamindars. A very large number of land grants came to him from Pahalwan Singh, the Raja of Rudrapur, Satari. These grants conferred on him during 1780, 1790, 1793, 1794, 1795, 1804 and 1805, gave jungles for the upkeep of his *dhooni*, orchards, cultivable lands and the *mauza* of Kosamhi. There were more grants from Raja Nawaz Singh in 1795 and 1796; from Rani Rup Narayani Devi in the year 1773; from Raja Ajeet Diwan in the years 1783, 1784, 1785; from Lala Bishan in 1784 and 1785; from Zulfiqar Khan in 1792 and 1793; from Babu Daan Singh, Babu Deen Singh and Pahalwan Singh in the year 1804; from Babu Teg Bahadur and Babu Shiv Bahadur in the year 1806; from Teeja Singh in the year 1807; from Bhawani Parshad in the year 1817 and so on and so forth. The most celebrated patron of the Sufi was the Nawab of Awadh, Asaf-ud-Daula (1775–1797). In an official document of the year 1797, one Golal Singh had mentioned that he worked for the Imambara of Roshan Ali and the lands which were granted to it by Asaf-ud-Daula, including the area of Pipraich. There are documents dated even earlier, during 1786 and 1789, which state that the areas of Mughlanipura, Jaleelpura and Haji Daud were granted to Roshan Ali by the Nawab. A document dated 1796 testifies to a grant of sixteen villages, a sum of Rs 10,000 and gold and silver *tazias* to the Sufi's Imambara.

According to a legend regarding his meeting with Asaf-ud-Daula, it is said that, once when Roshan Ali was meditating by his *dhooni* on a cold night, the Nawab who was out hunting, happened to pass by and seeing the faqir without any warm clothes, he gave him his own shawl, which was embroidered with gold thread and embellished with precious stones and pearls. The Sufi, instead of draping himself in the costly gift, dropped it in the *dhooni*. This took Asaf-ud-Daula by surprise and he inquired why his gift had been thrown to the flames. The Sufi replied that he had kept it in the safest of all places and could show the shawl to the Nawab if he so pleased; he thereafter picked up his *chimta* and took out innumerable shawls of the same kind from the embers of his *dhooni* until a heap of shawls lay before the speechless Nawab. Impressed by the display of miraculous spiritual powers, the Nawab requested him to conduct *Azadaari* in Moharram on his behalf. Roshan Ali agreed to this and as destiny would have it, his descendants still keep the promise that he had made to the Nawab.

Roshan Ali made a public appearance only during the Moharram processions. He wore a long white robe and a white amice over his shoulders. A turban like headgear covered his head and he did not cut his hair. The dress code for the Moharram procession, which evolved in his times, still continues.

Among the documents of Roshan Ali, I came across a *Niyaznamah-Hibanamah*, dated 1805, written in Persian in which one Mir Faulad Ali has stated that he, of his own free will and in a proper state of mental and physical health, was giving the custody of his five-year-old son, Ahmad Ali, to Syed Roshan Ali Shah and thereafter he would not have any claim over the property and wealth that the child may inherit as the adopted son of Roshan Ali. This is reinforced by an *Iqrarnamah* of Roshan Ali in which he states that his adopted child Ahmad Ali would be the sole inheritor of all his wealth and properties. Both these documents were meant for legal registration.

It is believed that Faulad Ali had also come from Bokhara and was himself a well-known Sufi faqir. Ahmad Ali was brought up under the supervision of Roshan Ali who trained him as a disciple. During Ahmad Ali's times, the fame of the Imambara and Miyan Sahib grew in leaps and bounds. The Moharram procession led by him became an elaborate affair and Miyan Sahib himself became a cult figure. The responsibilities, which came with this growing patrimony, were not always easy to handle. There were disputes and threats which made it difficult for the Miyan Sahib to retain his spiritual privacy. It was indeed a challenge for him to keep away from public view and yet attend to court cases, local disputes or activities like sale and purchase of properties etc., which had to be undertaken as part of managing such a huge trust.

Ahmad Ali proved to be an able disciple and lived up to the expectations of Roshan Ali. Even amidst rapid growth of wealth and property of the Imambara and the Miyan Sahib cult, the Sufi descendants of Roshan Ali ensured that the secular nature of the Imambara continued to flourish. Though all the Miyan Sahibs up to Wajid Ali were practically autodidacts, Ahmad Ali grew to be a man of letters and his command over Urdu and Persian was well-known. While translating his *Kashful Baghaavat Gorakhpur*, I comprehended the priceless treasure of his words and his control over their sound, meaning and impact. Like Roshan Ali, he too chose to remain a celibate and adopted his nephew Wajid Ali as his successor. Wajid Ali married at the age of forty. He passed away in the year 1915, leaving behind his wife and four children, the eldest of whom, nine-year-old Jawwad Ali Shah became the next Miyan Sahib. Like his predecessors, Jawwad Ali was tutored at home and he grew up to be a learned man, well versed in many subjects and languages. Jawwad Ali was the first of the Miyan Sahibs to have his hair cut. Eldest among his children was Mazhar Ali Shah, who grew up to be the next Miyan Sahib.

I met Mazhar Ali Shah during my first visit to Gorakhpur. Known for his patience, kindness and sense of humour, Mazhar Ali expanded the social welfare schemes undertaken by the Imambara Trust. He established and funded many educational institutions in the region. Today, his son Adnan Farrukh Ali Shah, a Sufi in his own right, continues to dispense his duties as Miyan Sahib with full dedication and passion.

Though the properties of Miyan Sahib have substantially decreased, compared to the pre-independence era, his prestige and fame as a cult figure remains unabated and transcends all man-made barriers of religion, caste and class.

II

At the beginning of the 18th century, most parts of the present district of Gorakhpur came under the *sirkar* of Gorakhpur in the *subah* of Awadh. The Mughal Emperor Bahadur Shah had appointed Chin Qulich Khan as the Faujdar of Gorakhpur in June 1707. However, Chin Qulich had to relinquish this post in 1710. Thereafter right up till the establishment of the Nawabi rule in Awadh, the local Rajput chieftains of the region, popularly known as the Rajas, dominated the socio-political order of the region through self-assertion.

However, things changed when Saadat Khan took over the charge of Awadh including Gorakhpur in 1722 and challenged the might of the local Rajas. To restrict the activities of Banjaras and Butwals, he supplemented the armed forces in the region and incidents of guerrilla warfare became a regular feature. After Saadat Khan's death in 1739, in the period of his successor, Safdar Jung, the confrontation with the local power lobbies continued. In 1754, Safdar Jung was succeeded by Shuja-ud-Daula. The economy of Gorakhpur, which had begun to show signs of prosperity during the reign of Saadat Khan, further improved despite the fact that large areas of arable land had still not been brought under cultivation. It was only somewhere around 1759 that the position of the Nawab of Awadh became comparatively invulnerable. However, this establishment of power was bought at the price of regular military assertions, and the common man had to bear the brunt of frequent warfare and instability in governance. Dispensation of justice remained the prerogative of the local lords.

After Shuja-ud-Daula's death in 1775, Asaf-ud-Daula succeeded him. In 1778, Colonel Hannay, was assigned the duties of revenue collection and commanding the Nawab's troops in the region. He proved to be an oppressive administrator and many peasants were forced to abandon their villages. Agricultural production hit an all-time low. Matters were made worse by the devastating raids of the Banjaras who started participating in local politics and at times instigated the local chiefs to fight among themselves. The position of the local Rajas was also greatly undermined by them; it was only with a great deal of effort that the latter were able to maintain their estates. By a treaty signed in 1801, Nawab Saadat Ali Khan ceded Gorakhpur and the neighboring tracts to the British East India Company to settle arrears of subsidies. John Rutledge assumed charge as the first British Collector of the area. The region had poor road connectivity and was infested with overgrown jungles. Robbers and other miscreants caused great havoc, and though troops were stationed in the district for organisation of a police force, the local chieftains and landholders were against any type of police administration.

During this time, the Gorkhas also started making aggressive inroads into the district, which ceased only after a settlement was reached with the Raja of Nepal in 1815. In 1829, Gorakhpur was made the headquarters of a division of the same name, comprising primarily the districts of Gorakhpur, Ghazipur and Azamgarh. In 1835, this division was abolished, only to be revived again in 1853. During this time, the East India Company drew up the revenue settlement of the region whereby unevaluated properties were brought under the settlement, particularly in the Northern Parganas. Ownership claims of forests and large tracts of lands by many landlords were dismissed, and these measures evoked antagonism and hostility against the British Raj.

In the year 1857, W. Patterson, W. Wynard and F. Bird were posted here as the Collector, Judge and Joint Magistrate respectively. The military force garrisoned in the district consisted of 21/2 companies of the 17th No. 1 whose headquarters were at Azamgarh, under the command of Captain Steel and ½ *resala* of the twelfth irregular cavalry.

Indications of restlessness surfaced in Gorakhpur on 25 May 1857 when the Indian infantry refused to take old greased cartridges. The police force was driven out of Barhalganj and the chiefs of Narharpur set approximately fifty prisoners free. They took possession of the ferry and stopped the conveyance of official letters to Azamgarh. On 5 June 1857, news arrived of the revolt at Azamgarh whereupon Captain Steel addressed the parade of sepoys. Soon, the sepoys at Gorakhpur not only refused to march to Azamgarh but also threatened to shoot any of the British servicemen who approached the district court. Some prisoners tried to escape and there were casualties as the law and order situation deteriorated.

Things came to a pass on 8 June when an armed confrontation ensued between the rebels and the British forces for the possession of the treasury. The chieftains of Narharpur and Satasi supported the rebels. Fugitives from Gonda reached Gorakhpur, supported by the Raja of Bansi, from where they proceeded to Azamgarh and then to Ghazipur, where they were joined by Gorkhas from Palpa. Meanwhile, the Gautam Rajputs who had been earlier dislodged from their lands, rose against the British under the leadership of the Raja of Nahar. The Rajas of Nurpur, Nagar and Satasi and the Babus of Pandepar also conspired against the British and by the second fortnight of July 1857, they together proclaimed that British rule had ceased to exist.

To quell this rebellion, the East India Company was forced to accept aid from Jung Bahadur, the ruler of Nepal. Meanwhile, revolt broke out at Sagauli on 26 July and Wynard, who had assumed the command of Gorakhpur, wrote to Colonel Wroughton for assistance. The latter was on his way to Gorakhpur via Nichlaul with an army of 3000 Gorkhas. Wynard also disarmed the 17th Native Infantry due to its blatantly rebellious tendencies and summoned all the European planters to Gorakhpur, from where they proceeded to Azamgarh. They were accompanied by the Gorkhas and had the treasure with them. The command of the district was handed over to a committee of Rajas belonging to Satasi, Gopalpur, Bansi, Majholi and Tamkuhi. Mohammad Hasan, the earlier Nazim of Gorakhpur, assumed the leadership of the rebels. On 18 August, he attacked the Gorkha camp, which was situated about 16 kms north of river Ghaghra, but suffered defeat. Only the Raja of Gopalpur assisted the British joint Magistrate F. Bird, because the others like the Rajas of Satasi, Bansi, Barhaiapar and Chillupar had made their hostilities known. The Raja of Gopalpur offered to remove what remained of the treasury to Gopalpur, but Bird turned down his offer and after the Raja left, all efforts of Bird to maintain law and order failed. Mohammad Hasan released all prisoners who joined his followers. Among the freed captives was Musharraf Khan who had been imprisoned on the orders of Bird. Musharraf Khan was appointed as the Naib-Nazim by Mohammad Hasan and in this new power equation Bird had to ultimately flee for his life. Had it not been for his knowledge of intricate jungle routes, he might not have made it at all. After a perilous journey, Bird reached Chapra in Bihar. It is believed that Ahmad Ali Shah was instrumental in organising Bird's escape from Gorakhpur.

Mohammad Hasan began his rule wherein the bungalows of Europeans and their supporters were burnt and looted. The Raja of Gopalpur, who had ventured to constitute a confederation to challenge Mohammad Hasan, was forced to retreat to Azamgarh.

However, Mohammad Hasan's command over the district was short-lived. A fresh contingent of Gorkhas advanced from the north under the command of Jung Bahadur and later under General Mac Gregor. From the south came British forces under the command of Colonel Rowcroft. Jung Bahadur reached Sagauli on the morning of 21 December 1857 with 10,000 Gorkhas. According to references in the *Kashful Baghaavat Gorakhpur*, it appears that Ahmad Ali arranged for the carriages and food and lodging of the Nepalese army in Gorakhpur. The huge army then marched towards Gorakhpur via Pipraich. The Gorkha artillery repulsed the attack by the rebels and in the violent assault that followed, the water of the river was said to have turned red with blood. Mohammad Hasan was forced to flee to Tanda, near Faizabad, where he tried to reorganise his forces. A fierce combat started on 26 December 1857 in which the British annihilated the rebels. Musharraf Khan, the rebel Naib-Nazim of Gorakhpur, somehow managed to escape alive from the battlefield. It is believed that later he was apprehended by the Rani of Basti, but was carted off by a powerful Zamindaar of her own district who wanted to curry favor with the British by handing him over to them.

Rowcroft then moved through Salimpur where the bungalows of Narain Dayal Qanongoh and his nephew Sangram Lal were plundered and torched to avenge their help to the rebels. The British also made attempts to recover the guns, which the rebels were believed to have hidden in some well or jungle in the environs of Sohanpur and Salimpur. The Gorkha army passed through Gorakhpur once again on its way to Bihar. The last contingent of the rebel sepoys of Mohammad Hasan was defeated on 20 February 1858. Mohammad Hasan himself was defeated by Rowcroft in June 1858.

On regaining authority, the British took their revenge against those who had directly or indirectly, supported or participated in the uprising against them. In a spate of retributions, the estates of Barhaiapar, Chillupar, Satasi and Shahpur were confiscated. Bird captured the opportunity for settling scores with Musharraf Khan, who had earlier been audacious enough to threaten him personally. Musharraf Khan, to be humiliated, was paraded in a cart through the streets of Gorakhpur before being hanged. The British thus began their system of rewards and punishments to equalize scores and set examples for the future. Prominent among the favored persons were the Raja of Gopalpur and Ahmad Ali Shah of Gorakhpur.

III

I strongly perceive that when Ahmad Ali Shah wrote *Kashful Baghaavat Gorakhpur*, more than one hundred and fifty years ago, he had substantial percipience that his narrative would assume immense worth when posterity would pause to revivify, retune and revalue the Revolt of 1857. The proximity of his intuition with realness is exciting.

Every generation cross-examines history in a manner peculiar to itself. For a fair trial of history by the contemporary, it is essential for revisionist agencies to decolonise and decolorise themselves. The passage of time changes the parameters of rationalization and sometimes in this dialogue between the past and the present, there is obtrusion of the future as well. There might be temptations to delude and confuse the present to cheer up the future. Often histories and historians have their dynamics, which change in accordance with the audience and the agendas that they cater to, but like a game of hide-and-seek, true research is fun only when the search is real.

Comprehending that there cannot be any full and final version of the revolt, I can safely say that *Kashful Baghaavat Gorakhpur* is indeed kaleidoscopic in the spectrum of dimensions that it touches upon. This revolt was one of the first major confrontations that the imperialists had faced in Asia. The novelty of this challenge was in itself so powerful that success or failure was relegated into the background. Multiple identities were acting as agencies of the rebellion; there were identities within identities, which were in a constant state of flux and metamorphosis. That is what makes the identification of motives and leaders dodgy. The generation, which witnessed the revolt, also looked at it from multifarious perspectives. There was simplification, complication, glorification, condemnation, romantisisation, fantasization and conceptualization of different things, by different people, in different ways. Some accounts were meant for official records, some for public discourses and yet others for personal aspirations. The ends could be emotional, religious, monetary, social or political. Thus sensitivity to ideas and people is essential to understand histories in their different dimensions. Flexible and wide-ranging possibilities of analysis is what makes this revolt an undying subject for researches and revisits. It would be bizarre to say that all Indians were fighting against all Europeans, or Muslims were fighting against Christians or that Hindus and Muslims stood united against Christians, or that all exploited classes revolted against the exploiting classes, or feudalistic powers rose against the imperialistic powers, and so on and so forth. Even though some intellectuals consider the revolt, the first War of Indian Independence, it is undeniable that indigenous exploitative classes like the moneylenders and some of the rich merchants were not spared by the fury of the revolutionaries for their support to the foreign rulers. On the other hand, to fancy that Muslims as a religious group were acting against Europeans like an anti-Christian, Jihadi lobby, or that the revolt was some kind of a religiously motivated conspiracy, is not only a piece of fantastic imagination, but also a dangerous invention. It is true that all Muslims do not perceive Jihad in homogeneous contexts. For some Jihad may mean war with one's own baseness; for example, I know of many Muslims who consider controlling outbursts of anger as some kind of Jihad; besides this, certain noble deeds which require immense self-control and self-sacrifice are assigned merits that are corresponding and synonymous to the merits of Jihad; for others it may mean war against oppression, irrespective of the oppressor being a co-religionist and for some others it may mean war against another religion per se. Proclamations of Jihad made in 1857 have to be dismantled and analysed in detail before jumping to any toxic deductions and breakneck verdicts: who were the people who gave the call for Jihad and how did they justify Hindu–Muslim unity against the Christians, given the presumption that the Hindus are not even *Ahl-e-Kitaab*? Who were the people who supported them? What was the number of people in these categories? What was the proportional ratio of these categories in comparison to the total of Muslim population? Who were non-Jihadis and yet Baaghis? Who were non-Jihadi, non-Baaghi, seemingly indifferent *Shurfa*? Who were the anti-thesis of the so-called Jihadis; who supported the British for political or monetary gains? Who were the people who stood up against violence towards any human being? It would be unfair to use Muslim and Jihadi as interchangeable and synonymous terms and to arrogate to all Muslims, ambitions of the conjectural clash of civilizations. Prisms of wholesale coloring have to be broken to see the singular brightness of truth.

Scholars have adopted different measures to understand the revolt. For some it was an assertion of introductory prototype of patriotic nationalism; for others, it was the uprising of feudal system against commercial system; for some, it was a Sepoy mutiny against the use of greased cartridges, for others it was a peasant revolt against oppressive taxation. Some look at it as the design of working classes against the bourgeoisie, for some it was one religion's war against another religion in context of their historical rivalry; for yet others, it was the war of all indigenous agencies put together against the octopus of imperialism which had tentacles of socio-economic, political-religious, cultural-ethical, emotional and psychological exploitation.

Practically, none of these arguments can be accepted or rejected in totality. There are abundant views to support and subvert these assumptions. If we very quickly take up examples in the above order, subversion can be effected by saying that the lack of coordination among the rebels and personal motives of some of their leaders is proof enough that the revolt was not national in character; it cannot be called a feudal uprising against a commercial system because all feudal elements were not participating in the revolt and were not anti-British in nature; some of those who participated, also did not have anything new to offer; saying that it was just a Sepoy mutiny against the use of greased cartridges is indeed oversimplification. The very fact that the mutiny spread out far and beyond the barracks and cantonments and involved multifarious anti-British groups besides the soldiers is proof enough that it was not just a sepoy reaction over greased cartridges. Some scholars opine that this idea was floated as the imperialist rationale for the revolt, because they wanted to camouflage and erase the ugly picture of economic exploitation; it cannot be called a peasant revolt in entirety, because all peasants were not anti-British and they did not have any methodical agenda of replacing one taxation scheme by another; it was not a working class revolt against the bourgeoisie, because all working classes were not participating in the revolt and those who were participants, targeted non-British bourgeoisie as well. The geographical extent of the revolt was expansive and its scale was incomprehensible; its impact was far-reaching and recklessly extravagant. Every rebel or rebellious group had its own dreams, plans and inspirations. Thus the revolt was not one single event, it was a multiplication of multidimensional and multi-directional tendencies with such remarkable potency that the possibilities and specifics within it became infinitely multipliable.

The *Ḳashful Baghaavat Gorakhpur* provides interesting insights into some of the controversies of 1857. A diacritical feature of the style employed by Ahmad Ali is that it is not at all argumentative, in fact it is more like an acutely innocent conversation; unpretentious and heart searching. He has not tried to equivocate or conceal any issues. His writing transforms into powerfully effective communication with the reader; his perspicuity and pellucid style of narration makes the description seem truthful. As an empirical work its value is great. The vividness and detailing, sketch such eidetic picture of the looting of his Imambara that one can visualize the shock and anguish. On the one hand, Ahmad Ali gives contesting ideologies and on the other, he breaks some icons and stereotypes; it is ironic that some hypotheses are concurrently proven by his pen. This work has points of departure and distinction. It effectively conveys that a single collapse of one British official's authority in one place was in fact symptomatic of plural collapses of authorities of officials at various levels. As far as the factual compilation of events is concerned, there is no discrepancy in his account. The unique configurations of socio-political networks, which the text reveals, are exciting.

Although Ahmad Ali finds the causes of the revolt quite abstruse and obscure, yet he understands that the revolt was not an adventitious development as far as its genesis goes. There were socio-political and economic dissatisfactions working towards its creation. There were many practical, everyday issues involved in it. However, he does not agree with the notion that the Europeans wanted to acculturate the Indians in any manner which would negate their religious beliefs and practices. The revolt was indeed an abiogenesis, whose birth could be traced to the economic plight of the common man. The moneylenders extorted compound interest on loans from the poor peasants whose properties were auctioned for the recovery of dues. Further accretion took place in this dissatisfaction because of cruel rack-renting of the peasants. Ahmad Ali is critical of the materialistic Mahajans and Tehsildars. The extortion that they subjected the average man to rendered the latter bankrupt. No moratorium was ever granted to him. Given the fact that even in the interregnum between the mighty Mughal Empire and the British Raj, the condition of the peasants never really changed, it is quite understandable that Ahmad Ali speaks of the depredations of the peasantry by the landed aristocrats and decries their dolorous condition. The abysmal state of the poor seemed the most plausible cause of the revolt to him.

Ahmad Ali was not directly involved in the larger political imbalances which were the cause and effect of the uprising, yet he is critical of the poor administrative set-up in the times preceding the British takeover of Gorakhpur. He praises the administrative stability and the Civil law and order that the British brought. During the early 19th century, Gorakhpur had begun to slide from its previous, relatively prosperous economy, he seemingly wrote with great vehemence against the rebels because at a personal level he considered it incivility to disrupt established governing authority. He felt that initially Azamgarh's rebels exerted influence on the people of Gorakhpur and instigated them to defy British authority. Once the fumaroles of revolt were set in motion, they engulfed the British dominions in a big way. If one analyses the loot and plunder of Ahmad Ali's Imambara and properties and the dialogues which were exchanged between him and the rebels, the latter's level of confidence reveals that the colonial state was robbed of its legitimacy very early on in the revolt and as the awareness of dilution of legitimacy of British authority seeped, turbulence and disobedience infiltrated quickly in the outlying areas too. The bold movements of rebellious bands in the countryside and regions far removed from the initial epic centers of the revolt were a proof that it had gorgonized the British administration and weakened it in at least some areas to paralytic impotency. The situation was bellicose and prominent persons were forced to make choices. Given his ambidexterity and the fact that his feet were deeply dug in the socio-cultural and eco-political plain of Gorakhpur, his choice was going to matter and he choose to support the British. Ahmad Ali was not ambiguous in his pro-British approach. He helped them quite directly and acted as a powerful, if not the only steering wheel of the events that took place in his town. He worked with promptitude to attenuate the rebellion at Gorakhpur. European families remained under his aegis till arrangements were made to transfer them to further secured venues. He also acted as a custodian of their belongings for which he paid a price not inexpensive. It is understandable that the rebels went berserk and wished to punish Ahmad Ali for the choices that he had made. Their diatribe towards him was only the beginning. His fortitude was tested when his personal belongings together with those of the British officials were looted; the properties of the sacred Imambara were also not spared. He writes that the rebels would have made off with the gold and silver *tazias* also, had they not feared that riots would break out as a repercussion of this act. His bungalows at Kosamhi and Mohiuddinpur were plundered and razed to the ground. His being a renowned mystic and ascetic might have shielded his life. In his work the baaghis are put forward as a bacchant lot. He refers to Mohammad Hasan as 'Dajjaal'; Antichrist/ great deceiver. Like the British records and the famous *History of the Indian Mutiny*, of Charles Ball, he too presents Musharraf Khan as an morbid, cantankerous and irascible character, who was a political and religious bigot and had a maleficent record behind him. Ahmad Ali does not uncritically let off the blue-blooded committee members also, who were made responsible for maintaining law and order in Gorakhpur, but turned rebellious or indifferent. He condemns their sloth and apathy and fearlessly lambastes them for their lassitude and lapses. There was a phase when he, despite his immense wealth and socio-cultural standing was treated as an outcast; this probably was an autotomy exercised by people to safeguard themselves from the ire of Mohammad Hasan, Musharraf Khan and their loyal followers who had become obvious enemies of Ahmad Ali. The latter's role as a supporter of the British in a district abandoned by them would not have been easy, he was a funambulist who had risked his all. Oppressed by the diktat of the rebels, he waited in maddening anxiety for either of the paradoxical elixirs–the British army or his death.

Ahmad Ali and rebel leaders of Gorakhpur, both did not perceive each other's actions as peccadillo. In Ahmad's case, even his personal mannerisms of observing Islam came under the scanner as he was accused of not offering Friday prayers in the mosque, which might have been so due to the tradition of seclusion that was imposed on him as being a successor of Roshan Ali. He was also accused of eating food cooked by the Hindus and trusting them greatly in all matters. He defended himself by saying that he is a Sufi and purity of heart is the greatest merit for him. He was not guilty of abnegation of Islam by freely intermixing with other religious groups. His acuity of the all embracing and humanitarian spirit of Islam is indeed impressive. He was critical of all those who over-emphasized ritualism and fanaticism and asserted that synthetic religiosity which violates human values is of no use. Established norms of Sufism seemed to be concretely institutionalised in his being. In fact some of his ideas were rooted in the conceptual category of Humanism, his slant towards which was rather pronounced. Religion was at no time a marker of differences or a defining category for Ahmad Ali. It goes to his credit that despite being a prominent religious figure of the district he did not allow lines of definition to be drawn by religious considerations. Nothing obfuscated his mind, neither his inelastic Sufism nor his inflexible Humanism. He was obdurate in his own way and was ready to embrace death with the usual panache with which he embraced life. He was unwavering as far as his commitment to his stand in the revolt was concerned. Religious fanaticism was never a watchword or a bench mark for him and he had obviated the need to prove his religiosity with adherence to formalism of any kind. In some of his verses, Sufism and formalism have been juxtaposed against each other. He adduced to the examples of Mansur and Sarmad to remind how Sufis had been persecuted by earlier, fanatically oppressive bigot authorities and the subtle point that he makes here is that these authorities were non-Christian. His own latitudinarianism towards orthodoxy was restricted due to principles of sufistic secularism and his social and religious ideas did not contradict each other. His oriflamme is not formalistic synthesized religiosity. It is interesting that rebel leaders at Gorakhpur were also Muslims but the faith-religion continuum of Ahmad Ali and the rebels did not make them coterminous with each other. Both Muslims, both loyal to their respective cause and paradoxically, the convoluted subject of their loyalty made them deleterious for each other. They never coalesced as a religious group and never came together for commination against the British. In fact, religion seemed like an unidentifiable indicator. Ahmad Ali's acerbic criticism of Mohammad Hasan and Musharraf Khan is in itself abortifacient of any assumption that religious identities defined inclinations in 1857. It is worthy of notice that on the one hand, Ahmad laments that Mohammad Hasan who was proud of his Shiism was the one who had the Imambara looted with ruthless indifference, while on the other hand, his own beginning of his narrative with a doxology cannot be used as any parameter of anticipation and guesses, because after all his personal religious beliefs did not at all ensure his political or economic support to his co-religionists. Ahmad Ali in fact displays tranquility and indifference as far as the paradoxical juxtaposition of his religious beliefs with those of the rebel leaders go.

The book has many pages of long-winded encomium of the British rulers. The unction that he sets in motion to praise the British is sometimes uncomfortable, but it should not be underrated as meaningless eulogy or mere balderdash, because it helps us figure out some unsaid fears and unfaceable phobias, of what displeasing the white rulers could mean. It is common knowledge that the revolt unleashed behemoth violence and terror. Restoration and reestablishment of authority was the real challenge for the British and they were prepared to do anything to achieve that end. The rebels were excoriated and castigated in such a merciless manner that the memory of it acted as a deterrent to ensure the non-repetition of any uprising of this genus and magnitude. The magnum of revenge and the macabre violence, which was used to execute it, benumbed the anti-British enthusiasts. Blinded with hubris, British vengeance engulfed the guilty and innocent alike; like molten fire which burned all that came in its way. There ensued foudroyant reclamation of power. They realized that the revolt had fibrillated legitimacy of their authority in a big way and if they wished to restart their powerful machine of imperialism once again they would necessarily have to service or replace its components; big or small. Monopolization of power gave a befitting engagement to the company. Their eco-political policies had already cut the roots of older systems, now they had to plug in and interlace with the local elements and stress their power in a more positive manner. They wished to normalize relations with those local power magnates who would help them in upholding the rule of law; after all the laws were their's and so what if they were exploitative. Denial of vindication to all would have been politically unwise and incorrect. Being the victors they had the privilege to report the revolt to the world in their own words; Reports were structured and moulded in accordance with requirements. In the eirenicon offered by them the British did have to include land restoration and land grants in some cases, but it came as an act of charity to the grantees. They had realized that they could not possibly administer the colony with autarky and support of local elements was a must. At times they had no choice but to act benignant; it was a compromise, which did not taste too good, but had to be swallowed to keep the monster of imperialism alive. On the other hand all the aristocrats who supported the British were not just carpetbaggers, in fact more often than not, loyalty to those in authority seemed like an integral part of the value system of these families. They hung on to their fidelity with absolute certitude in the goodness of their decision. Besides, on the face of it the British seemed only as exploitative as the earlier regimes had been; the deadly difference that the drain of wealth made was yet to be fully comprehended.

Despite the risk of being accused of zooming to yare deductions, I dare to say that minus the mirage of nationalism as a backdrop and the archetypical presumption of high moral values of all the rebels, Ahmad Ali does not come across as an anti hero. He should not be misprisioned as an anti-national because the concept of nationalism as we understand it today was rather nascent at that time. Given the determinant certainty that he had deliberately fenced off his personal religious beliefs by wires of toleration and understanding and barely had any pressing political or economic stakes in the revolt; he appears as a maverick, who did his own thing; whatever the cost may be. He was ready to pay any price for an idea that he valued. Once evaluated and chosen, hardly did he care about the consequences of his choices; reevaluation was not his style; even if it implied self-destruction. He rated his survival through the revolt as an anabiosis of sorts. He has narrated the events pertaining to the threats that he received and the looting of the Azakhana and other properties with such minutiae of details that the readers can actually visualize emotions; And pronounced, among those emotions is unyielding persistence with which he held on to his convictions. His determination to stand by his decisions was inelastic and inflexible. There appears no antimony in his value system, which is tested against the greatest odds. His rock solid loyalty could not be moulded by shrewd bends of any hypothetical assumptions. It is to be remembered that it was not just by chance that the rebels were countervailed successfully in his town.

Kashful Baghaavat Gorakhpur is definitely not a fabulist's fictitious account, its historicity is irrefragable and its simplicity nonpareil. I consider it fortuitous that I happened to read it.

Bismillah-ir Rahmaan-ir-Raheem

In the name of God, the Most Gracious, the Most Merciful

1. Karun pehle tauheed Rabb-e-Jaleel
Kiya jis ne paida kaseer-o-qaleel
First I praise the great God
Who has created all big and small

2. Khudawand maah-o-najum-o-sipahar
Khudawand arsh-o- Khudawand meher
Lord of moon, stars and the vault of sky
Lord of heavens, Lord of the sun

3. Woh Haajat-rawa hai woh hai Beniyaaz
Wohi apne bandon ka hai Kaarsaaz
He grants wishes, He is independent
Only He is the true accomplisher for His subjects

4. Kareem-o-Raheem aur Razzaaq hai
Do aalam ka laaraib Khallaaq hai
He is kind, merciful and the ultimate sustainer
He undoubtedly is the creator of both worlds

5. Zamin se falak tak hai ek shaan-e-Haq
Pur az khawane nemat hain chaudah tabaq
From earth to sky there is nothing but the glory of God
Filled with his blessings are the fourteen stratums

6. Gada ko woh karta hai ek dam mein shah
Jo chahe kare pal mein shah ko tabaah
He makes a beggar a king in a moment
If He so wishes, in a moment He can destroy a king

7. Kisi ko woh deta hai zar beshumaar
Koi fakhr-o-faaqaa se hai sogwaar
To some He gives boundless wealth
Some due to poverty and starvation are crestfallen

8. Koi mubtalaa-e-gham-o-ranj hai
Koi maalik-e-daulat-o-ganj hai
Some are embroiled in sorrow and suffering
Some are the masters of wealth and treasures

9. Woh karta hai jo usko manzur hai
Esi ja pe insaan majboor hai
He does whatever He approves of
On these decisions, humans are helpless

10. Woh Rabbus Samad hukm jab tak na de
Kahaan shaakh-e-ashjar mein phal lage
Until and unless that Almighty God orders
How can stems of trees bear fruits?

11. Nahin koi gul aisa khush rang-o-ruh
Ke us baaghbaan ki na kahta ho bu
There are no such flowers, colourful and beautiful,
Which do not possess the fragrance of that Gardener

12. Gulistaan mein Bulbul jo hai naghma saaz
Usi ne diya us ko sooz-o-gudaaz
That Bulbul which sings melodiously in the gardens
Was granted passionately burning tune by Him, to delight hearts

13. Agar jism-e-insaan hai ya jism-e-moor
Diya mukhtalif usne har ek ko zoor
Whether it is the human body or the body of a peacock
To all, He has granted specific capabilities

14. Usi Rabb ne ajsaam-e-insaan kiye
Banaye hain ajza azdaad se
That God has created bodies of humans
Has made parts with paradoxical variety

15. Jo dariya ke hain zeer-e-charkh-e-kuhan
Usi ki mohabbat mein hain moojzan
Those lakes which have been in motion since ages
Are flowing in waves for His love

16. Guhar aabroo pake chamka do chand
Sadaf qatra-e-faiz se behramand
On being honoured the pearl shines like moon
The oyster shell has become fortunate by a drop of his mercy

17. Falak ko sitaaron se zevar diya
Bashar se zamin ko muzzaiyyan kiya
The sky has been bejeweled with stars
With living beings lands have been bedecked

18. Jala nur se uske jab Koh-e-Tur
Toh ankhon ko sabke mila us se noor
When the mount of Tur burnt with His light
Vision was then granted to all with that

19. Joh hain khaaksaaraan-e-raah-e-Khuda
Unhen ikhtiyaar juz-w-kul diya
Those who serve the ways of God
They have been granted total potential

20. Jo chaahen toh mitti ko sona karen
Samandar ki aab ek qatra ko deyen
Like alchemists they can convert dust into gold
Can capture the waters of the ocean in a drop

21. Yeh hai qudrat-e-Paak Parwardigaar
Ke Sane hai masnooah mein aashkaar
This is the nature of Pure Providence
That the Creator is reflected in his creations

22. Parastish ke qabil tu hai aiye Kareem
Teri zaat hai benazeer-o-saheem
You deserve to be worshipped, O kind Lord
Your Being is incomparable and unsurpassable.

Naat Hazrat Mohammad Mustafa SallAllaho Alaihe Wassallam

Verses in praise of Hazrat Mohammad Mustafa; Peace be upon him

23. Karein baad uske nisaar-e-Rasool
Jo hain durrey yakta be bahar-e-qabool
After Him, I praise His messenger
Who is a rare, singular pearl in the ocean of acceptance

24. Unhi se hai umeed-e-bakhshish mudaam
Salaat un pe din raat hai aur salaam
Due to him exists the hope of emancipation always
Benediction and obeisance are sent to him day and night

25. Karimul sajaayaa nabi-ul-umam
Sakhi-o-shuja-o-muali himam
Merciful in nature, the Prophet of races
Generous, brave, supremely courageous and bold

26. Pas az naat-e-ashaab-e-Hazrat hain chaar
Khuda ke woh nazdeek hain bavaqaar
Therefore worthy of encomium are the four companions of the Prophet,
Close to God, they are honorable

27. Rahe din-e-haq par sada mustaqeem
Unho se hai raazi Khuda-e-Kareem
Always remained consistent with the true faith
The benevolent God is pleased with them

28. Hain aale Rasool safa ba safa
Durood unpe wajib hai kahna sada
The family of the Prophet is pure and shining
It is mandatory to always say Durood on him

29. Khuda dil mein de unki ulfat ka josh
Ke hain woh jawanmard aur aib posh
May God grant enthusiasm of his love to the heart
For he is brave and concealer of others' faults

30. Khudaya bahaq-e-Mohammad Rasool
Dua mujh gunahgaar ki kar qabool
O God! For the sake of Mohammad, the Prophet
Accept the prayers of myself, a sinner

31. Mera dil ho ganjeena-e-noor-e-haq
Mujhe de tu imaan mein sab par sabaq
May my heart treasure the light of truth,
In faith give me excellence over all others!

Maddah Malika Muazzama

Praise of the Exalted Queen

32. Pila saaqiya saaghar-e-iftikhaar
Karun midhat-e-Malika-e-bavaqaar
O cup bearer, serve the cup of honour
To praise the Highly-exalted Queen

33. Hai kis Shah ke wasf mein ye asar
Qalam ban gaya nezaa-e-neeshkar
Qualities of which king have such an impact?
That the pen obtains the sting of a spear!

34. Qalam Khizr aab-e-baqa hai madaad
Hai maddaah beshak Attaar-e-nehaad
The pen is like Khizr and elixir is the ink
The eulogist undoubtedly has the qualities of Attaar

35. Falak martabat Malika Victoria
Hai shaq dar se ada ka qalb dariya
Queen Victoria has the stature of the skies
Fear has fissured the sea of the enemies' soul to a stream

36. Khadiiv-e-jahan Shah-e-aafaaqgeer
Hai jis ka laqab adl mein benazeer
Sovereign of the world, Universal Empress,
Whose reputation of justice is unsurpassed,

37. Nahin koi aisa khadiiv-e-jahan
Ke hain aish-o-ishrat mein khurd-o-kalan
There is no such sovereign in the world
That all, small and big, are living in luxury and pleasure

38. Jo pichle zamaane ke the baadshah
Na thi un ki insaaf pe kuch nigaah
Those who were emperors in earlier times
They did not have a vision for fairplay

39. Jahan adl se uske aabaad hai
Gharibon faqiron ka dil shaad hai
The world is flourishing due to her justice
Cheerful is the heart of the poor and the mendicants

40. Hamari ye beja nahin qeel-o-qaal
Sataye kisi ko koi kya majaal
My conversation is not senseless
How can anyone dare to trouble another?

41. Hai ba yak digar har jagah raaste
Sada sher ke paas bakri rahe
Everywhere the roads of outlook are broad
The feeblest too are unfazed by the powerful

42. Raheem-o-kareem aur raaya nawaaz
Woh hi bevaseelon ki hain kaarsaaz
Kind, benevolent and caring for her subjects
She is the helper of the vulnerable

43. Ye roshan hai har dil se maanus hai
Woh hai shama toh khalaq faanus hai
She is enlightened; understands every heart
If she is a flame of light, then the subjects are her protective canopy

44. Adaalat mein sharminda Nausherwan
Sakhavat mein Hatim khajal harzman

In justice, Nausherwan is put to shame
In generosity, Hatim is surpassed every time

45. Shujaat ka uske yeh hai zoor-o-shoor
Larazti hai haibat se Rustam ki goor
Such is the name and fame of her bravery
That the grave of Rustam trembles in fear

46. Gharaz hai woh es waqt mein bandobast
Hue pastaani jise dekh past
Such is the administration at this time
On seeing which the progenitors seem weak

47. Shah-e-Rome aur mulk-e-Iran ka shah
Riyo Ruus ke shah kardoon kulah
King of Rome and King of the country of Iran
The Emperor of Russia who could accomplish all

48. Yeh sab us ke hazman ke hai khoshaachin
Hai halqa bagosh unka faghfur-e-Cheen
They are all inspired by her resolution
The Emperor of China is her devoted slave

49. Har ek mu-e-tan se zabaan ho ayaan
Aur ek ek dahan mein ho sau sau zabaan
From every hair over the body may a tongue appear
And every pore may have hundreds of tongues

50. Kamayambaghi vasf ta ham na ho
Bayaan us ki taareef ka kam na ho
Eulogy as it ought to be, cannot be compressed
Description of her praises will never cease

51. Governor Bahadur hain vala guhar
Hain khaas ardalee unke shams-o-qamar
Governor Bahadur is a precious pearl
The sun and the moon are his special attendants

52. Wazir-ul-Mumaalik aqeel-o-faheem
Kareem-o-raheem-o-raees-o-nadeem
Minister of countries, wise and intelligent
Kind, benevolent, rich and friendly

53. Dua hai yeh Ahmad ki aiye Kirdgaar
Rahe hashr tak sultanat payedaar
This is the prayer of Ahmad, O Creator!
Till the last day may the empire remain stable!

54. Hawakhah Malika ke hozam rahen
Jo hain unke dushman woh bagham rahen
May the well-wishers of the Queen flourish!
Those who are her enemies may remain sorrowful

55. Mere yahaan zila ke jo hukkaam hain
Raaya ke khuwahaan-e-aaraam hain
At my place, administrators of the district
Are concerned about comforts of the subjects

56. Rahen khush yeh hukkaam aali tabaar
Rakhe shaad-o-khurram unhe Kirdgaar
May these administrators of the grand dynasty remain happy!
May the Creator keep them happy and mirthful!

57. Adaalat ka amla bhi hai daadgar
Police ka bhi amla hai sab khush siyar
The staff of the court is also praiseworthy
All staff of the police too are good-natured

58. Hain sarrishta-e-maal ke amalgaan
Buland iqtidaar-o-rafiul makaan
Worthy administrators of the department of property
Highly powerful and of exalted position

59. Raeesaan-e-shahri hain sab basifat
Nihaayat farotan hain aur nek zaat
The plutocratic of the town are endowed with good qualities
They are extremely enlightened and gentle.

Bayaan Vajh Tasneef-e-Kitaab

Account of reasons for writing this book

60. Sabab es ketaalif ka kar bayaan
Jo dil mein nihaan hain use kar ayaan
Describe the cause of this writing
Whatever is hidden in the heart, make it apparent

61. Bajuz aish ke gham na tha zeenahaar
Raha mujh pe afzaal-e-Parwardigaar
Nothing except pleasure; there was no sorrow at all
Grace of the Creator was upon me

62. Saubat aziyat se hum paak the
Aur aafaat-e-duniya se bebaak the
I was free from distress and pain
And was fearless of worldly calamities

63. Phanse panja-e-zulm mein nagahaan
Yaqeen tha ke hargiz bachegi na jaan
Was caught in the claws of tyranny unexpectedly
Was sure that definitely my life will not be saved

64. Magar fazl-e-Khaliq se payee nijaat
Dobarah hui az sar-e-nauhayaat
But by God's grace I got respite
As if again I was granted a new life

65. Kaha dil se kuch tazkirah kar bayaan
Karen yaad to tuj ko khurd-o-kalan
Said to my heart, narrate some instance
So that all small and big may remember you

66. Yeh nuskha rahega qayaamat talak
Kareynge sana jin-w-ins-o-malak
This description shall survive until Doomsday
Genii, humans and angels will praise it

67. Sukhan se tera naam hoga buland
Kareynge teri maddah sab aqalmand
Your name will be exalted due to these verses
All intelligent ones shall praise you

68. Karega tujhe yaad har khaas-o-aam
Kahenge raeesoon mein tha nek-naam
All elite and commoners would remember you
Would say that you, among noblemen, were reputed as of good-character

69. Yeh nuskha tera dilkusha baagh hai
Khizaan ka nahin dakhl bedaagh hai
This description of yours is an attractive garden
There is no interference of fall and decay; it is spotless

70. Hai pur mewah shaakh-e-sukhan doostoon
Jo hain lazzateen us mein haasil karo
Friends, stems of the description are laden with fruits
Relish the tasteful delights available in them

71. Hain es baagh-e-dilchasp ke baaghbaan
Miyan Shah Ahmad Ali khush-bayaan
The gardener of this enchanting garden
Is Miyan Shah Ahmad Ali, the sweet-tongued

72. Bhara sahv-o-nisyaan se hai aadmi
Nahi aib-jui hai kuch mardumi

Man is full of omissions and forgetfulness
Malignant criticism is not manliness

73. Hai umeed mujhko khiradmand se
Hunar aur firasat ke paband se
I have hope from the intelligent
From those who are disciplined by talent and foresight

74. Agarche nahin sahv se main bari
Nahi aib se harf khaali koi
Although I am not unconstrained from oversight
No word or speech is free of blemish

75. Mussanif pe lekin na ho taanaazan
Baraaye Khuda-o-Rasool-e-zaman
But please do not animadvert the writer
For the sake of God and the Prophet of the age

76. Hai Raavi pe lazim karam ki nazar
Amal Shaikh Saadi ke kar qaul par
Taking a kind view of the narrator is necessary
Do follow the instructions of Shaikh Saadi

77. Shunidam ke dar rooz umeed-o-beem
Bad an raba neykan ba bakhshad Kareem
I have heard that on the day of hope and fear
The kind Lord will forgive the bad, like the noble ones

78. Tu niiz ar khataa bini andar sukhan
Ba khalq Jahan-Aafreen Kaarkun
If you find faults in other person's narrative
Then remember that Creator of people and souls is the greatest worker

79. Chal aiye ish-hab-e-khaamah chalaak-o-chust
Na ho inqalaab-e-zamaana se sust
Move the grey pen with wit and speed
Do not slacken due to the vicissitudes of times

80. Raqam kar kuch ahwaal-e-Hindustan
Jise kahte hain Hind jannat-nishaan
Narrate something about the conditions of Hindustan,
Which is called Hind, 'The Heaven like'

81. Woh chalaaki-o-tezi kar aashkaar
ke ho paa-e-auhaam jis se figaar
Exhibit such intellect and speed
So that it may lacerate the feet of apprehensions

82. Raah-e-raasti mein woh khushgaam ho
Ke aaghaaz ka nek anjaam ho
Move as such on the path of goodness
That the genesis may have a noble culmination

83. Tu kar haal tajdeed-e-dauraan raqam
Par es shart se ta na ho besh-o-kam
You narrate the novel circumstances of the times
But with such parameters that it is neither exaggerated nor understated

84. Haqiqat bayaan ki jo hai mu-ba-mu
Madad se main teri likhun hu-ba-hu
Truth, which is narrated in its absolute entirety
With your help may I write it with exactitude

85. Zamaane ke haalaat kuch hon raqam
Jise sun ke shunwa ho gosh-e-asam
Some conditions of the times may be indited
On hearing them, the ears of the deaf shall also respond

86. Hamesha se duniya ka ye haal hai
Ajaayeb tilismon ka janjaal hai
State of the world has always been such
That it is a network of bewildering sorceries

87. Zari es mein bu-e-wafaa kuch nahin
Bhara sum se hai aasmaan-o-zamin
There is not the least fragrance of loyalty in it
The skies and lands are full of venom

88. Mithai mein zahir hai poshida sum
Siyaahru qalam hai bawaqt-e-raqam
In sweets also is apparent the hidden poison
The pen too is black-faced at the time of narration

89. Wafaa es ajoozah se hargiz na chaah
Jhuka we gi Harut san warna chaah
Do not at all wish for loyalty from this hag
Or else this Tartarus will make you stoop like Harut

90. Ayaan haal ka kiyjiye kya bayaan
Bayaan kiyjiye tab ke jab ho nihaan
How should one describe conditions which are apparent?
Description is required when the matter is concealed

91. Yehi aaqiloon ko hai taabeer-e-khwaab
Ke duniya to jifah hai taalib gulaab
This for the wise is interpretation of dreams
That the world is a carcass, seeker of rose

92. Bas ab yahaan se tahreer-e-haalaat hai
Sikander ko darpesh zulmaat hai
From here onwards starts the narration of conditions
Sikander is confronting the darkness

93. Karun sanihaa Hind ka aashkaar
Qalam ka bhi ho jis se seena figaar
I am divulging the occurences of Hind
Which would wound the pen's heart as well

94. Yeh hai qudrat-e-Khaliq-e-Zulminan
Pada Hindiyon par ye ranj-o-mehan
This is the will of the Creator of the world
That this sorrow and tribulation befell the residents of Hind

95. Hua har bashar par ye ranj-o-taab
Pada yak ba yak yeh Khuda ka ghazab
This sorrow and fatigue engulfed every creature
All of a sudden befell this wrath of God

96. Ke afwaaj-e-Sultan-e-walahimam
Sar-e-afsar-e-Rome-o-Chin-o-Ajam
That the armies of the bravest of emperors
The overlord of Rome, China and India

97. Baaghi apne sardaar se ho gayi
Kamaai hamesha ki sab kho gayi
Revolted against their own commanders
Earnings accumulated over the years were lost

98. Woh shaadi-o-neki-o-naamaawari
Bayak gardish-e-chashm sab mit gayi
That happiness, nobility and fame
Suddenly, in the blinking of an eye, all was erased

99. Na samjhe zara kuch bhi shart-e-namak
Yeh shohra hai ab az sama ta samak
Did not understand any of the conditions of loyalty, attached with salt and service
This is now publicized from the skies to the depth of oceans

100. Ajab nutfabad the laain-e-Khuda
Kab aison ka munh dekhna hai rawa
Strangely ill-born were those accursed by God
When is it advisable to look at such people's faces?

101. Mere haal par raham-e-Laulaak ho
Ke aison se iqliim sab paak ho
May the raison d'etre of creation have mercy on my state,
May the whole world be cleansed of such people,

102. Khuda in ke aamaal ki de saza
Ke aamaal-e-bad ki hai bad hi jaza
May God punish them for their deeds,
Because the repercussion of bad deeds is surely bad

103. Bhala kis tarah yeh na hon naabkaar
Ke mohsin-kashon mein hai unka shumaar

After all how can they not be notorious,
When they are listed among the benefactors' betrayers?

104. Magar pahle Meerut se aaghaaz hai
Ayaan hum pe akhbaar se raaz hai
But the embryonic initiation is from Meerut
This information reached me through the newspapers

105. Maee ka mahina tha aiye hoshiyaar
Thee tareekh dusween ye hai aashkaar
O clever one! It was the month of May
The date was tenth, it is well-known

106. The adad barah sad-o-shust chaar
Esi Fasli san mein hua khalfshaar
The number was twelve hundred and sixty-four
In this Fasli year happened the conflict

107. Sane Hijri barah sau huftad-o-seh
Ishara hua do sanon ka to yeh
The Hijri year was twelve hundred and seventy- three
This is in the context of two dating systems

108. Munasib hai ab Isvi san likhun
Hai sattawan attharah sau par fizoon
It is advisable that I should now use Isvi dates
Fifty-seven (years) had passed from eighteen hundred

109. Mahina tha roozon ka garmi ki fasal
Hui shahar Meerut se jhagdon ki asl
It was the month of fasting in summer season
Dispute began from the town of Meerut

110. Yakayak yeh Sultan se baaghi hue
Ke sab fauj Dehli ko raahi hue
Suddenly they revolted against the Emperor
All the troops started moving towards Delhi.

Khabar Zila Azamgarh, Mauqa Taarikh-e-Sowum-Maah June, Attharah Sau Sattawan Isvi

News of the town of Azamgarh, Time: Date 13th; Month-June; Year – 1857 Isvi

111. Azamgarh ka ahwaal aagee suno
Zara baaghiyon pe taassuf karo
Hear the news of Azamgarh now
Pity the rebels a little

112. Yeh Shaitaan ne unko dee hai daghaa
Ke aaqa-e-nemat se ki yeh vaghaa
This is their deception by Satan
That they have begun war against the master of grace

113. Mukhaalif yahaan ka bhi lashkar hua
Misaal-e-shutar woh bhi Dehli chala
The army of this place also became an adversary
That too like a camel left for Delhi

114. Woh jab aath lakh naqad-o-zar le chuke
Toh seedhe woh Dehli ko raahi hue
When they had taken eight lakhs (rupees) of cash and gold
Then they straight away fled to Delhi

115. Har ek shahr-o-qariya ko taaraaj kar
Ziyada hue buzdil-e-khiraahsar

They ravaged every town and village
Became increasingly cowardly and immodest rebels

116. Himaqat ke aasaar sab the ayaan
Bhala daakuon ka thikana kahan
All signs of foolishness were apparent
Where could dacoits find a refuge?

117. Na the aql-o-danish se woh kaamiyaab
Khuda ne kiya unko aakhir kharaab
They had not acquired wisdom and intelligence,
Finally, God ruined them

118. Ali Bakhsh Nazir the ek khairkhah
Samajh kar woh hukkaam ko baadshah
Ali Baksh Nazir was a well-wisher
He considered the officers as rulers

119. Sar pur-ataat se tasleem kar
Rahe unke farmaan mein sarbasar
Saluted them with respectful obedience
Remained totally under their command

120. Dam har dam ataat ka bharte rahe
Bure kaam ko naam dharte rahe
He always sang praises of obedience
Kept on condemning bad deeds

121. Sharafat ka jo muqtaza tha kiya
Najaabat ko dhabba na lagne diya
Did whatever came under the exigency of gentleness
Did not let nobility be sullied

122. Sharifon se aisa hi hota hai kaam
Taraazi se aaqa ki karte hain naam
This is how gentlemen behave
They work with the consent of their masters

123. Hamesha ho aison pe rahm-e-Khuda
Urooj aur izzat hai inki baja

May God always be benevolent towards such people,
Their high status and respectability are well justified

124. Shujaat se apni gaya Ghazipur
Kiya arz ye haakimon ke huzoor
Due to his valour he went to Ghazipur
Stated this to the officers

125. Ke be-khauf hon aap raunaq furooz
Yeh aasi hai hukkaam ka kafashdooz
That you may fearlessly grace your position
This sinner is a cobbler of the masters

126. Hamesha hatheli pe rakhta hun sar
Ataat mein hun mustaid sarbasar
I am forever ready to lay down my life
Am heedlessly enthusiastic about compliance

127. Kisi tarha ka kuch na keeje khatar
Khuda par faqat rakhiye apni nazar
Do not entertain fears of any kind
Just look up to God's mercy

128. Hua tab ye irshaad hukkaam se
Ke ghafil nahin hum bhi anjaam se
It then happened that the officers said
That we too are not unaware of the expected consequences

129. Hum hukkaam sab yahaan hain padar rakaab
Faqat etni taakhir mein hai sawaab
We, all commanders here, have our feet in the stirrup
But just this much of postponement has appropriation

130. Ke tum chalke aage karo sab durust
Raho kaar-e-haakim mein chalaak-o-chust
That you proceed first and put everything in order
Be smart and quick-witted in executing master's work

131. Chale aate hain paashnaakoob hum
Mitate hain sab in ka jaur-o-sitam
We will follow thumping our feet
We will erase all their cruelty and tyranny

132. Raiyyat ko aabaad karte hain hum
Dilon se sabhon ke mitate hain gham
We would rehabilitate the subjects
We would erase sorrow from everyone's heart

133. Sab afwaaj le kar bafazl-e-Kareem
Wahaan aake hote hain phir hum muqeem
With all the troops by the grace of the Merciful
We shall then be stationed there

134. Sarrishta ke afsar hain Safdar Husain
Dayaanat amaanat se karte hain chaain
Safdar Husain is an officer of a department
By honesty and integrity he remains in peace

135. Bahut khoob hain mard-e-danish guzeen
Hazaar aafreen sad hazaar aafreen
He is excellent, a chosen man of intellect
Thousand applauds, a hundred thousand applauds!

136. Jawanmard-o-dana-o-khush-ru haseen
Shujaat ke hatim ke goya nageen
Youthful, intelligent, good-natured and beautiful
He is like a jewel of bravery and generosity

137. Rifaqat mein hukkaam ke woh bhi the
Jo pesh aaya ranj-o-alam sab sahe
He was also a friend of the rulers
He endured all the pain and calamity that eventuated

138. Ali Baksh ke saath woh bhi gaye
Ghazipur mein chand din woh rahe
He too went with Ali Baksh
And stayed in Ghazipur for a few days

139. Ijaazat se hukkaam ke aud kar
Azamgarh ke the muntazim sarbasar
On returning with the permission of the rulers
He fully managed the affairs of Azamgarh

140. Sab anjaam jo chahiye tha kiya
Kuch ilzaam hargiz na aane diya
He executed whatever was required
Did not at all allow any accusation of lapses

141. Unhi ki maeeyyat se tha intizaam
Sab iqbaal-e-haakim se tha ye nizaam
All arrangements were because of their association
All this set up was due to the good fortune of the rulers

142. Jo Pulwaar ki qaum bigdi thi sab
Uthani padi unko ranj-o-taab
All those people of Pulwaar who had gone astray
They had to bear sorrow and fatigue

143. Saza ye bad-aamaal paane lage
Jo bad the woh aakhir thikane lage
They started receiving retribution for bad deeds
Those who were blameworthy, eventually met their end

144. Burai se kismet ki gumraah the
Hazaaron azeeyat mein aakhir phanse
Due to ill fate they had deviated
Finally they were engulfed by a thousand calamities

145. Adab se jo baahar rakha tha qadam
Gulogeer hote the tegh-e-do dam
Since they had stepped beyond the limits of decorum
They were put to end by the running edge of the sword

146. Burai ki aakhir ye paayi saza
Ke sab nang-o-naamus ghaarat kiya
Ultimately they received this punishment for misconduct
That they eroded all prestige and honour

147. Gharaz apne aamaal ki ab saza
woh paate hain milte hain jo ja-ba-ja
Therefore, now the vengeance for their deeds
Those receive, who are caught here and there

148. Ajab log hain haakim-e-zee-sho'oor
Ke hai shohra-e-adl nazdeek-o-dur
The very sensible rulers are indeed marvellous people
That the fame of their justice is spread near and far

149. Sakhi-o-shuja-o-diler-o-qavi
Nihaayat jawanmard hain aur jari
Generous, brave, daring and mighty
They are extremely youthful and courageous

150. Adaalat se rakhte hain din raat kaam
Raiyyat nawaazi se karte hain naam
They dispense justice day and night
Earn fame by granting favours to their subjects

151. Nihaayat ba tafteesh maalaa kalaam
Saza dene mein bhi hai yeh ehtimaam
They conduct extremely detailed investigation and interrogation
In awarding punishments also, they exercise vigilance

152. Liya mujrimoon se iwaz jurm ka
Jo laaiq the unke wohi dee saza
Took from the culprits recompensation for their crimes
Gave punishment in scrupulous correlation to what was deserved

153. Na chaahaa kisi ghair se intiqaam
Bakhubi kiya mulk ka intizaam
Desired no revenge from any innocent
Made excellent arrangements for governance of the country

154. Jo hukkaam bhi karte kuch kajravee
Jo bachta yeh taqat bhala kis mein thi

If the rulers tried some unprincipled actions
Who had the power to escape them then?

155. Agar bar jafaa pesha bashtaafte
Ke az dast-e-qahar-ash aman yaafte
If they had fought with the oppressive
Then they would have gained immunity from the cruelty of their hands

156. Magar unko aabaad rakhe Khuda
Ke insaaf se adl-e-Kisra kiya
But may God keep them prosperous
With absolute fairness they dispensed the justice of Kisra

157. Saza mujrimon ko hui begumaan
Raha unke insaaf se khush jahan
The culprits were punished undoubtedly
The world was pleased with their justice

158. Raiyyat sab aabaad hone lagi
Hui har bashar ko nihaayat khushi
All the people started getting rehabilitated
Every human being was extremely happy

159. Rabistaan birun raft-o-aamad bahaar
Bar aaurda sabza sar az ju-e-baar
Winter has passed and spring has come
Lush greenery has sprung by the rivers

160. Hamesha rahen wahaan pe haakim muqeem
Ba haqq-e-Mohammad ba fazl-e-Kareem
May the rulers always reside there
In the name of Mohammad and by favour of the kind God!

161. Dua hai ye Ahmad ki har subh-o-shaam
Rakhe khush unhun ko Khuda-e-Karaam
This is Ahmad's prayer every morning and evening
May the kind God keep them euphoric!

Hikayat Zila Gorakhpur

Report of the Town of Gorakhpur

162. Gorakhpur ka aage ahwaal hai
Yahaan ki haqiqat mein yeh qaal hai
Following is the news of Gorakhpur
These are the facts about its condition:

163. Yahaan ki bhi afwaaj baaghi hui
Shararat se apni woh daaghi hui
The armies here also rebelled
Due to their mischief they became soiled

164. Yahaan par jo do Company fauj thee
Bahut bhid se mauj dar mauj thee
The two Company armies which were here
Were swarming in layers

165. Azamgarh ka ahwaal usne suna
Ke haakim se sab ne baghaavat kiya
They heard of the conditions of Azamgarh
Where all had rebelled against the rulers

166. Luta maal-o-asbaab hukkaam ka
Baghaavat ki dil mein samayee hawa
Wealth and belonging of the rulers were looted
The idea of rebellion entered their hearts

167. Khazana ke lene pe taiyyaar ho
Hue mustaid woh ke paikaar ho
They were set to capture the treasury
So they were prepared to stir up a war

168. Yahaan par jo haakim the zee-izz-o-shaan
Karun un ki jurrat ka kya main bayaan
The high stature rulers who were here
What can I say to describe their daring?

169. Nihaayat shujaat ki hukkaam ne
Ke jana use pukhta-o-khaam ne
The rulers acted with extreme bravery
The experienced and inexperienced realized this,

170. Kiya agarche afwaaj ne inhiraaf
Rausa magar yahaan ke the paak-o-saaf
Though the armies did deviate
The aristocrats of this place were clean and innocent

171. Muawin the hukkaam ke es qadar
Na aane diya un pe hargiz zarar
They were such worthy followers of the rulers
They did not allow any harm at all to come to them

172. Hue yahaan jo hukkaam raunaq furooz
Shab-e-tira meri hui misl-e-rooz
When the rulers graced this place by their presence
My dark night became like a bright day,

173. Tab hukkaam ne aake maskan kiya
Azakhana maawaa-o-malja bana
When the rulers came to reside here
The mourning house became their shelter and asylum

174. Zan-o-mard-o-atfaal-o-khurd-o-kalan
Rahe shaad-o-khurram basad izz-o-shan
Females and men and children and small and big
Were happy and cheerful with lots of respect and honour

175. Mila chain-o-aaraam hukkaam ko
Zara dekho aaghaaz-o-anjaam ko
The rulers were peaceful and comfortable
Just look at the beginning and the end

176. Munawwar woh chehre bayaazi rahe
Ataat se woh meri raazi rahe
Those white faces remained illuminated
They were pleased with my services

177. Duago-e-hukkaam hun main faqir
Bhala mujh se raazi na ho kyon amir
I am a mendicant, praying for the rulers
Why should the governors not be happy with me?

178. Yahaan se phir kothi mein Kosamhi ke ja
Hue saare hukkaam raunaq faza
From here they proceeded to the mansion of Kosamhi
All the rulers graced that place with their presence

179. Hue kothi mein mem-o-ladke muqeem
Guzarti thi har waqt bekhauf-o-beem
The madams and children resided in the bungalow
Every moment passed without any fear or danger

180. Tha garmi ka mausam sama khub tha
Sab hukkaam ko bas woh marghub tha
It was summer season, the weather was good
All the rulers found it pleasant

181. Ataat ki humne bhi aisi wahaan
Ke raazi hue haakim-e-qadardaan
I too rendered such service there
That my patron rulers were highly pleased

182. Bird Sahib us ja pe maujood the
Razamand the hum se khushnood the
Bird Sahib was present at that place
He was agreeable and happy with me

183. Hum har waqt khidmat ko istaadah the
Gharaz jaan-nisaari pe aamaadah the
At all times I was vigilant in their service
In short, I was ready to lay down my life for them

184. Kiya intizaam hum ne aisa wahaan
Ke haakim rahe raazi-o-meherbaan
I made such arrangements there
That the rulers remained gratified and agreeable

185. Rausa ataat mein haazir rahe
Paye jaan-nisaari woh maujood the
The rich were present in reverence
Due to loyalty, they were in attendance

186. Yeh hai Vinet Sahib pe bhi aashkaar
Nahin hai mera qaul beaitbaar
This is well known to Vinet Sahib also
That my narrative is beyond any doubt.

Intizaam Hukkaam-e-Aalishaan

Arrangement by the Grand Officers

187. Yahaan ke Collector bahut hain diler
Dileri-o-saulaak mein hain misl-e-sher
The Collector of this place is very courageous
In bravery and awe is like a lion

188. Bahut aman unke sabab se raha
Raiyyat ko aaraam un se mila
Great peace reigned because of him
The subjects received comfort from him

189. Nihaayat qavi-dil hain aur zeekhirad
Nigah par chadha rahta hai nek-o-bad
He is very strong-hearted and wise
His eyes can very well judge good or bad

190. Sar Farqadaan par hai paaye kamaal
Atuft se sharminda baad-e-shumaal
His head is positioned higher than the Farqadaan stars
The pleasant winds of the north are put to shame by his endowments

191. Session Judge jo hain yahaan ke aali tabaar
Governor ke nazdik hain bavaqaar
Session Judge of this place who is of noble descent
Is dignified in the eyes of the Governor

192. Nihaayat khiradmand-o-sahib sho'oor
Shujaat mein mashhoor nazdeek-o-dur
Extremely wise and master of competence
He is famous for bravery near and far

193. Khajal un se hai adl-e-Nausherwan
Ke sach hai kahan ye hain aur woh kahan
The Justice of Nausherwan is humbled by him
For it is true, there is no comparison between the two

194. Sakhaawat se Hatim ko sharmindagi
Hukumat mein Jam ko sarafkandagi
Hatim is embarrassed by his extreme generosity
Jamshed is worried on seeing his administration

195. Hain Vinet Bahadur Session Judge yahaan
Bahut himmat aali wa waalaa makaan
Vinet Bahadur is the Session Judge here
He is very courageous and highly placed

196. Aur Captaan Estabal shamil rahe
Arastu manash woh bhi aaqil rahe
And Captain Estabal is an accomplice
Like Aristotle he too is very wise

197. Patterson Magister Bahadur rahe
Har ek tarha se daad-e-gustar rahe
Patterson is the Magistrate Bahadur
In every way he dispensed justice

198. Un hi se hai ab adl ko zindagi
Sakhaawat ko unse hai deh-chandagi
Now equity is vivified because of him
Generosity is augmented ten times due to him

199. Koi sikhe ilm-o-hunar un se aa
Aristu manash kahiye to hai baja
One should come to acquire knowledge and skills from him
It is appropriate to call him one with Aristotle's temperament

200. Balinas kyon kar na shagird ho
Sabaq deven Buqraat-o-Suqraat ko
Why should Balinas not be his pupil?
He can impart lessons to Hippocrates and Socrates

201. Gaye pehle hukkaam pesh-e-sipah
Kaha apni chodo na tum sidhi raah
First the rulers went before the troops
Said do not leave your correct path

202. Kaji ka na pesha karo ikhtiyaar
Yehi tum se kahte hain hum baar-baar
Do not adopt fraudulent profession
This is what we tell you repeatedly

203. Ho jis ke muti us ke taabeh raho
Jo kehna ho tumko woh hum se kaho
Whoever's subordinate you are, remain obedient to them
Whatever you have to say, say to us

204. Qadam had se baahar na apne dharo
Abas aap se beajal mat maro
Do not set your foot beyond limits
Do not unnecessarily die without arrival of the hour of death

205. Ataat se aaqa ki baahar na ho
Tumhi sab khazana ke hafiz raho
Do not leave the services of your master
Persist in being protector of all treasures,

206. Agar uzr-e-beja koi laaoge
Baqaul-e-Nizami saza paaoge
If you will bring forth any improper plea
You will be punished as Nizami has said

207. Wagar na chunaanat daham gosh pech
Ke daani tuhichi wa kamtar zahech
If you do not listen to and ponder over this
Then you would be reduced to nothing and even worse

208. Chunanat daham malish az tegh-e-tez
Ke ya marg khwahi zaman ya guureez
I have sharpened my sword
So either be ready to die by my hands or escape

209. Yahaan tak sujhaya nasheb-o-faraaz
Ke aakhir ko raazi hue kinasaaz
Explained them the declivity and acclivity to this extent
So finally the malicious became somewhat agreeable

210. Muhaafiz hui maal ki woh sipah
Hui tab Gorakhpur mein kuch panah
Those troops became the protectors of wealth
Then Gorakhpur became a comparitively safe asylum

211. Lage sab ke sab rahne aaraam se
Lage kaam rakhne woh sab kaam se
Everyone started living comfortably
They all were busy with their own respective chores

212. Jo hukkaam aaye Faizabad se
Yahaan aman paya to bas shaad the
The officers who came from Faizabad
Were extremely happy to find peace here

213. Bahut Lucknow se bhi aaye chale
Woh Bansi ke Raja se aa kar mile
Many arrived from Lucknow also
They came and met the king of Bansi

214. Mila un ko aaraam wahaan beshtar
Na kuch jaan pe un ke aaya zarar
They derived extreme comfort there
No danger fell on their lives

215. Woh Raja-e-Bansi woh Gopalpur
Madadgaar ho kar rahe dar huzoor
That King of Bansi and that of Gopalpur
Became helpful and remained available for service of their masters

216. Padrona ka Raja madadgaar tha
Hamesha se hukkaam ka yaar tha
The King of Padrona was helpful
He had always been a friend of the rulers,

217. Hamesha ataat mein bandhe kamar
Raha mustaid kaam mein sarbasar
Was always ready for obedient service
Remained entirely active in his duties.

Kaifiyat Taaluqah Ganeshpur wa Bidat Qaum Gautam

State of the Taaluqah of Ganeshpur and heresy of the people of Gautam

218. Gorakhpur mein ek Ganeshpur hai
Yeh mauza bahut dur mashhoor hai
In Gorakhpur there is one Ganeshpur
This village is famous far and wide

219. Woh sabiq mein Gautam ke tha dakhal mein
Kuch haakim ne behtar samajh aql mein
In the past it was in possession of Gautam
The rulers, due to some better administrative understanding

220. Qadarbaksh Jamadaar ko de diya
Toh qabze se Gautam ke khaali kiya
Gave it to Qadarbaksh Jamadaar
So it was relieved of the occupation of Gautam

221. Bahut khoob the aadmi benazeer
Shreef-o-najeeb-o-sakhi-o-ameer
He was a very fine matchless man
Gentle, of noble birth, generous and rich

222. Amanullah ek unke dilband hain
Bahut maal-o-hashmat se khursand hain
One Amanullah is his son
Possessor of a lot of wealth and dignity, he is happy

223. Padi un pe bhi gardish-e-aasmaan
Kiya charkh ne un ko bekhanma
On him also fell the vicissitudes of fortunes
The heavens rendered him homeless

224. Yakayak nazar aaya jab inqalaab
Liya loot bar Gautamon ne shitaab
When an unexpected revolution came in sight
The followers of Gautam looted him

225. Badi se sipah ke khabardaar ho
Chale lootne unko taiyyaar ho
Being aware of the evil intentions of troops
They proceeded with preparations to loot him

226. Liya cheen mauza basad zoor-o-shoor
Jataya har ek gaunwale ko zoor
They seized the village very forcefully
Every villager was intimidated with violence

227. Sab asbaab aur maal ghaarat kiya
Khash-o-khaar tak le gaye behaya
All property and wealth was destroyed
The shameless took away even hay and thorns

228. Toh Amanullah ne aa kar hukkaam tak
Kiya arz aaghaaz-o-anjaam tak
So Amanullah came up to the rulers
Narrated details from the beginning till the end

229. Karega yeh jis waqt haakim khayaal
Talaf hoga us qaum ka jaan-o-maal
When the rulers shall take cognizance of this matter
Life and property of those people (Gautam's followers) shall be destroyed

230. Saza paawenge apne kirdaar ki
Saza paawenge apni raftaar ki
They will be punished for their character
They will be punished for their conduct

231. Bas ab aiye qalam mukhtasar kar bayaan
Ab aage khabar aur kuch kar ayaan
Enough now, O pen! Make the account brief
Now narrate some other news.

Kaifiyat Pandeypaar

Condition of Pandeypaar

232. Pandeypaar ka Babu azbas hai bad
Kiya loot par usne bhi jadd-o-kad
The Babu of Pandeypaar is quite notorious
He also made serious attempts to loot

233. Vinet Sahib ka maal kashti pe tha
Use us ne bekhauf ghaarat kiya
Vinet Sahib's belongings were on the boat
Which he fearlessly plundered

234. Aur Buran ka bhi maal sab le liya
Khataawaar hukkaam-e-aali hua
And by taking the goods of Buran also
He became a culprit of the lofty rulers

235. Kiya tang Raja-e-Betiyah ko bhi
Raaya ko us se azeeyat hui
He troubled the King of Betiyah too
Subjects were tormented by him

236. Hain Rajpurpaniya ke Babu kharaab
Zaroor un pe howe ga naazil azaab
The Babu of the Rajpurpaniya is bad
Definitely divine wrath will descend upon him

237. Bahut shorish un sab ne ki ja-ba-ja
Sitam aur balwa nihaayat kiya
They all created a lot of disturbances everywhere
Committed extreme atrocities and rioting

238. Baghaavat ke uski bhi azbas hai dhoom
Kharaabi ka baais hai jun boom shum
His rebellion is quite a popular talk of the town
The reasons for of this calamity are cycles of vicissitude, land and niggardliness

239. Badi par hua mustaid es qadar
Ke har ek ne us se kiya alhazar
He was so very prompt in evil
That every one became cautious and asked for God's protection

240. Baghaavat pe tha apni usko ghuroor
Woh jaayega ab Kalepani zaroor
He was arrogant about his rebellion
He shall definitely go to Kalapani now

241. Ajab tarha ka zulm us ne kiya
Ke ban kal ke jaane ke laaiq hua
He committed bizarre kind of brutalities
And easily deserves exile in darkness.

Khabar Zila Ghazipur Waghairah

News of the district of Ghazipur and other places

242. Aur aashoob se jo ki khaali raha
Use bhi batafseel maine likha
And that which remained free of uproar
That too I have written in detail

243. Sabhon par muqaddam raha Ghazipur
Bahut us ki shohrat hai nazdeek-o-dur
Ghazipur remained superior among all
Its fame extends near and far,

244. Wahaan ke rausa-e-aali nasab
Safadeed azla wala hasab
The nobles there are of high birth
Visionaries in those parts are of exalted lineage

245. Dilon se bhi hukkaam ke khairkhah
Nasibon mein un ke rahi waah-waah
From their hearts too they are well-wishers of the rulers
They are destined to get applauds and appreciation

246. Bulandi ka taaraa chamakta raha
Gul-e-shaadmaani gamakta raha
The star of elevation kept shining
The flower of happiness continued echoing fragrance

247. Doyum shahar aabaad tha Mirzapur
Hamesha barasta raha uspe noor
The second flourishing town was Mirzapur
Brilliance always kept raining upon it

248. Rahe apne sultan ke khairkhah
Duago-e-Haakim the shaam-o-pagah
Remained well-wishers of their sovereign
Prayed for the rulers dusk and dawn

249. Banaras jo Kaashi bhi mashhoor hai
Bahut naqd-o-daulat se maamur hai
Banaras, which is also famous as Kashi
Is entrusted with a lot of money and wealth

250. Yahaan ke bhi the log farmanpazeer
Ataat mein maujood the naguzeer
People of this place too were obedient
In submission they were also compliant

251. Balam teer paltan the wahaan par muqeem
Baghaavat par thi mustaid woh laeem
A spear-arrow troop was stationed there
That sordid lot was ready for rebellion

252. Khabar jab hui us ki hukkaam ko
Ghanimat samajh apne aalaam ko
When the rulers learnt of that
They considered their notification benedictory

253. Diya saari paltan ko fauran uda
Jo bach kar ke bhaage chupe ja-ba-ja
They immediately crushed the entire troop
Those who escaped alive hid hither and thither

254. Unhin shahroon mein haq ka afzaal tha
Ke English Bahadur ka iqbaal tha
In those towns, justice was excellent
For the English Bahadur were flourishing there

255. Ba fazl-e-Khuda khub tha intizaam
Ke hukkaam-e-English ka tha yahaan maqaam
By the grace of God, arrangements were excellent
Because the British rulers were stationed here

256. Rausa pe yahaan ke rahe fazl-e-Rabb
Riza-ju-e-hukkaam the sab ke sab
God's favours may remain on the rich here
All of them were seeking the good offices of the rulers

257. Ki do company Aare ne sarkashi
Abas apne haakim se baaghi hui
Two companies of Arrah revolted
Uselessly mutinied against their commander

258. Danapur mein teen paltan jo thi
Woh jab mustaid sarkashi par hui
The three troops which were at Danapur
When they became ready for rebellion

259. Toh ek fauz gore ki thi jo muqeem
Kiya saikdon ko unhoon ne doneem
One army of whites which was stationed there then
Slaughtered hundreds of them

260. Tillange bahut un se aari hue
Jo bach kar ke bhage faraari hue
Many native soldiers were rendered ineffectual by them
Those who decamped alive became fugitives

261. Aur Patna mein do company jo rahi
Raiyyat ko unse azeeyat mili
And the two companies which were in Patna
Subjects were traumatized by them

262. Kunwar Singh Babu tha Jagdishpur
Hua dur us ke bhi chehre ka noor
Kunwar Singh was the Babu of Jagdishpur
His face also lost its radiance

263. Muqabil na sarkaar se ho saka
Toh Dilli ka usne bhi rastaa liya
He could not confront the government
So he too took the route to Delhi

264. Bhatija jo uska tha ek Har Kishan
Khasumat ki uske hui dil mein daman
One Har Kishan who was his nephew
A detritus of antagonism grew in his heart

265. Gaya apne kaka ke humraah woh
Ab aage ka ahwaal jo ho so ho
He went along with his uncle
Now whatever shape circumstances may take, let them take.

Bayaan Himaaqat-e-Rajgaan

Narrative of the foolishness of Kings

266. Batafseel likhun chand ashkhaas ko
Mumaiyyaz karun aam se khaas ko
I am writing in detail about some persons
To differentiate the ordinary from the extraordinary

267. Unhun ki himaaqat karun ab raqam
Jise likh ke sharminda howe qalam
I am now describing their irrationality
In writing which the pen is embarrassed

268. Narharpur ka Raja hai bekhirad
Nihaayat safih abla-o-pur hasad
The King of Narharpur is unwise
Very mean, gullible and full of jealousy

269. Hai Neelpur ka Raja bhi waisa hi
Hamesha hai shaitaan ka dil se rahi
The King of Neelpur is also the same
His heart has always pledged loyalty to Satan

270. Abhi toh bahut khurram-o-shaad hain
vale thode hi din mein barbaad hain
Currently they are very euphoric and cheerful,
But in a few days they will be ruined

271. Bahud jald paawen woh ab intiqaam
Karen asfalus safilin mein maqaam
May they now soon enough suffer vengeance
May they take up residence amongst the most mean!

Hikayat Mushtamil Barchand Kawaif

Narrative based upon certain circumstances

272. Yahaan se hai ab chaudhween ka bayaan
Hua hum pe zahir jo raaz-e-nihaan
From here starts the description of the fourteenth
When hidden facts came to my knowledge

273. Mahina tha ziqaad ka sahibo
Kuch us rooz ki kaifiyat ab suno
O Sahibs! It was the month of ziqaad
Now listen to the situation of that day,

274. Kaha hum se sahib ne ye besh-o-kam
Ke afwaaj-e-haakim se hai yeh sitam
Sahib said this to me, more or less
That this tyranny is due to the armed forces of the rulers

275. Ab un fitna keshoon ki hai justaju
Unhi ki hai talaash ab chaar su
Now the hunt is on for those mischief mongers
They are now being pursued in all four directions

276. Jo hai bhi koi yahaan toh ruposh hai
Har ek misl-e-tasveer khaamosh hai
If anyone at all is here, he is absconding
Everyone is silent like a picture,

277. Magar yeh to Meerut se eijaad hai
Dil-e-Company jis se naashaad hai
But this is a contrivance from Meerut
With whom the Company's heart is displeased

278. Doyum bar Dehli se mashhoor hai
Zabaan par sabhon ke yeh mazkoor hai
The second phase is well-known to be from Delhi
This is on everyone's tongue

279. Magar pahle Hindu se eijaad hai
Hunudoon se awwal mein buniyaad hai
But first the Hindus concocted it
The Hindus are at the foremost foundation

280. Vale yeh na tahqiq hum ko hui
Ke baais kharaabi ki kya baat thi
Though I did not research this issue
What was the problem that caused this destruction?

281. Sabab kaun sa barhami ka hua
Qadam had se kyun sab ne baahar dhara
What was the reason for this antagonism?
Why did everyone step beyond their limits?

282. Kiya dushmani apni kyun jaan se
Mubaddal kiya dil ko kyun shaan se
Why did they become adversaries of their own life?
Why did they take pride in their change of heart?

283. Magar es qadar zehan mein aa gaya
Ke jo kuch kiya fahm-e-bad ne kiya
However, this much my mind was able to understand
That whatever happened was due to misunderstanding

284. Woh samjhe ke tonti mein kuch tha laga
Agarche haqiqat mein woh saaf tha
They thought something was stuck on the spout
Although in reality it was clean

285. Daghaa aur daghal ki zaroorat na thi
Na thi dain par khwahish-e-Company
There was no need for betrayal and hypocrisy
The Company did not wish to be a liability

286. Hamesha se haakim ko hai yeh khayaal
Ke mazhab kisi ka na ho paimaal
The rulers have always had this consideration
That no religion should be crushed

287. Hamesha aanat hai hukkaam se
Ke bigde na Hindu-o-Islam se
The rulers have always enforced that
There be no unpleasantness with Hinduism or Islam

288. Alawah dalilon ke samjho zara
Meri baat mein kuch nahin hai daghaa
Understand the reason for my arguments
There is no deception in my narrative

289. Haqiqat ko karta hoon main aashkaar
Zara esko dil mein samajh bavaqaar
I am disclosing the truth
Do understand the gravity of the matter in your heart

290. Ke lisai mazhab mein aiye zeesho'oor
Jehadat-e-saifi nahin kuch zaroor
O sensible one! That in the Christian religion
There definitely is no concept of religious wars of malediction

291. Faqat daawat-o-iltimaas sareeh
Bafahwaiye Injeel aaya sahi
There is only invitation and outright entreaty
In the pages of the Bible it is mentioned correctly

292. Paye mazhab-e-lisi ba safa
Sabhi zulm-o-bidat hue narawa
In the pursuit of Christian religion with immaculateness
All tyranny and heresy become unjustified

293. Toh ab puchta hai yeh tum se faqir
Ke kya baat thi unki mafiz zameer
So now this mendicant asks of you,
What was the substance in their design?

294. Magar haan ye nahaq ki ek ched thi
Dilon ki thi khwahish hui jo hui
But of course this was an unnecessary vexation
It was the whim and fancy of hearts, whatever it was,

295. Shikaayat hai nahaq ye sarkaar ki
Tillangon ne ki raah paikaar ki
This is an unjustified grievance against the government,
The native soldiers went on a warpath

296. Jo log aake aise hue muttafiq
Unhon ne bhi samjhi na kuch us ki shaq
Those who came to be agreeable with this
They too did not comprehend its flaw

297. Khabar sunte hi sahib-e-shar hue
Musalman bhi misl-e-akhgar hue
On hearing the news they at once became masters of wickedness
Muslims also became like live ashes

298. Namak-khaar-e-sarkaar jo log the
Unhi se yeh sab fitne barpa hue
Those who were bred by the government's money
Were the ones who caused these seditious mischiefs

299. Namak ka nahin paas aaya zara
Nahin dil mein un sab ke khauf-e-Khuda
Did not have any regard for allegiance at all
None of them have any fear of God in their hearts

300. Magar baaz un mein se the khairkhah
Chale apne siyar se sadaaqat ki raah

However some among them were well-wishers
Because of their character they trod the path of fidelity

301. Chale jitne hi woh baraah-e-nifaaq
Sabhon ko hai es amr par ittifaaq
All those who have started on the path of hypocrisy
Have consensus of opinion in this affair

302. Bache baaz, baaz unmen mare gaye
Magar Hinduon mein toh sare gaye
Some were saved and some among them were killed
However, among the Hindus all were liquidated

303. Dilon se bhi badkhaah sarkaar hain
Vale sab ke sab ab giraftaar hain
From the core of their hearts, they are also ill-wishers of the government
But now all of them have been arrested

304. Yeh un sab ke naamon ki tafseel hai
Bura kyon na jaane jo koi sune
These are the details of their names,
Why should any listener not consider them to blame?

305. Baaghi Munsifon mein Salamat Ali
Khabar hum ko aiye sahibon ye mili
Among the Munsifs, Salamat Ali is a rebel
O Sahibs, I got this information

306. Allahabad ka yeh toh Munsif raha
Tillangon ka damsaaz yeh bhi hua
He was a Munsif of Allahabad
He too became a companion of the native soldiers

307. Rahe Murtaza Khan Allahabad mein
Qadam apna rakha tha afsaad mein
Murtaza Khan was in Allahabad
He had set his foot in quarrels

308. Abul Qasim tha ek Sadr-us-Sudur
Dipty Hikmatullah Khan tha Fatehpur
Abul Qasim was one Sadr-us-Sudur
Hikmatullah Khan was a Deputy in Fatehpur

309. Woh Kanpur ka Dipty tha Ramlal
Abas apna khote the sab jaah-w-maal
That Ramlal was the Deputy of Kanpur
Suddenly they were squandering all their life and property

310. Rahe ek Dipty jo Sardaar Khan
Tu bhai ko bhi uske baaghi mein jaan
There was one Deputy called Sardaar Khan
You can count his brother also among the rebels

311. Ke ban kar ke haakim hue sab kharaab
Namakkhar ho ke phanse dar azaab
In spite of being administrators they all became guilty
Despite being faithful earlier, they were trapped in misfortune

312. Jo mulla-o-pundit ke dam mein pade
Aql aur faham kya na rakhte rahe
Those who were duped by the boastfulness of Hindu and
Muslim priests
Did they not possess any intellect and perception?

313. Nana Rao Bithur ka hai shareer
Thode rooz mein woh bhi hoga asir
Nana Rao of Bithur is mischevious
In a few days he too shall be imprisoned

314. Raha ahle pension bhi sarkaar ka
Woh mardud bhi ziyadah baaghi bana
He was also a pensioner of the government
That reprobate too became an extreme rebel

315. Jagah yeh hai thodi si insaaf ki
Bhala unko zeba yeh hi baat thi

This is an occasion which calls for some justice
Was this behaviour elegant enough for him?

316. Ke ahsaan-e-nemat ko ekbargi
Dilon se bhula deven sun kar sabhi
That impulsively the favour of blessings
May be erased from everyone's benumbed hearts on hearing

317. Es tarha kufraan-e-nemat karen
Khusumat se dushman se ja kar milen
That in this manner they should be thankless
Due to enmity, they should align with the contenders

318. Rahen mustaid qatal-e-hukkaam par
Dilon se bhula den karam sarbasar
That they should be ready to annihilate the rulers
That they should entirely dismiss graciousness from their hearts

319. Magar haan jo likha tha taqdeer ka
Woh sab hone wala tha aakhir hua
But yes! Whatever was written by divine fate
All that had to materialize, eventually it happened

320. Magar us ka mansoob hai aadmi
Siwa us ke kuch gardish iflaak ki
But it is attributed to man
Besides that, to some rotational positioning of heavenly spheres

321. Karoon ataf yahaan se anaan-e-qalam
Karoon mukhtasar ab main tul-e-raqam
From here I turn the reigns of the pen
Now I make cursory the prolixity of narrative

322. Khasumat talab jo hain sarkaar ke
Sar unke sazawaar hain daar ke
Those who are soliciting enmity of the government
Their heads deserve the gibbet

323. Sare jahilaan bar sar-e-daar ba
Ke jahil bakhwari giriftaar ba
Heads of the uncouth deserve to be hung on the gibbet
It is appropriate to dishonor and arrest them

324. Rahe jab talak gardish-e-aasmaan
Munawwar hai khur se zameen-o-zamaan
Until the moment the sky is in motion
Earth and times are illuminated by the sun

325. Rahe mulk qabza mein sarkaar ke
Raiyyat ko aaraam un se mile
May the state remain in possession of the government
May the subjects receive comfort through them

326. Sar-e-daar par khasam ho sarfaraaz
Yeh hai khwahish-e-Ahmad paakbaaz
May the enemies' head be raised to hang on a gibbet
This is the wish of Ahmad, the undefiled one

327. Yahaan par hua jab ke khatm-e-bayaan
Toh Sahib gaye yahaan se apne makaan
When the narrative ended here
Then Sahib went from here to his house

328. Toh phir haakimon ne kiya sarfaraaz
Raha mustaid main baijz-o-niyaaz
So then the rulers exalted me
I remained prompt with humbleness and deference

329. Laga karne main unse baaham salaah
Ke maalum hoti hai es mein falaah
I started mutual consultations with them
This appears to be the means for accomplishment

330. Bahut khub ye amr hai beguzand
Kahun aap ko garche aawe pasand
This matter is indeed very interesting and harmless
I may articulate it if you like

331. Na do ikhtiyaar aisa tum fauj ko
Munasib hai goron ko afsar karo
You do not give such power to the army
It is expedient that the whites be appointed as officers

332. Subedaar na aur Jamadaar ho
Koi Hindiyon mein na sardaar ho
Should neither be a Subedaar nor a Jamadaar
No one among the Hindustanis should be a commander

333. Rahen gore har mulk mein beshtar
Es tarha har shahar mein ho guzar
In every state let there stay numerous whites
In this manner let every town have arrangements

334. Hindustani paltan jahan ek ho
Wahaan panch sau gore hon sahibon
Wherever there may be one Hindustani platoon
Sahib, at least five hundred whites may be posted there

335. Bandobast es dhab ka daayam rahe
Na daawa koi humsari ka kare
This type of arrangement may be perpetual
No one may make any claims of equivalence

336. Kisi shah ko raja ko sarwat na ho
Ke bandhe kamar apne taaraaj ko
No monarch or king may have riches
That he may set out to plunder

337. Jo hum kar chuke haakimon se bayaan
Woh hi hum ne captaan se ki ayaan
Whatever I have expounded before the rulers
The same I elucidated before the Captain

338. Jo es waqt mein khairkhahi kare
Maraatib-o-ezaaz us ka rahe
Those who wish well at this juncture
Offices and awards may be endowed upon them

339. Aur do company jo khazana par hain
Karo bartaraf naukri se unhen
And the two companies which have the treasure
Should be dismissed from service

340. Talab de ke un sab ko rukhsat karo
Batadbeer aalaat-e-jungi ko lo
Give their salary and discharge them
With tactful strategy seize weapons of war

341. Kaha maine jo kuch woh aaya pasand
Kaha sab ne yeh baat hai beguzand
Whatever homily I gave was appreciated
Every one said that this suggestion is salubrious.

Hikayat Sawaraan Sogoi

Report of the Cavalry of Sogoi

342. Sogoi mein bhi ek risala raha
Risala ne bhi wahaan ke fitna kiya
There was one squadron in Sogoi too
The squadron of that place also undertook devilment

343. Bigad kar Salimpur aaye chale
Khazana ke lene pe dil ko dhare
By rebelling they came away to Salimpur
With a heartfelt desire to seize the treasure

344. Sawaaron ne haakim se ki hai daghaa
Hue mustaid woh baraah-e-vaghaa
The cavalry has betrayed the rulers
They are speedily set on the path of battle

345. Khazana ko chaha ke ghaarat karen
Zard naqad haath aaye to raah len
They wished to plunder the treasury
And set out after securing the gold and cash

346. Salimpur mein jangi jo thi sipah
Hui apne sarkaar ki khairkhah
The military troops which were in Salimpur
Became approbative of their government

347. Sipahi jo pahra pe maujood tha
Khazana ko unko na lene diya
The soldiers who were present on guard
Did not allow them to capture the treasure

348. Kiya khairkhahi se anjaamkaar
Ke jurrat se unki hue sab faraar
With solicitousness they successfully terminated
And because of their courage, all fled

349. Pashemaan ho kar ke raahi hue
Khuda jaane aage kidhar ko gaye
On being disgraced they became vagabonds
God knows where in future they did go!

Hikayat Afwaaj-e-Nepal

Report of the Armies of Nepal

350. Suno thodi Nepal ki kaifiyat
Yahaan se hai uska bayaan-e-sifat
Listen to some incidents from Nepal
From here starts the description of its attributes

351. Hamesha se hai rasm-e-Shahanshahaan
Mohabbat se karte hain kaar-e-jahan
It has always been the manner of emperors
To execute worldly business with fondness

352. Madad ek ki ek karta raha
Hamesha se yeh qaida hai bandha
Each one helps the other one
It has always been an established practice

353. Aanat talab jab hui Company
Toh afwaaj-e-Raja wahaan se chali
When the Company was in need of support
Then the armies of the King proceeded from there

354. Adad mein woh paltan hai sab chaar dah
Jo yeh rashq-e-khur hain toh woh rashq-e-maah
In numbers that troop is all four tens
If these are the envy of the sun, then those are the envy of the moon

355. Chali fauz Nepal bejadd-o-kad
Toh pahuncha mere paas hukm-e-rasad
The army of Nepal set off effortlessly
Then an order for provisions reached me

356. Rasad ke liye ek shuqqah likha
Jo kuch tha zaroori so maine diya
Wrote a letter for supplies
Thus whatever was necessary I provided

357. Hua jab ke Pipraich mein aa maqaam
Bakhubi rasad ka kiya intizaam
When there was a sojourn at Pipraich
I made excellent arrangements for rations

358. Bahut fauj ko maine raazi kiya
Zaroori jo kuch chahiye sab diya
I made the army very happy
Provided whatever essentials were required

359. Talab gaadiyon ko bhi mujh se kiya
Aur shuqqah mein mazmoon aisa likha
Asked me to supply vehicles also
And wrote such matter in the letter

360. Jo mumkin ho gaadi ilaaqah se do
Ke es waqt sarkaar ka kaam ho
If obtainable, arrange for vehicles from the region
So that the government's mission may be accomplished at this time

361. Kiya main ne gaadi ka bhi intizaam
Bakhubi kiya us ka bhi insiraam
I arranged for the vehicles too
Managed that also very well

362. Sowum maah Zilhijja es shahar mein
Hua hukm kuch rooz es ja rahen

On the third of the month of Zilhijja, in this town
It was ordered that they stay here for a few days

363. Yeh Nepal se yoon hi aayee chali
Ke kaali ghata jaise chayee chali
They had forged ahead from Nepal in such a way
As if black clouds had overcast the sky

364. Sawaaron ka captaan humraah tha
Azakhana se mere aagaah tha
The Captain of the cavalry who came along with them
Was aware of my mourning house

365. Hifazat ki payee jo us ne jagah
Toh sab aa gaye meri pesh-e-nigah
When he found a secure place
They all came under the umbrella of my protection

366. Kahun kya main afwaaj ki kaifiyat
Karun kis zabaan se main un ki sifat
What should I say about the features of the army?
With what words can I convey their praise?

367. Har ek rashk-e-Sohrab ba-zhiyaan sipah
Jise dekh Rustam kahe waah-waah
Each one is the envy of Sohrab; very ferocious troops
On beholding whom Rustam would exclaim: Excellent! Bravo!

368. Chali aayee thi fauj sab joq-joq
Khushi se bajati hui tabl-o-boq
Multitude after multitude of the army began to enter
Playing clarions and tambourines with exhilaration

369. Za naqqara aawaaz aamad biroon
Ke gar doon-doon ast gar daun-daun
Their arrival is announced by the sound of the drum
The drummer is boastful and bragging, even though the way
is scorching hot

370. Kaha zer se bam ne bahre shakoon
Na doon doon khushi se khabar kyon na doon
From the low to the high, every beat said
Not muffled-murmurs, why should I not announce with happiness?

371. Sowum ko to ek paltan aayi yahaan
Ke jiska kiya maine aage bayaan
On the third, one troop reached here
Which I have described earlier

372. Batareekh panjam wagar paan sad
Jo peeche se unke woh the be adad
On the fifth came additional five hundred troops
Those following them were innumerable

373. Ba maidaan shud istaadah khiyaam
Dar unja giraftah hamah ha qiyaam
Tents have been put up in the grounds
Where everyone has encamped

374. Shudah dast-e-afwaaj za an jumla tan
Pur az nafa-e-mushk Cheen-o-Khutan
Hands of the bodies who came in those armies
Had fragrance of the musk of China and Khutan

375. Shusham ko chali aayi yahaan sari fauj
Koi fard-fard aur koi zoj-zoj
On the sixth, the whole army came here
Some one by one and some couple by couple

376. Pade tambu shamiyane baham
Gaye sare dushman ba-su-e-adam
Tents and canopies were put up together
All enemies were reduced to nothingness

377. Sab aalaat-e-jungi maujood the
Jo us dam zaroori-o-maqsood the

All instruments of war were available
Which at that moment were essential and objective

378. Bhujali jo khaas un ka hathiyaar hai
Bure waqt mein un ka woh yaar hai
Bhujali, which is their special weapon
In adverse times it is their friend

379. Har ek ke hai kandhe pe jungi tufang
Girane mein dushman ke hai bedirang
On each one's shoulder is a fighting musket
In laying the enemies its speed is reckless

380. Siyaah paijama siyaah mirzai
Yeh Nepaliyon ki hai wardi bani
Black trousers, black loose-sleeved quilted waist-coat;
This is the uniform of the Nepalese

381. Siyaah unke sar ke bhi dastaar hain
Siyaah qalb dushman se paikaar hai
The turbans on their heads are also black
In war they are pitted against black-hearted enemies

382. Woh chota sa qad aur chandi ka chand
Jise dekh khursheed rah jaye mand
That short height and silvery forehead
On viewing which the sun would also be left weary.

Hikayat Shujaat Hukkaam

Report of the Bravery of Rulers

383. Karun maajra-e-nahum ab raqam
Dikhaun zara apna zoor-e-qalam
Now I narrate the occurrence of the ninth
Let me reveal some power of my pen,

384. Nahum maah-e-Zilhijja thi aiye basher
Ke di Ramjimal ne mujh ko khabar
It was the ninth of the month of Zilhijja, O men!
That Ramjimal gave me the information

385. Yahaan ke sab hukkaam hain purkhirad
Hukumat mein hain vaaqif-e-nek-o-bad
All the officers of this place abound in intelligence
In governance they are well acquainted with good and bad

386. Hain Vinet Bahadur Session Judge Diler
Patterson Magister bhi hain misl-e-sher
Vinet Bahadur Session Judge is courageous
Patterson Magistrate also is like a lion

387. Hain Captaan Astayal Rustam khisaal
Bird Sahib hain gent bas bemisaal
Captain Astayal has the traits of Rustam's character,
Bird Sahib is simply an incomparable gentleman

388. Aur hain Brackley Sahib hoshmand
Aur hain Padri Sahib arjmand
And Brackley Sahib is sensible
And Padri Sahib is noble

389. Kiya hoshiyaari se woh ehtimaam
Hua khair-o-khubi se sab intizaam
With intelligence they made such arrangements
That the administration was managed with goodness and safety,

390. Jo bigde hue the khazana pe log
Laga jaan jaane ka har ek ko rog
Those who had become debauched over the treasure
In fact they all were masochistically nursing a fatal illness

391. In hukkaam ne ja ke afwaaj ka
Sab aalaat-e-jungi ko bas le liya
These officers embarked towards the armies
Simply seized the entire weaponry of war

392. Tillangon se aalaat-e-jungi ko le
Aur farkhandagi se talab un ki de
Acquired the weapons of war from the native soldiers
And with opportuneness gave them their emoluments

393. Khushi se Tillangon ko rukhsat kiya
Tillangon ne bhi dam na mara zara
Disbanded the native soldiers buoyantly
The soldiers too were unable to protest at all

394. Khazana pe Gorkha ka pehra kiya
Muhaafiz unhen maal ka kar diya
Deputed the Gorkhas to guard the treasure
Made them the defenders of riches

395. Bahut khoob yeh ho gaya intizaam
Yeh hukkaam ke wasf ka hai maqaam
Thus a very brilliant arrangement was made
This is an occasion to eulogize the rulers

396. Jawanmardi-o-buzdili dekh kar
kachahri ko barkhwast amlon ne kar
On weighing well, gallantry and dastardliness
The staffers dismissed the courts

397. Khatarnaak ghar apne aaye chale
Khazana ke dar par the Munshi khade
Came back to their home in danger
The clerk was stationed at the portal of the treasury

398. Aur daftar ke hafiz bhi the woh bashar
Bila shaibah yeh qissa hai mukhtasar
And that man was also the guardian of the office
Without doubt this narrative is laconic

399. Khuda ka sawaaron pe tha kuch gazab
Bigad kar woh purab chale sab ke sab
God was also angry with the cavalry
After vitiation they proceeded eastwards

400. Bahut us mein dhau suthra maare gaye
Jo baqi the bhaage woh jaan ko liye
Many among them were killed in the wheel of massacre
Those who survived fled to save their lives

401. Magar woh gaaye taabe Mansurganj
Nahin aage malum kuch unka ranj
But they went upto not less than Mansurganj
I do not know more of their toil

402. Kiya un sawaaron se har ek ko dur
Magar woh jo thode se the dar huzoor
Everyone of those cavalry men was dispelled
Except some who were in attendance

403. Rahe unse hukkaam khushnood sab
Dilon se mita unke ranj-o-taab
All the rulers were pleased with them
Agony and exhaustion was erased from their hearts

404. Woh sab khairkhahi mein haazir rahe
Har ek kaam mein apne maahir rahe
All of them were present in well-intentioned spirit
Remained adept in each of their assignments

405. Nihaayat dileri ki hukkaam ne
Ke jana unhen khaas aur aam ne
The rulers exhibited extreme courage
So that everyone, exceptional and unexceptional acknowledged them

406. Satrahween thi jab maah-e-Zilhijja ki
Toh Gorkhon ki paltan rawaana hui
When it was the seventeenth of the month of Zilhijja
Then the troops of Gorkhas set forth

407. Azamgarh rawaana hue paanch sad
Adu se chali ladne be jadd-o-kad
Five hundred departed for Azamgarh
Proceeded to fight the enemy without exertion and stress

408. Chale unke peche se phir paanch sad
Rahi haakimon par Khuda ki madad
After them set off another five hundred
The rulers were backed by God's assistance

409. Na rakhenge yeh log peeche qadam
Khuda ka rahe unpe fazl-o-karam
These people will never step back in their gait
May God's mercy and benevolence persist on them.

Hikayat Rubkaar Committee

Report of the Warrant Committee

410. Attharah sai sattawan thi Isvi
Ke hukkaam ne rubkaari likhi
The year was eighteen hundred and fifty seven Isvi
When the rulers composed legal orders

411. Aur taarikh thi seezdah yaar ghaar
Mahina tha us dam August aashkaar
And the date was the thirteenth, O sincere friend!
It clearly was the month of August

412. Woh Bansi ke Raja jo hain bavaqaar
Satasi ke Raja duvam purghayaar
That King of Bansi who is dignified
Secondly, the King of Satasi who has a keen sense of honour

413. Sivum Raja jo yahaan hain Gopalpur
Safai se hain dil ke woh darhuzoor
Thirdly, the King of Gopalpur who is here,
Being pure of heart, he is in attendance

414. Chahaarum Majholi ke Raja jo the
Khushi dil se haakim ke taabe rahe
Fourth was the King of Majholi
Remained obedient towards the ruler with beatific heart

415. Namkoi ka Raja raha paanchwaan
Committee mein hukkaam ne yak zabaan
The King of Namkoi was the fifth one;
In the Committee the rulers unanimously

416. Unhi ko zila ka diya ikhtiyaar
Ke taa mere aate raho hoshiyaar
Gave the management of the town to them
That until we arrive remain prudently cautious

417. Hui rubkaari yeh hukkaam ki
ijaazat di Raja ko anjaam ki
This was the decree of the rulers
The kings were empowered for governance

418. Bahut maal-o-daulat khazana mein tha
Raaya pe baqi tha kuch ja-ba-ja
A lot of wealth and money was in the treasury
Some arrears were due from subjects here and there

419. Diya hukm-e-tahsil be jadd-o-kad
Bahut naukaron ki hai dee thi madad
Gave orders for revenue collection without exertion
A lot of help had been granted through employees

420. Diya hukm jo kuch zaroorat rahe
Bamujib zaroorat ke naukar rakhe
Gave directives that whatever may be the requirements
In accordance with those necessities, servants may be employed

421. Karen eska anjaam hoshiyaar ho
Ke ta aate haakim ke sab kaar ho
This must be executed with circumspection
So that before the arrival of the rulers all tasks should be accomplished

422. Hua munkashif jab committee ka haal
Hui sab ke dil ko musarrat kamaal

When the particulars of the Committee were disclosed
Everyone's heart was extremely pleased

423. Ke hukkaam goo chodte hain zila
Karenge phir aakar ese muntaza
That even though the rulers are evacuating the district
They shall again come back to manage it

424. Humari sipar honge rajwade paanch
Kisi tarha ki ab na aayegi aanch
Our shield would be the five kings
No harm of any kind shall come now

425. Diya unko har tarha ka ikhtiyaar
Muti unke hain sab saghaar-o-kabaar
Granted them all kinds of powers
All inferiors and dignitaries are submissive to them

426. Kisi par karega na koi sitam
Rahega Khuda ka hamesha karam
No one shall behave tyrannously towards another
God's mercy shall always remain extant

427. Chalenge wohi log sabiq ki chaal
Bandobast agla rahega bahaal
The same people will work in the former manner
Earlier arrangements shall remain unaltered

428. Jo ban kar ke Nazim yahaan aaye ga
Sazaa apni sabqat ki woh paye ga
Whoever will come here as a self-proclaimed administrator
He shall be punished for his initiative

429. Ba waqt-e-muhim honge hum sab shareek
Samayee thi dil mein bhi yeh baat theek
At the time of an enterprise, we all shall cooperate
This idea also was rightly accommodated in the heart

430. Magar haif-o-sad-haif wa hasrata
Na aamaadah raja hue mutlaqa

But Alas! For shame! How unfortunate!
The kings were not persistent in the least

431. Agar kaash aa jate es shahar mein
Yeh haq hai na padta koi qahar mein
Only if they had come to this town
It is true that no one would have been entrapped in catastrophe

432. Jo aamaadah rajwade hote zara
toh kyon aata yahaan Nazim behaya
Had the kings made a little steelier preparations
Then how would have the shameless Nazim dared to come here?

433. Woh haibat se dariya ke us paar tha
Idhar aane mein usko inkaar tha
Due to fear he was on the other side of the river
He disapproved of coming towards this side

434. Faqat teen sau aadmi the udhar
Taarruz jo hota na aata idhar
Merely three hundred men were there
Had there been opposition he would not have come this side

435. Jo aaya yahaan zalim badgumaan
Sarasar yeh hai ghaftal-e-rajgaan
The fact that the distrustful brute came here
This entirely is resultant from the negligence of the kings

436. Kahenge yeh munsif jo hain ghaur kar
Hai rajon ki es mein khataa sarbasar
Those who are fair-minded shall say after pondering
That the kings were completely at fault in this

437. Kiya rubkaari ke baraks kaam
Kisi ne na dala idhar ek gaam
Executed an antithesis of the warrant,
No one set a single foot here

438. Wahin raj mein aish karte rahe
Yahaan zulm se log marte rahe
Kept luxuriating there, in their kingdoms
Here people were dying of brutality

439. Taghaaful kiya nazm mein es qadar
Macha unki susti se yeh sab ghadar
Were so very apathetically detached from the arrangements
That all this mutiny was caused due to their lethargy

440. Magar jaa-e-afsos hai doostaan
ke jab reh ke raja sab yakzabaan
But this is a grievous situation, O friends!
That all the kings despite being unanimous

441. Taarruz mein zalim ke yakbargi
Yeh ghaflat unhoon ki sarasar hui
In confrontation with the cruel, suddenly
They were absolutely negligent

442. Yeh ghaflat hai raja ki bas aashkaar
Nahin jurm kuch doosroon ka hai yaar
This indifference of the kings is very obvious
O friend!
There is no misdemeanour on the part of anyone else

443. Kamarbasta dil se woh rahte agar
Toh aabaad rahta zila sarbasar
Had they been enthusiastic from the core of their hearts
Then the town would have remained in a state of flourish always

444. Satasi ka Raja tha sab mein shareer
Phira hukm-e-haakim se woh naguzeer
The King of Satasi was most notorious
He acted in contravention of the orders of the rulers, indispensably

445. Musharraf Khan tha ek qaidi yahaan
Ke muddat se tha qaid-e-bekhaanumaan

Musharraf Khan was a prisoner here
For ages he had been a captive of vagabondness

446. Makaan us ka Balwa ke mauza mein tha
Nihaayat safi abla-o-behaya
His house was in the village of Balwa
He was extremely daft, unreasonable and shameless

447. Woh raja ki janib se mukhtaar ho
Gaya pesh moozi ke sardaar ho
He, as an agent from the side of the king
Went before the obnoxious as a leader

448. Zila ke the maalik yehi paanch-chah
Raha hanth mein sab sufaid-o-siyaah
These five-six kings were the proprietors of the town
In their hands lay absolute power

449. Satasi ka Raja hua purghuroor
Woh haakim se karne laga makr-o-zoor
The King of Satasi became arrogant
He began exerting deceit and power over the rulers

450. Rahe muntazir uske hukkaam sab
Na haazir hua haif woh beadab
All rulers were awaiting him
But, alas! That impudent one did not present himself

451. Musharraf ki had se shararat rahi
Wohi baat us se bhi zahir hui
Musharraf's mischievousness was beyond limits
The same concept was displayed through him also

452. Nahin zeher mein qand ka kuch maza
Miyan Shaikh Saadi ne sach hai kaha
In poison, there is no taste of sugar at all
Miyan Shaikh Saadi has truly stated

453. Darakhte Zaqqoom az bajaan parwari
Mapandara hargiz kazo bar khuri

No matter how much of effort you put in gardening the Cactus tree
You can never ever eat its fruit!

454. Woh tha jaisa waisa kiya usne dol
Hai es jaa pe Firdausi Tusi ka qaul
He acted in a fashion complementary with his personality
Appropriate for this situation is an utterance of Firdausi Tusi:

455. Darakht ke talkh ast-o-yara sar shust
Gar arsh bar nishaani ba baagh-e-bahisht
Qualities of a bitter tree shall not change
Even though it may be a souvenir of the garden of heaven

456. Daraaze ju khuldash ba hungamee aab
Bebayakh angbeeni rezi wa sheer naab
Even if you water its roots with the liquid of heavenly streams
And with the sweetest honey and purest milk

457. Sar anjame gauhar bakar aawarad
Human mewa-e-talkh bar aawarad
The final result of this superficial care will be nothing
Lacking natural flow of sweetness the fruit shall still be bitter

458. Zabad asal chashm bhi daashtan
Bood khaak dar deedah apnaa shatan
No matter how beautiful a base born person's eyes might be
Nevertheless they would be full of the dust of evil.

Hikayat Baghaavat Taman-w-Ghaaratgaraan

Report of the Revolt of Troops and Plunderers

459. Naya ek ghazab us ne barpa kiya
Taman ke na logon ko jaane diya
A new dilemma was created by him
He did not allow the troops to go

460. Bird ka yeh tha qasad aiye sahibo
Ke gorkhon ke lashkar se chalkar milo
O Sahibs! This was the proposal of Bird
To go and join with the armed forces of Gorkhas

461. Taman ne Musharraf se saazish kiya
Bird ke na humraah koi gaya
The troops conspired with Musharraf
No one proceeded with Bird

462. Bura kaam sab par ziyaadah kiya
Ke aaqa ko naukar na bayyine diya
The worst of all the things done
The servant gave no reason for noncompliance to his master

463. Chale jab ke hukkaam aali maqaam
Chute yahaan ke mahbas ke qaidi tamaam
When the senior rulers departed
All the captives in the prison here became free

464. Bahut rahzan-o-saariq-o-badmaash
Lage maal mardum ke karne talaash
Many highway robbers, thieves and immoral rogues
Started scrutinizing the belongings of people

465. Kiya tabetra mein ghaaratgari
Hui haanth se unke wahaan abtari
Saturated with power, they plundered
Their hands caused ruination

466. Siwa unke tha ek unka chacha
Ke shaitaan bhi us se sharminda tha
Besides them, there was an uncle of their's
Such that the Satan was also ashamed of him

467. Yahaan se suno aur logon ka haal
Bas ab doosre haal mein hai yeh qaal
From here on, listen to the news of other people
So now in the other situation, these are the facts:

468. Madapaar Balwa ka Babu jo tha
Bahut usne Kosamhi ko ghaarat kiya
One who was the Babu of Madapaar Balwa
He ransacked Kosamhi to the extreme limit

469. Mawari bhi tha Talibabad ka
Bhavabarh ka Babu humraah tha
Mawari of Talibabad was also there
Babu of Bhavabarh was an accomplice

470. Woh Domri ke Babu jo the naabkaar
Bandhu Singh maa apne sab pattidaar
That Babu of Domri who was wicked
Bandhu Singh with all his supporters

471. Batarghib-e-shaitaan baaghi hue
Shararat se apni woh daaghi hue
Became rebels by inducement of the Satan
Due to their roguery they became satanic

472. Ataat se haakim ki bezaar hain
Ab es waqt woh laaiq-e-daar hain
They are disgusted with obedience towards the rulers
Now at this time they are worthy of the gibbet

473. Unhi sab ne Kosamhi ko ghaarat kiya
Jo asbaab tha mera sab le liya
They all ravaged Kosamhi
Whatever provisions I had, they looted

474. Jala phunk kar khaak sa kar diya
Jo kuch maal-o-asbaab tha le liya
Burnt, carbonized it; razed it to the ground
They seized whatever money and goods were available,

475. Luta jo ki kothi ka asbaab-o-maal
Main tashrih karta hoon kijiye khayaal
Whatever property and wealth of the bungalow was plundered
I shall elucidate, do ponder over it

476. Zar-o-naqd do sai bahattar raha
Ke ho waqt-e-haajat ke haajat rawa
Money in cash was two hundred and seventy two
So that at the time of need, the requirement may be met

477. Jo chamcha waghaira raha nuqrai
Woh ninyanwe us ki qeemat rahi
The spoons, etcetera, which were of silver
Their price was ninety nine

478. Missi aur baranji zarufaat the
Bahut cheeni shesha ke aalaat the
Red lead and brass vessels were there
There were many utensils of Chinese glass

479. Rahi qeemat uski hazaar aath sad
Aur saintees zaayid kar aiye zeekhirad
Their price was one thousand eight hundred
And count thirty seven extra, O sensible one!

480. Woh almariy-o-kursi-o-maize hum
Hua do hazaar panch sad nau baham
Price of those almirahs, chairs and tables also
Became two thousand five hundred and nine, all together

481. Aur asbaab chandi ka jo tha dhara
Shamul uske raavi ne usko likha
And the articles of silver which were kept
The narrator has included those in this narrative

482. Firosh aur hathiyaar the beadad
Do alif uski qeemat thi aur haft sad
The seller's different weapons were innumerable
Their price was two thousand and seven hundred

483. Raqam panch ki uspe zaayid dharo
Nahin farq es mein baawar karo
Add an amount of five over and above that
There is no alteration in this; do trust

484. Kahan tak bayaan uska karta rahe
Agar sab likhe ek daftar bane
How much of these can be narrated?
If all of it is written, it will become a volume

485. Bird Sahib se sab kiya iltimaas
Liya maal mardudon ne beharaas
Everything was petitioned to Bird Sahib
The reprobates have looted assets, fearlessly

486. Yeh farmaya Sahib ne kuch gham nahi
Milega sab asbaab tum ko kabhin
Sahib said, do not be disheartened
At some point of time all possessions shall be retrieved by you

487. Hui mukhtasar yeh hikayat tamaam
Luta maal-o-asbaab mashoor-o-aam
These reports have been concluded succinctly
Fortunes and assets of the eminent and ordinary were looted alike.

Hikayat Gagaha

Report of Gagaha

488. Azamgarh ka jab qasd haakim hua
Maqaam apna Gagaha mein jaa kar kiya
When the rulers had designs on Azamgarh
They went and stationed themselves at Gagaha

489. Liya aariyat hum se ek toop ko
Karenge inaayat humein toop do
Borrowed one cannon from me
Shall later grant me two cannons

490. Collector, Session-Judge rawaana hue
Ba humraah ek toop meri liye
Collector and Session Judge proceeded
Together with one of my cannons

491. Mohammad Hasan wahaan par warid hua
Tama se khazana ke aakar lada
Mohammad Hasan appeared there
He fought for the greed of treasure

492. Yeh jab dekha afwaaj-e-haakim ne haal
Kiya khasam ko khub sa paimaal
When the armies of the rulers witnessed this situation
They thoroughly ravaged the assailants

493. Yahaan tak hue sab woh zer-o-zabar
Kisi ko na thi paun sar ki khabar
They were shattered and smashed to such an extent
That no one was cognizant of their own feet or head

494. Hue jab na sarbar to raahi hue
Woh mardud sab pur tabaahi hue
When defeated, in humiliation they fled
All those reprobates were squandered

495. Thi baandhi kamar usne mubaaf se
Hadaf ho ke atka tha woh kaaf se
He had tied his waist with woven hair
Like a target of aim, he was entangled with Caucasians

496. Nafa ki tamanna se nukhsaan hua
Nahin yeh sukhan shayad usne padha
Due to the over ambition for profits, deficits materialized
Probably he did not read this speech

497. Kalagh tak Kubuk dar gosh kard
Nak khoshiyatan ra faramosh kard
When the crow wishes to speak in Kubuk's rhyme
He forgets his own insipid rhyme as well

498. Chu kasar dambadi maarkhuee gayee
Ke baazdaha jang juee kuni
When you adopt habits of the scorpion and the snake
Then you will have to fight the python as well

499. Hama saal gauhar na kheezo za sang
Jahan sulah saazo gahegaah jung
Every year, sharpness of the sword is not increased by stone
Where there is peace and concord, rarely is the need for fighting

500. Zakhaake ke bar aasmaan afkani
Saro chashm khudraaz maan afkani

If you throw mud towards the sky
It is obvious that automatically it will fall back on your head and eyes

501. Kiya jake Gagaha mein sab ko doneem
Narharpur mein ja hue tab muqeem
On reaching Gagaha, slaughtered every one
Then they sojourned at Narharpur

502. Hua khoob taaraaj woh bhi makaan
Hui fauj raja ki sab benishaan
That place was also thoroughly ravaged
All the army of the king was wiped out

503. Azamgarh mein jaa kar kiya intizaam
Rahi fauz Nepal sab shaad kaam
Made arrangements on reaching Azamgarh
All the army of Nepal was happy and successful

504. Hua Rajajilal aamaadah jung
Kiya kaafiya uska Gorkha ne tang
Rajajilal was in preparedness for war
He was pushed in desperate straits by the Gorkhas

505. Gira unpe chaapaa liya toop do
Bas ab se zawaal uske aafaal ko
Raid was conducted on them and two cannons were seized
From this instant began the waning of his ascendant acts

506. Abhi tak na tha shahar mein kuch fasaad
Ab hukkaam-e-English ko karte hain yaad
Till now there had been no disturbance in the town
Now they remember the English rulers

507. Khud hukkaam English ne es shahar ka
Zara chod kar imtehaan tha liya
This town, the British administrators themselves
Had tested, by deliberately abandoning it

508. Ke dekhen toh es jaa ke bashindagaan
Khare ya ke khote hain dar imtehaan
Let us just evaluate the people of this place
Whether they are genuine or insincere in an appraisal

509. Jo achche the achche rahe aaj tak
Daghal sab siyaah ru hue barmahak
Those who were good, remain incorruptibly good till today
All the criminals turned into hypocrites with a touchstone test.

Kaifiyat-e-ittalai Bahuzur Khudawand-e-Nemat

Story of communication with His Honour, The Beneficient Master

510. Zara qissa-e-bist-o-hashtam suno
Mahina tha Zilhijja ka doostoon
Now, listen to the account of the twenty eighth
Friends, it was the month of Zilhijja

511. Kaha Jaan Ali se ke ab zudtar
Bird gent Sahib se jaa arz kar
Told Jaan Ali: now as soon as possible
Go to gentleman Bird Sahib and convey respectfully

512. Moharram ka darpesh hai intizaam
Ke Ashrah mein hota hai pas izdehaam
The time for organizing Moharram is advancing
That on Ashrah there finally is a colossal crowd

513. Sipahi milen hasb rasm-e-kuhan
Rahe aap par saya-e-Panjtan
Soldiers may be allocated as per the earlier norms
May the grace of the Panjtan remain upon you

514. Usi waqt Sahib ne baad az talab
Jamadaar se kah diya jald ab
On hearing the request Sahib instantaneously
Asked the Jamadaar to act expeditiously

515. Sipahi ko maamul se bhej do
Jo irshaad hota hai usko karo
Dispatch soldiers as per the convention
Do whatever is being commanded

516. Na baaz aayaa woh zasht kirdaar se
Hua munharif apne sardaar se
The Jamadaar did not abandon his repulsive character
Rebelled against his leader

517. Phira hukm-e-haakim se woh naabkaar
Usi se hua hai sazawaar-e-daar
That wicked one transgressed the commandment of the rulers
That is why he deserves the gibbet

518. Musharraf se ja kar ke sab kah diya
Nahin hukm tameeyl haakim kiya
Communicated everything to Musharraf
Did not execute the orders of the ruler

519. Yeh sun kar woh mardud barham hua
Sukhan haai behuda bakne laga
On hearing this, that reprobate became furious
Started speaking in an obscene language

520. Kaha Jaan Ali ne jo yeh ched chaad
Gira mujh pe ranj-o-alam ka pahaad
When Jaan Ali narrated this vexatious incident
A mount of sorrow and torment fell upon me

521. Kaha humne asla na taakheer ho
Abhi ja ke Sahib ko aagah karo
I said that there should be no delay at all
Go and warn Sahib just now

522. Husain Baksh Cheyda ko humraah lo
Haqiqat jo hai sab guzaarish karo
Take Husain Baksh Cheyda along with you
Make a submission of the truth

523. Karo uski bad baatini aashkaar
Rahen unse Sahib bahut hoshiyaar
Divulge his malicious wretchedness
Sahib should be very cautious of him

524. Bad andesh-o-badkaar-o-makkaar hai
Woh moozi nihaayat sitamgaar hai
He is malevolent, sinful and cunning
That tormentor is extremely oppressive

525. Nahin us se hai kuch umeed-e-wafaa
Woh badasl hai us se hogi khataa
There is no hope of fidelity from him
He is born mean and can certainly commit wrong actions

526. Yeh sun kar ke Sahib ne hans kar kaha
Hai malum hum ko taman phir gaya
On hearing this Sahib laughed and said
I know that the army has revolted

527. Magar baad sab haakimon ke yahaan
Rahe ek Sahib Bird begumaan
However, after all the officers left this place
Only Bird Sahib remained fearlessly

528. Dileri-o-mardi ko raunaq diya
Jo mardaangi chahiye so kiya
Brought splendour to bravery and manliness
Accomplished whatever was expected of a man

529. Dilawar bahadur hain Sahib Bird
Jo aata yahaan us ko dete ulat
Sahib Bird is courageous and bold,
Would have toppled down whoever dared to come here

530. Nahin un ke saani koi doosra
Raaya bhi hai jaan-o-dil se fida
There is no one like him
The subjects are also wholeheartedly devoted

531. Jo Gorkha ki thodi bhi rahti sipah
Na aata koi shahar mein rusiyah
Even if some armed forces of the Gorkhas had remained
No criminal would have dared to come to the town

532. Bamajboori Sahib yahaan se gaye
Madadgaar raja na babu hue
Sahib left this place due to compulsion
Neither kings nor clerks were helpful

533. Thi us rooz taarikh unteeswin
Bird jab gayee es makaan ke makeen
On that day, the date was twenty-ninth
When Bird, the Resident of this place, left

534. Ke hukkaam se sab ko aaraam tha
Hai afsos yaaron ye kya ho gaya
For everyone had reassurance from the rulers
O alas, friends! Whatever happened is regrettable

535. Nazar mein jahan tira-o-taar hai
Sarasar yeh ab qahar-e-Jabbaar hai
The world in my sight is quite gloomy and dark
Now this undoubtedly is the wrath of the Forceful One

536. Gaye baad arsa ke par kya karen
Na haakim na yaavar yeh kyon kar rahen
Left after a considerably long time, but had no choice
Neither officers nor supporters, how could he stay?

537. Yahi un ke jaane ka mojib hua
Taman ke sipahi ne sazish kiya
This became the reason for his departure
That the soldiers of the army turned betrayers

538. Rahe muntazim Raja Gopalpur
Hue kaam sab behtar unse zahoor
The King of Gopalpur became the manager
All work was managed well by him

539. Nahin sath Sahib Bird ke gaye
Su-e-khana apne yahaan se phire
He did not go with Bird Sahib
Returned towards his house from here.

Hikayat Mohammad Hasan Naib Dajjaal

Report of Mohammad Hasan, the Vice-Regent of Dajjaal

540. Hilaal-e-Moharram ki yeh baat hai
Chehattar the Hijri ke sun barah seh
This is an occurance of the new moon of Moharram
The Hijri year was twelve hundred and seventy-three

541. Ke makkar ek shaks aayaa yahaan
Woh Nazim na tha afsar-e-dakuaan
When a deceitful fellow came here
That officer of dacoits was not any Nazim

542. Siyaahfaam tha rukh pe chechak ka daagh
Kiya saikdoon ghar ka thanda chiraagh
He was dark complexioned with small-pox marks on his face
He extinguished the lights of hundreds of houses

543. Kashidah qad-o-sar ba mu-e-siyaah
Jise dekh ke aql maange panaah
Tall-statured with a head full of black hair
On glimpse of a sight of him, wit seeks asylum

544. Alam se mushaba tha woh namuraad
Nizami ke ashaar hain mujh ko yaad
That unfortunate one was analogous to torment
I recall some verses of Nizami

545. Alam deedah-e-parchame bar sarash
Namigasht yak mu-e-azpaikarsh
Over notorious eyes flew his banner
It did not make even a hair's difference

546. Garinja bud Taash ke sarnagun
Do deedah baro bud chun Taash khoon
Someone as brave as Taash would also have hung down his head
If such murderous bloodshot eyes stared upon him

547. Bazaahir woh Nazim yahaan aa bana
Haqiqat mein jaali-o-masnui tha
Evidently by usurpation he became the Nazim here
In reality, he was fake and false

548. Aur uska tha ustad Abbas Ali
Bali Singh ki raae usse mili
And his master was Abbas Ali
Bali Singh's opinion matched with him

549. Sharik un sabhon ka hai raja magar
Ke English Bahadur se tha bekhabar
The king is an accomplice of them but
Because he was ignorant of the English Bahadur

550. Narharpur ka Raja us se baham
Yeh sab mil ke karte the jaur-o-sitam
The King of Narharpur was also with them
They all together used to terrorize and oppress

551. Unhi sab ne fitna ko barpa kiya
Maeeyyat se unke woh Nazim bana
All those who engineered the revolt
Due to their fellowship he became the Nazim

552. Woh mardud dariya ke us paar tha
Idhar aana sakhat us ko dushwaar tha
That reprobate was on the other bank of the river
Crossing over to this side was very difficult for him

553. Na aata tha haibat se zalim idhar
Hazeemat se Gagaha ke tha dil mein darr
Due to horror the tyrant did not dare come this side
The defeat of Gagaha had created terror in his heart

554. Gaye peshwai ko yeh mardumaan
Suna humne logon se aiye doostaan
These persons went for his reception
I heard this from people, O friends!

555. Karun us ki tashrih es ja raqam
Rawaan es bayaan mein ho mera qalam
I am noting its details here
In this description, may my pen run smoothly

556. Musharraf-o-Pundit rahe peshwa
Khataawaar yeh log hain barmala
Musharraf and Pundit were the guides
These people are conspicuously guilty

557. Maa aqriba apne Sardar Ali
Aur Aali Hasan bhi basad khush dili
Sardar Ali with all his allies
And Aali Hasan also with an extremely euphoric heart

558. Rahe un ke humraah Nawandah Rai
Taasuf hai aur aql par unke vae
Nawandah Rai was together with them
Deprecate their actions, and doubt their intellect

559. Aur Mirza Fateh Ali manind-e-barq
Maa aqriba pahunche ba zeb-o-zarq
And Mirza Fateh Ali like lightning
Reached with allies in all adornments and glitter

560. Rahe sath sab ke Mohammad Sayeed
Sirf donon bhai the unse baeid
Mohammad Sayeed was with everyone
Only the two brothers were distant from him

561. Ba targhib Sardar Ali ke gaye
Abas sab khataawaar English hue
They went due to the inducement of Sardar Ali
Uselessly they became culprits of the English

562. Rahe sath Rajhye ke Tehsildaar
Mere shahar mein the bade hoshiyaar
The Tehsildaar of Rajhye was also together
In my town were many discreet ones

563. Siva unke the chand kas badsheaar
Siva zulm-o-bidat ke rakhte na kaar
Besides them were some ill-mannered individuals
Except tyranny and heresy had no other business

564. Koi jaa ke azlam ka chaakar hua
Musharraf ka bhi koi naukar hua
Some went and became servants of the most cruel one
Some became servants of Musharraf also

565. Hain Sardar Ali Khan toh baaghi kamaal
Maa aqriba apne daaghi kamaal
Sardar Ali Khan is an utmost rebel
Together with his allies he is exceedingly spoiled

566. Yahaan jis qadar ahle Shia rahe
Woh darbaar-e-azlam mein behtar hue
As many Shiites as were here
They were best placed in the court of the cruel

567. Kiya us ne qadr unki sab se seva
Pe naukar nahin koi uska hua
He honoured them the most
But no one became his servant

568. Faqat Mirza ke ghar ke naukar hue
Jo hum jins the log sab jaa mile
Only from Mirza's house became servants
Those people who were genetically same, united

569. Aur Ulfat Ali bhi mulazim hue
Khataawaar English ke woh bhi hue
And Ulfat Ali also became an employee
He too became a culprit of the English

570. Amir-e-Ali jo Muharrir raha
Tamandaar badkaar woh bhi hua
Amir-e-Ali who was a Muharrir
He too became a centurion of the sinful

571. Risaaldaar the uske Mohammad Sayeed
Kiya kaam usne khirad se baeid
Mohammad Sayeed was his Risaaldaar
He acted in a manner bereft of wisdom

572. Kamaan Khan Jamadaar thana ka tha
Yeh naamard thana pe nahaq raha
Kamaan Khan was a Jamadaar of the police station
This coward remained in the police station in vain

573. Bandhu Singh Tamandaar badkaar tha
Maa khandaan woh madadgaar tha
Centurion Bandhu Singh was sinful
Together with his family he was helpful

574. Woh ghaaratgari mein yeh mashhoor hai
Bayaan uska sabiq mein mastoor hai
He is infamous for plundering
His account has been written in the past

575. The Imdad Ali aur Abid Ali
Aur Mazhar Ali aur Wajid Ali
There were Imdad Ali and Abid Ali
And Mazhar Ali and Wajid Ali

576. Ahmad Khan Risaaldaar sab mein kalan
Yehi baaghi the sarkaar ke doostaan
Ahmad Khan Risaaldaar is the greatest of all
Friends, these were rebels against the government

577. Ibrahim Beg aur the Kallu Beg
Yehi Raja ke janib se lete the neg
There were Ibrahim Beg and Kallu Beg
They used to collect cash on behalf of the king

578. Raha Brij Mohan bhi unka sharik
Raaya ki karte the haalat rakik
Brij Mohan was also their accomplice
They reduced the subjects to a state of impropriety

579. Anup Bari raja ka dildaar tha
Fehrist mein sharah hum ne sab ki likha
Anup Bari was the beloved of the king
In the list I have written details of them all

580. Aur Mansoor Ali aur Maqdoom Baksh
Taman ke Subadaar the Faiz Baksh
And Mansoor Ali and Maqdoom Baksh
And Faiz Baksh who was a Subadaar of the army

581. Hue munharif az raah-e-buzdili
Hui unse hukkaam ko bekali
Became rebellious by way of cowardice
The rulers became restless due to them

582. Subadaari ka rutba rakhte rahe
Ataat yeh haakim ki karte rahe
Were possessors of the status of governorship
They always attempted to obey the rulers

583. Mulazim yeh ho kar ke baaghi hue
Musharraf ke kahne se daaghi hue
Despite being employees they became mutineers
On Musharraf's incitement they became tarnished

584. Us zalim ke kahne se Bansi gaye
Sazawaar yeh log phaansi hue
Went to Bansi on the instigation of that brute
They came to deserve the hangman's noose

585. The maare khushi ke woh jhund tamaam
Basaan-e-gul surkh khandaa tamaam
Due to happiness in that whole group
Every one was cheerful like blooming red flowers

586. The jis rooz aaye Mohammad Hasan
Kiya unke refaqaa ne ziyaadah jashan
The day on which Mohammad Hasan had arrived
His comrades indulged in great celebration

587. Khazana wa atwaap-e-maujood ko
Musharraf ne de dala mardood ko
The available treasure and cannons
Musharraf gave away to the reprobate

588. Madar Baksh ahaata ka woh Najaf Ali
Unhi se toh haakim ko toopen mili
That Najaf Ali of Madar Baksh compounds
It was from him that the commander obtained cannons

589. Magister ne dariyah mein ki theen nihaan
Ke paawen na uska pata baaghiyaan
The Magistrate had hidden them in the river
So that the rebels may not get wind of it

590. Nikala toh inaam ek sad liya
Usi ne pata toop ka bhi diya
Took one hundred as prize for retrieving it
He revealed the whereabouts of the cannon also

591. Bahut log kamzarf naukar rahe
Kahan tak sharah uski raavi likhe
Many malicious people were servants
How many of their details can the narrator write?

592. Sawaaron ki tafseel karta hoon main
Jo malum hai usko likhta hoon main
I am giving detailed particulars of the cavalrymen
I am writing whatever is known to me

593. Sawaaron ke maalik the Sardar Ali
Buri baat ko usne jaani bhali
Sardar Ali was the master of the cavalry men
He considered a malevolent thing as benevolent

594. Nawaban-o-Gauhar-o-Shamsheer Ali
Sawaaron mein bhi baat yeh thi chali
Nawaban and Gauhar and Shamsheer Ali
This was also a topic of discussion among the troops

595. Aur kahta tha Ahsan Ali yeh pukaar
Ke ho jaayenge ek rooz un par nisaar
And Ahsan Ali proclaimed this boldly
That one day we shall sacrifice ourselves in devotion

596. Aur Khursheed Ali Khan bhi tha lafezan
Waziran tha us se bhi ziyadah magan
And Khursheed Ali Khan was also boastful
Warizan was even more engrossed than him

597. Daffadaar aswaar tha Kallu Beg
Padi chashm-e-Dildaar Khan mein bhi rek
Kallu Beg was a newly commissioned officer of cavalry
Dildaar Khan's eyes were also blinded by dust

598. Chadha asp idbaar par naamdaar
Yeh shiddat se nadaan tha naabkaar
The famous mounted the horse of misfortune
This wicked one was extremely irrational

599. Sawaaron mein naukar Hasan Khan hua
Usi pesha mein Ram Behel bhi raha
Among the knights Hasan Khan became a servant
Ram Behel was also in the same profession

600. Aur Ghaziuddin Khan bhi mulazim hua
Pisar uska bhi saath uske raha
And Ghaziuddin Khan also became an employee
His son was also with him

601. Maa apne bhai Walidad Khan
Mulazim yeh azlam hue badgumaan
Together with their brother Walidad Khan
These distrustful ones became servants of the diabolic

602. Rahimdad Khan bhi hua munsalik
Musarrat hui us ko sabse adhik
Rahimdad Khan also became attached
He was the most exhilarated

603. Aur Abid Ali bhi sawaaron mein tha
Woh gumnaam naami hazaaron mein tha
And among the knights Abid Ali was also present
That obscure one was lionized among thousands

604. Taman ka sipahi bhi humraah tha
Mulazim yeh azlam ka sab ho gaya
Soldiers of the army were also accompanying
They all became servants of the tyrant

605. Aur the chand kash aur bhi badsheaar
Mulazim the sarkaar-e-aali tabaar
And there were some more ill-mannered individuals
Were servants of the government of noble descent

606. Gopalpur ke Raja se phir gaye
Nazar se khalayiq ke sab gir gaye
Rose up against the King of Gopalpur
They all fell in the estimation of the people

607. Yeh hi log badraah gumraah the
Badil Company ke woh badkhah the
These very persons were wicked and apostate
From the core of their hearts they wished ill of the Company

608. Jo achche the uski na ki naukri
Kisi ne mohabbat na azlam se ki
Those who were good, did not work for him
None of them loved the tyrant.

Hikayat Mushtamil Barchand Kawaif

Report inclusive of some details

609. Bula kar ke logon se maine kaha
Ke es baat mein hai sarasar bhala
Calling the people, I said
There is absolute goodness in this point

610. Agar thode se log hoowen shareek
Abhi kardoon zalim ki haalat rakeek
If only a few people participate
At this instance I would bring the brute to his knees

611. Do dil yak shud bash kand koh ra
Paragandagi aarad abnooh ra
If two hearts become one, mountains can be cut
With double-fold fire they can be reduced to flour

612. Kisi ne na mana yeh kahna mera
Raza par main raazi-o-shakir raha
Nobody adhered to my plan
I remained agreeable and thankful in the general will

613. Agar saath dete toh kya khoob tha
Ke yeh amr haakim ko marghoob tha
If they had cooperated it would have been superb
Because this scheme was desired by the rulers

614. Yeh hi mujh ko andesha tha har ghadi
Yeh hi fikr subh-o-masa thi badi
This was my perpetual apprehension
From morning till evening I was very worried on this account

615. Ke kuch log gar saath deven mera
Ladai pe aamaadah hoven zara
That if some people become my confederates
They become poised for a confrontation

616. Toh azlam se chal kar ke main jang loon
Use khoob zer-o-zabar main karoon
Then I would have a battle with the barbarian
I will thoroughly degenerate him

617. Saza uske aamaal ki khoob doon
Sabhon ko liye haakimon se miloon
Shall give him loads of retribution for his deeds
I would meet the rulers with my colleagues

618. Musharraf ko bhi khoob doon main saza
Chakhe woh bhi aamaal-e-bad ka maza
I would inflict a lot of punishment upon Musharraf as well
Let him too have a taste of the yield of ill deeds

619. Usi ka tha din raat mujh ko khayaal
Usi ka nihaayat tha ranj-o-malaal
This is what I pondered over day and night
This made me extremely distressed and disheartened

620. Kisi ne diya saath mera na jab
Saha dil hi par maine ranj-o-taab
When no one accompanied me
My heart was inflicted with pain and debility

621. Gar ma nisyat rozi rafahar kasaan
Khuda ast razzaaq rozi rasaan
We do not get subsistence by anyone's mercy
Only God is the Sustainer and giver of daily bread

622. Faqat teen sau aadmi saath the
Magar woh bhi sakna-e-dehaat the
Just three hundred men were with me
But they too were residents of the village

623. Agar kuch bhi aajata ghaiz-o-jalaal
Bhaga deyna azlam ka kya tha mohaal
Had any infuriating anger and rage materialized
Making the tyrant flee was not an impossible task

624. Jo es shahar mein log maujood the
Mile ja ke azlam se mardood the
Those people who were present in this town
Joined the tyrant, were reprobates

625. Kiya ja ke Dajjaal se ittifaaq
Lage dil mein mohsin se rakhne nifaaq
Joined hands in concordance with the Dajjaal
Started bearing maliciousness towards their benefactors

626. Bilachargi dast-e-afsos mal
Likha maine hukkaam ko barmahal
Rubbing my hands in melancholy helplessness
I wrote to the rulers very opportunistically

627. Ke thode se mujh ko sipahi milen
Idhar ko maa toop jaldi chalen
That I should get some soldiers
With cannons they should proceed here quickly

628. Siwa uske kuch aur bhi qaal tha
Areeza mein azlam ka kuch haal tha
Besides there were a few evidential facts
In the representation were some reports of the brute

629. Magar un dinon qaum-e-Pulwaar se
Ladai thi darpesh sarkaar se
But in those days with the people of Pulwaar
The government was confronting a hostile situation

630. Hua Rajaji Lal bhi kinasaaz
Kiya fauz ne usko narm-o-gudaaz
Rajaji Lal also became malicious
The army made him mellow and deliquescent

631. Mukhaalif se har waqt tha saamna
Aanat ka us waqt mauqa na tha
There was constant confrontation with opponents
At that time there was no possibility of assistance

632. Aanat ka us dam na tha kuch khayaal
Nahin ab hai gunjaish-e-qeel-o-qaal
There was no thoughtfulness for help at that moment
Now there is no scope for any polemic debate

633. Mili jab na sarkaar se kuch madad
Dua ki ba dargaah-e-Rabb-us-Samad
When no support was received from the government
I prayed at the royal court of the Eternal Lord

634. Buzurga Buzurgi duhaai qasam
Tu hai yaawari bakhsho yaari rasam
O Great One! I cry for mercy from your greatness
You are the helper, grant help as per custom

635. Chu kardi charagh mera noordaar
Zaman baad mashal kashan doordaar
When you have enlightened my lamp
You do not take away my eyesight from me

636. Tu haafiz-e-izzat-o-jaan-o-maal
Tujhe bekason ka hai hardam khayaal
You are protector of life, property and honour
You are always concerned about the helpless ones

637. The jo log hukkaam ke khairkhah
Unhi ka woh dushman hua rusiyah
Those people who were well-wishers of the government
That criminal became an enemy of those very persons

638. Faqat ek akele ka kya bas chale
Na de saath jab koi kaise lade
What power would just a solitary individual have?
When none collaborates, how can he fight?

639. Hua jab woh es shahar mein mutmaeen
Hua yeh taqaazaa-e-tab laain
When he was settled in this town
It was the demand of his accursed temperament

640. Kiya baad Ashrah ke yeh ishtehaar
Ke haazir na ho jo woh ho dilfigaar
After the Ashrah he made this notification
That whoever does not present himself may be grief-stricken

641. Sab asbaab ghar ka bhi taaraaj ho
Har ek tarha barbaad usko karo
All property of their house should also be plundered
They should be destroyed in everyway

642. Laga hone har tarha ranj-o-taab
Phanse ek zalim ke panja mein sab
Were engulfed in all kinds of pain and fatigue
All were trapped in the clutches of the beast

643. Kisi ka bacha maal us se na haif
Magar haan jo the saath mein ahl-e-saif
Alas! No one's property was saved from him
Except those who were accompanying the swords-men

644. Gharibon ko pamaal karne lage
Dilon par ajab daagh dharne lage
Started trampling the poor under their feet
Began loading hearts with an eerie pain

645. Esi ka agar naam Islam hai
Toh aison hi par qaaf aur laam hai
If Islam is the name of this
Then such are the ones who deserve critical revilement

646. Musalman-o-Hindu the donon kharaab
Hue hanth se unke laakhon azaab
Both, Muslims and Hindus were corrupt
Lakhs of atrocities were committed by their hands

647. Musharraf jo Naib tha uska bana
Woh sabiq se shaitaan ka ustaad tha
Musharraf who had become his deputy
He had always been the master of Satan

648. Hua nasl-e-Adam pe jab dastaras
Toh aawaaz-e-aah aayi misl-e-jaras
When he asserted power over the race of Adam
Then the sound of lamenting came like a bell

649. Kiya khub barbaad har ek ko
Na chooda tha usne kisi nek ko
Ravaged everyone thoroughly
He had not spared any noble person

650. Lavaahiq mein raja ke jo log the
Woh sardaar ghaaratgaron ke hue
Those people who were in subordination of the king
They became leaders of the plunderers

651. Toh soncha sabhon ne yeh tadbeer kaar
Ke behaaziri hoonge sab zaar-o-khwaar
So they thought of this plan of action
That all absentees should be wounded and disgraced

652. Lavaahiq bhi sab mard-o-zan hain yahaan
Nahin aisi jaa taa rahen sab nihaan
All men and women are also dependents
There is no such place where they could remain hidden

653. Na haakim koi apni hai pusht par
Ke hum log apni bana den sipar
There is no officer behind us
Whom we could make our shield

654. Yeh ek aur bidat ziyaadah hui
Ke dastak bhi un sab par hone lagi
This was yet a further heresy
That they all were issued warrants also

655. Muiyyan hue unpe jab Chobdaar
Hue jab ke bahaal zaar-o-nizaar
When a Chobdaar was appointed over them
Then their state was full of weakness

656. Toh laachaar ho ahle hurmat gaye
Paye hifz-e-izzat woh haazir hue
Being vulnerable, the dignified people went
For the sake of protecting their honour they attended

657. Agarche bazahir woh laachaar the
Magar dil se English ke sab yaar the
Although apparently they were powerless
But from the core of their hearts they were friends of the English

658. Diya zar toh laachaar ho kar diya
Ataat na dil se unhon ne kiya
Gave money only because of helplessness
They never obeyed him with their heart and soul

659. Magar haan jo saazish mein azlam ke the
Batafseel naam unke maine likhe
But yes, those who were participants in the conspiracy of the tyrant
I have written their names in detail

60. Hai pehle risala mein taarif sab
Bane baaghi do chaar un mein se ab
All elucidation is available in the first brochure
Some of them became mutineers now

61. Jirah wasf sabiq mein hai narawa
Woh sabiq mein jaise the waisa likha

Any remonstration in favour of their earlier virtues is unjustified
I narrated just as they were in the recent past

662. Session Judge ko phir maine arzee likha
Zabaani bhi qaasid se kuch tha kaha
Then I wrote a petition to the Session Judge
Had also conveyed something verbally through the messenger

663. Ke es shahar ka woh to bashinda tha
Bahut hoshmand aur dil zindah tha
After all he was a resident of this town
He was very sensible and lively

664. Yahaan se gaya tez aur bekhatar
Kiya arz wahaan ja ke sab ki khabar
From here he went fast and undaunted
There he narrated everyone's news

665. Session Judge ne izhaar sab ka liya
Kachahri mein tasdeeq usko kiya
Session Judge took everyone's testimony
And verified it in the court

666. Yeh sunkar ke azlam hua khashamnaak
Raha zulm se uske har ek ko baak
On hearing this the beast was enraged
Everyone feared his cruelty

667. Hamesha main likhta tha sab kaifiyat
Magar kaifiyat woh jo thi basehat
Invariably I wrote about all occurrences
But only those reports which were accurate

668. Rifaqat mein moozi ke jo shaks tha
Batafseel naam usme unka likha
Those who were comrades of the tyrant
In detail I wrote their names therein

669. Brabar araiz main bheja kiya
Kawaif sada yahaan ke likha kiya
I regularly sent applications
Always wrote the particulars of this place.

Hikayat Zulm-e-Dajjaal

Report of cruelty of the Dajjaal

670. Ab ek aur turfa suno maajra
Ke yeh hukm Dajjaal ne ab diya
Now listen to another strange happening
That now the Dajjaal gave this order

671. Maveshi sabhon ki giraftaar ho
Jahan gaadi paaoo use cheen lo
Everyone's cattle should be apprehended
Wherever you see a cart seize it

672. Karega koi hukm mein gar iba
Toh pavega inkaar ki woh saza
If anybody desists from following orders
Then he will be punished for denial

673. Jahan paaoo jis tarha ho cheen lo
Sifarish ho harchand hargiz na do
Wherever you find, by whatever means wrench away
There might be any amount of intercession but do not return

674. Magar thode hi din yeh jaari raha
Tashaddud se har shakhs aari raha
However this was operational only for a few days
Everyone was tired of severity

675. Ke hai dil mein zalim ke ab yeh khayaal
Ke talaash ghar-ghar ho English ka maal
Now there is this scheme in the tyrant's heart
That all houses should be searched for goods of the Britishers

676. Har ek ja pe mashhoor aur faash hai
Ke ab maal-e-English ki talaash hai
Everywhere it is well-known and egregious
That now the search for belongings of the Britishers is on.

Taayyun Pahra ba-azm-e-Ghaaratgari Mohammad Hasan Dajjaal

Inception of vigilance; Mohammad Hasan Dajjaal's intention of plundering

677. Bayaan ab main karta hoon takleef-e-khesh
Hua sanihaa us ko karta hoon pesh
Now I describe the agony of the people
There occured a catastrophe which I present

678. Idhar khana si yaum ka pakta raha
Jo dekha to ek ghol aaya chala
The meal of the third day was being cooked here
I noticed that a mob had come unannounced

679. Bahut tursh karte the woh guftagu
Jama ho gaye log har chaar su
They conversed in a very rude manner
Crowds had gathered in all directions

680. Khade ho ke karne lage yeh kalaam
Firistaadah Dajjaal the jo tamaam
They stood and started saying this:
All those who were envoys of the Dajjaal

681. Azakhana mein maal jo hai dhara
So lay jaeynge esko hum barmala

The goods which are kept in the mourning house
So those we shall take away openly

682. Abbot Sahib us waqt baithe rahe
Woh sab kaifiyat unki sunte rahe
Abbot Sahib was sitting at that time
He kept listening to all their statements

683. Yahya Khan Darogha aur Himmat Ali
Suna jisne jisne hui bekali
Darogha Yahya Khan and Himmat Ali
Whoever heard of it became restless

684. Rahe jo yahaan log aamaadah jung
Jawaab unko humne diya bedirang
Those people who were psyched up for a battle here
I replied to them unhesitatingly and instantaneously

685. Azamgarh ko qaasid rawaana kiya
Sab kaifiyat haakimon ko likha
Sent a messenger to Azamgarh
Wrote of all these conditions to the rulers

686. Jo khaayin the sab maal-o-asbaab ke
Woh mardood sab hamla-aawar rahe
Those who were the embezzlers of all the wealth and property
Those reprobates were invaders

687. Jawaab unko raavi ne aisa diya
Ke hargiz main maalik nahin maal ka
The narrator gave them such an answer
That I am definitely not the owner of the wealth

688. Nahin humko dene ka kuch ikhtiyaar
Amaanat hai sarkaar-e-aali vaqaar
I have no authority to give it
It is the entrusted property of the highly prestigious government

689. Na kuch ched hum ko tu aiye naabkaar
Ke beshubha hoga sazawaar-e-daar
O wicked one! Do not harass me
For definitely you shall be worthy of gallows

690. Woh jo maal hai waqf-e-nazr-e-Imam
Shar-o-khair mein kya karun main kalaam
That wealth which is an endowment as offering to the Imam
In turmoil and welfare what can I say

691. Baroozo gar aaya Aali Hasan
Ghazabnaak behuda bakta sukhan
Perforce and trickily came Aali Hasan
Prattling in a wrathful and obscene language

692. Sipahi tha humraah apne liye
Sab asbaab par mere pehra kiye
Had brought soldiers along with him
Keeping a vigilant eye on my belongings

693. Kaha maine us se yeh karte ho kya
Batarz-e-amaanat hai yeh sab rakha
I said to him: What are you doing?
All this is kept by way of entrusted property

694. Agar hukm ahle committee ka ho
Ke asbaab-e-hukkaam tum unko do
If the members of the committee order
That you give the belongings of the rulers to them

695. Toh banda main asla jisaarat nahin
Amaanat mein jaiyz khiyaanat nahin
So not in the least am I an audacious man
It is not appropriate to embezzle an entrusted deposit

696. Bhala aise hote ho tum bekhatar
Bahut jald hukkaam lenge khabar
How have you become so very undaunted
Very soon the rulers will come to question

697. Azamgarh yahaan se nahin dur hai
Jo karte ho tum log sab zoor hai
Azamgarh is not far from here
Whatever you are doing is all violence

698. Paiyadon ko barkhwast kar deejiye
Munasib yeh hi baat hai keejiye
Dismiss the foot soldiers
This suggestion is decorous, follow it

699. Bade aap daana-o-hoshiyaar hain
Purane hawakhah-e-sarkaar hain
You are very sagacious and intelligent
Are an old sympathizer of the government

700. Namak ka nahin paas karte ho tum
Khuda ke ghazab se na darte ho tum
You are not discharging your obligations of loyalty
You do not fear the wrath of God

701. Bhala tum namak-khaar-e-sarkaar ho
Ke masnui Nazim ke tum yaar ho
Are you a well-wisher of the government
Or are you a friend of the fake Nazim?

702. Haqiqat mein yeh sab tilismaat hai
Yeh khwaab-o-khayaalaat ki baat hai
In fact all this is a magic spell
It is a thing of dreams and hypothetical fancy

703. Daraan khisht zarrin Shadaad Aad
Che aamad bajuz mardane namuraad
Those golden bricks that Shadaad and the people of Aad had seen
They got nothing but misfortune and death from them

704. Daryan baagh-e-rangeen darakhte tar ast
Ke manind az jafa-e-badtareen dar ast
The trees of this beautiful garden are not green
They are tarnished like unfaithfulness in a bad woman

705. Karo kaam aisa ke kuch naam ho
Ke es kaam mein bhi tera kaam ho
Do such work that you may become distinguished
So that in this task also your end may be served

706. Namak ka karo paas aiye ghaafilon
Uthao na tum asla asbaab ko
O negligent ones! Have some regard for your committment to loyalty
Do not impound any possessions at all

707. Hai lisaiyon par Khuda ka karam
Bhala kis mein taqat hai jo maare dam
There is God's graciousness over the Christians
Who has the power to protest against them?

708. Sare gar tu gardo bulandi garaaye
Ba fakandane kas nafitad za paaye
If you are proceeding towards height and exaltation
Then ensure that you do not trample anyone under your feet

709. Yeh shahi ke laaiq hain haq hai gavah
Rahenge yahi hashr tak badshah
They deserve royalty, equity is a witness
Till the day of resurrection they shall remain sovereign

710. Hai awwal hi para mein Quran ke
Likha hai tajaahul na kar jaan ke
It is in the very first chapter of the Quran
It is stated - do not feign ignorance consciously

711. Bas itna hi maine kaha tha ke bas
Ese sun ke Nazim jala misl-e-khas
Just this much had I said, that impetuously
The Nazim blazed with anger like a straw on hearing it

712. Woh ghussa se shola-bhuka hua
Yeh aakhir ko phir hukm usne diya
He fumed and flushed with fiery rage
Finally he gave this order

713. Ke jaawen taman le ke Fazle Ali
Karen zabt amwaal-e-Ahmad Ali
That Fazle Ali should go with the armed forces
Should seize the properties of Ahmad Ali

714. Siwa us ke jo kuch ho sarkaar ka
Diya ho wa ya ho amaanat rakha
Besides it, whatever that belongs to the government
Be it gifted or kept in trust for security

715. Sab asbaab le aao yahaan loot kar
Na bach jaye us mein se ek zarrah bhar
Loot all the possessions and bring them here
Out of that not even a particle must escape

716. Bade tadke aaya woh ghar par mere
Bahut sar mein tha baad-o-nakhwat bhare
Very early in the morning he came to my house
His head was choc-a-bloc with conceit

717. Takkabbur azaazil ra khwaar kard
Ba zindane laanat giraftaar kard
Arrogance makes even an angel satanic
Arrests him in the prison of rebuke

718. Kuch Aali Hasan ne jo humraah tha
Ho us waqt sargosh us se kaha
Something, Aali Hasan who was together with him
Whispered to him at that time

719. Tab uth kar ke donon lage dekhne
Sab asbaab mera lage phenkne
Then both of them got up and started searching
Began throwing all my things

720. Woh sab maal-e-hukkaam lene lage
Mulazim ko apne woh dene lage
They started taking all the possessions of the rulers
And handed them over to their servant

721. Phir Aali Hasan se yeh maine kaha
Yeh laaiq na tha jo ke tum ne kiya
Then I said this to Aali Hasan
What you have done is not proper

722. Jo puchega mujh se koi kaifiyat
Karoonga yehi aap ki main sifat
If someone enquires about the conditions from me
I would reveal these attributes of yours

723. Zara baawar kar esko aiye naabkaar
Jaza bad ki bad dega Parwardigaar
O villainous one! Do trust this to be credible,
Providence shall give you a malevolent retribution for malevolent deeds

724. Amini ko meri na barbaad kar
Iwaz es ke zar le tu aiye bekhabar
Do not devastate my custodianship
Take gold as a substitute for this, O benighted one!

725. Kiya ja ke zalim se usne bayaan
Ghazab mein bhara woh bhi aaya yahaan
He went and informed the brute
Buoyed with rancour he also came here

726. Pata mera paya ke hain baagh mein
Nihaayat hain woh maal ke daagh mein
Got to know that I was in the garden
And was in extreme shock over the loss of property

727. Mere ghar par aaya tha jo Fazle Ali
Usi ne diya tha mujhe bekali
That Fazle Ali who had come to my house
He was the one who made me restless

728. Ali Baksh Darogha ne aakar kaha
Ke badraah hai zalim-e-behaya
Darogha Ali Baksh came and said
That the shameless barbarian is sinful

729. Mukarrar phir Hafiz ka pahuncha payaam
Ke zahir hai yeh baat har khaas-o-aam
Again Hafiz's message reached here
That this issue is apparent to all, elite and commoners

730. Woh aakar ke baithta na tha koi meet
Ali Baksh-o-Hafiz se kee baat cheet
No friend came over and sat
Talked to Ali Baksh and Hafiz

731. Jo kahte the woh sab yeh dete jawaab
Na thi raae un sab ki hargiz sawaab
To whatever they all said, these people responded
Their opinion was definitely not respectful

732. Bachi jaan raaqim ki unke sabab
Paye qatl aaya tha woh beadab
The writer's life was saved due to them
That impudent had come in pursuit of murdering

733. Bahut sakht mujhse woh karta tha baat
Har ek baat mein apni karta tha ghaat
He used to speak to me very rudely
Through every dialogue of his, he brought into effect an ambush

734. Woh kahta tha English ke tum yaar ho
Agar Lucknow bhej den kya karo
He said, you are a friend of the English
If we send you to Lucknow, what shall you do?

735. Jo Aali Hasan se kiya tha kalaam
Rafa humne hujjat ki us se tamaam
Whatever conversation had taken place with Aali Hasan
I tried to set at rest all altercation with him

736. Usi ko yeh kahta tha kyon yeh kaha
Na tha khauf Aali Hasan ko zara
He was remonstrating why I said this
Aali Hasan was not at all fearful

737. Meri guftgu ka eadah kiya
Mukarrar muqabil mein phir sab kaha
He revised my conversation
Repeated all of it again in front of me

738. Main khaamosh baitha tha baitha raha
Bula kar Kamidaan ko usne kaha
I was sitting in speechless quietude, kept sitting
He called the commander and said:

739. Makaanaat par inke pahra karo
Tamandaar ki unpe dastak bhi ho
Keep a watch on his houses
A centurion of the army should also patrol over him

740. Jab aaya to ek hashr barpa hua
Qayaamat se din sahibo kam na tha
When he arrived a tumult was generated
Sahibs that day was no less than the doomsday

741. Zara dekhna gardish-e-aasmaan
Hua said rubah sher-e-ziyaan
Just look at the vicissitudes of fate
That the truculent tiger has become a prey of the fox

742. Do rangi zamaana ki mashhoor hai
Kahin saayaa hai aur kahin noor hai
Paradoxical duplicity of the world is proverbial
Somewhere there are shadows and somewhere light

743. Hai andeshaa-e-neesh humraah nosh
Hai paihum takhallul bhi humraah hosh
There always is a fear of sting along with honey
Fantasy and sense oscillate along with each other

744. Woh hain kaun duniya ki jo chah mein
Na khaaya ho thokar ko es raah mein
Who are those, desirous of the world
Who have not stumbled on this zesty path?

745. Hai baad-e-khizaan ka guzar dar chaman
Satata hai mehtaab ko bhi gahan
The breeze of withering fall passes through the garden
Even the moon is afflicted by eclipse

746. Nahin gard se saaf koi sehan
Sada abr par raad hai barqzan
No courtyard is free of dust
Always thunder strikes with lightning of clouds

747. Nahin bahar ki ek tar char nami
Kahin hai tarraqi kahin hai kami
The moistness and current of the ocean is not always the same
Sometimes there is enhancement and sometimes reduction

748. Hai Bulbul ke dil ko sada gul se laag
Magar gaah khush hai gahe dardnaak
The nightingale's heart is always attached to the flower
But it is sometimes happy and occasionally sad

749. Jo phirte the kal aaj hain goor mein
Hai zoof unko rahte the jo zoor mein
Those who had a free gait yesterday, are today inert in graves
Those suffer from weakness who once exercised power

750. Kahin nooriyaan hain kahin hain taleel
Hai sabit shab-o-rooz se yeh daleel
Somewhere is brilliance and darkness somewhere
This argument is proven by night and day

751. Zamaana chu-aajiz nawaazi kunad
Be taz azdaahaa mor baazi kunad
If the world starts treating the weak with goodness
Then a dangerous python will also play with an ant

752. Musharraf kuja aur Aali Hasan
Kuja banda-e-Hazrat-e-Zulminan
Where are Musharraf and Aali Hasan?
And where is the servant of the Great Bountiful One?

753. Yeh hai inqalaab-e-zamaana ki baat
Lage munh chidhane jo khaate the laat
This is a matter of revolutionary times
Those dare to tease who earlier were kicked

754. Hua hamla-aawar Mohammad Hasan
Bekhauf-e-Khuda-o-Rasool-e-Zaman
Mohammad Hasan became an assailant
Fearless of God and the Prophet of the age

755. Musharraf aur Aali Hasan saath the
Taman ke sipahi bhi hai haath the
Musharraf and Aali Hasan were along with him
Alas! Soldiers of the army were also present

756. Asiraan-e-mahbas bhi humraah the
Muaawin mere nala-o-aah the
Captives of the prison were also along with them
Laments and sighs were my companions

757. Aur Jafar Ali mard bepir tha
Bana sabka yaaron main nakhcheer tha
And Jafar Ali was a merciless man
Friends, I had become everyone's target

758. Woh darrana aaya azakhana mein
Na baaqi tha kuch mere mar jane mein
He came rushing into the mourning house
Zilch was left in my dying

759. Hue hamla-aawar yeh sab naabkaar
Shararat pe bandhe kamar ek baar
All these beasts became aggressors
They were singularly determined on notoriety

760. Lage ghul machane jo woh charm dooz
Main samjha qayaamat ka hai aaj rooz
When those cobblers started making cacophonous noises
I felt that today is the day of resurrection

761. Jo asbaab hukkaam ka tha dhara
Aur jo kuch ke asbaab raaqim ka tha
The possessions of the rulers which were kept
And whatever was the property of the writer

762. Lage lootne us ko maalun sab
Khuda ki gire unpe barq-e-ghazab
All these people started plundering it
May the lightning of God's wrath fall upon them!

763. Har ek saariq-o-rahzan-o-purfasaad
Shaqawat mein the misl-e-ibn-e-Ziyad
Each one was a pilferer, highway robber and seditious
In villainy they were like the son of Ziyad

764. Hai dushwaar karna raqam sab ka naam
Na mauzoon kabhi hota mera kalaam
It is difficult to write down everyone's names
Or else my narrative would never have been agreeable

765. Sukhan hai moojaz wa sharah buland
Hamesha se hai aaqilon ko pasand
The account is compendious and highly explanatory
This style is always liked by intellectuals

766. Mujhe yawahgooi se raghbat nahin
Tawalat ki asla zaroorat nahin
I do not have the inclination to speak of minute details
Actually there is no requirement of protraction at all

767. Musalman gumraah sab saath the
Rifaqat mein woh log haihath the
All the apostatical Muslims were accomplices
Alas! These people were in comradeship

768. Kamar basta jo log the bar fasaad
Rahe sab ke sab woh toh ibn-e-Ziyad
Those who were in a state of readiness for discord
Each and everyone of them was the son of Ziyad

769. Samajh boojh kar woh gire chaah mein
Hue mubtala qahar-e-Allah mein
With deliberative understanding they jumped into the well
Were entangled in the wrath of Allah

770. Kawaif yeh sab dekh kar haazireen
Yeh kahte the dil mein ke hain sab laain
The audience on witnessing these circumstances
Would say in their hearts that all are sordid

771. Azakhana mein jab hua yeh sitam
Rausa hue shahr ke chashm-e-nam
When this violence took place in the mourning house
The nobles of the town had tearful eyes.

Bayaan Taaraaji-e-Asbaab

Description of the plundering of possessions

772. Satrahween ko asbaab uthne laga
Mera huzn se zoor ghatne laga
On the seventeenth, the lifting of goods began
Due to grief my strength started diminishing

773. Taman ke sipahi jo the sath-sath
Liya maal maujood ko hanthon-hanth
The soldiers of the army who were along with them
Snatched the available goods with swiftness

774. Nusrat Beg bhi yak Hawaldaar tha
Ke masnui Nazim ka woh yaar tha
Nusrat Beg, a Hawaldaar was also there
As he was a friend of the fake Nazim

775. The Mirza Humayun wa Ramzan Khan
Yehi maal ke sab the ghaaratgaraan
There were Mirza Humayun and Ramzan Khan
They were the plunderers of all the possessions

776. Miyan Abde Khaliq bhi gumraah the
Allahdad Khan uske humraah the
Miyan Abde Khaliq was also misguided
Allahdad Khan was also along with him

777. Woh Sardar Ali Khan aur Fazle Ali
Diya un sabhon ne bahut bekali
That Sardar Ali Khan and Fazle Ali
They gave a lot of discomfort

778. Mohammad Faqir aur Aali Hasan
Mutaiyyan hue leke apne taman
Mohammad Faqir and Aali Hasan
Were assigned with their armies

779. Bihari bhi ek mard-e-mardood tha
Bahut dil mein apne woh khushnood tha
Bihari was also an unprincipled man
Indeed he was very pleased in his heart

780. Ho Qahhaar ka unpe nazil ghazab
Rahen hashr tak mubtala-e-taab
May the wrath of the Vanquisher descend upon them!
May they suffer from fatigue until the day of judgement!

781. Sitam bar zaeefaan-e-miskeen makun
Ke zalim ba dozaq ravad be-sukhan
Do not be cruel towards the poor and the weak
Because the cruel will be sent to hell without a dialogue

782. Karon uski tafseel gar main raqam
Toh ek juz se hargiz na hove ga kam
If I write the details of that
Then it will not be less than a chapter

783. Jo tha maal mera wa hukkaam ka
Jahan tak bana khub ghaarat kiya
Whatever were mine and the ruler's belongings
They ravaged as much as they could

784. Jo cheezen ke hukkaam ne mujh ko deen
Batarz-e-amaanat woh sab theen rakheen
Those things which the rulers had given me
They all were kept as entrusted property

785. Har ek kothri se woh laye nikaal
Rakha tha jahan sone chandi ka maal
They brought out from every cabin
Where articles of gold and silver were kept

786. Siwa mere asbaab ke aur bhi
Azakhana ki us mein sab cheez thi
Besides my goods, others too
There were all things of the mourning house

787. Woh sab bakhshi Nawab Asaf ki thi
Paye zeenat-e-Karbala thi rakhi
All those had been granted by Nawab Asaf
Were kept for the adornment of the Karbala

788. Zamaana mein sabiq ke Nawab ne
Buzurgon ko mere diya tha use
The Nawab of earlier times
Had given them to my noble elders

789. Mohayyaa kiya tha buzurgon ne sab
Muhaafiz tha main unka vaaqif hai Rabb
All was furnished by my ancestors
God is cognizant of the fact that I was its protector

790. Siwa uske kuch main ne bazaat-e-khesh
Mohayyaa kiya tha sab asbaab-e-aish
Besides that, some things I myself
Had made available, all articles of luxury

791. Tha pachpan baras mein ekaththa kiya
Khuda ne mujhe tha yeh sab kuch diya
Had collected it over a period of fifty-five years
God had bestowed all these things upon me

792. Raha haakimon ka bahut iltifaat
Kahan tak likhun haakimon ki sifaat
There persisted a lot of courtesy of the rulers
How much can I write of the praises of the rulers?

793. Baiqbaal-e-hukkaam paida kiya
Bahaal usko sab haakimon ne rakha
This property was created by the bonanza of the rulers
And all the officers kept it intact

794. Bahut maine izzat imaarat kiya
Yeh sab haakimon ki badaulat hua
I commanded a lot of respect and authority
All this materialized with the help of the rulers

795. Muhaafiz raha main dil-o-jaan se
Nahin sadma pahuncha kisi aan se
I persisted as a guardian with all my heart and soul
Did not receive a shock at any instance

796. Khiyaanat na kuch us amaanat mein thi
Woh sab cheez thi jaisi thi waisi hi
There was no defalcation in that entrusted property
All those things were, just as they were

797. Nahin faraq aaya bamikhdaar-e-khas
Sada mujh ko uska raha pesh-o-pas
Came no difference in quantity, even of a straw's quantum
I always had hesitation over it

798. Main daulat se hukkaam ke tha ghani
Na dekha kabhi humne aisa dni
I was rich by the power of the rulers
I had never witnessed such ignominiousness

799. Musalman-o-Hindu se hain yeh juda
Hai bidat har ek deen mein narawa
They are different from Muslims and Hindus
In every religion blasphemy is unlawful

800. Meri aql es jaa pe hairaan hai
Ke in sab ka kaisa yeh imaan hai
At this point my intellect is amazed
That what kind of faith do these people have?

801. Amini ko mere kiya hai kharaab
Saqar mein yeh paawenge laakhon azaab
They have undone my guardianship
They would suffer from lakhs of torments in hell

802. Amaanat ka main kaam karta raha
Diyanat ki baaton pe marta raha
I was discharging the duties of a guardian
Was ready to lay down my life on issues of honesty

803. Khiyaanat na ki maine asla zari
Har ek shai ko dil se amaanat rakhi
In fact I did not misappropriate at all
Heartily considered everything as an entrusted deposit

804. Muhaafiz raha naqad-o-ajnaas ka
Taraqqi ka din raat durr pai raha
I was the trustee of cash and commodities
Was in pursuit of the pearl of progress day and night

805. Yeh makhfi nahin amr mashhoor hai
Har ek shahar mein uska mazkoor hai
This point is not a secret but is well known
It is discussed in every town

806. Rausa-e-shahri hain vaaqif tamaam
Hai azhar minash shams nizde awaam
All the noblemen of the town are well aware
To the common man it is crystal clear

807. Amaanat samajhta tha usko mudaam
Hifazat se uski hamesha tha kaam
I always used to consider that a trust
Was always engaged in its security

808. Siwa uske hukkaam-e-English ne bhi
Bahaal unko jaise thi waise rakhi
Besides that the English rulers too
Upheld them immutably just as they were

809. Tha hukkaam-e-English ko mera khayaal
Woh sab mulk-o-miraas rakha bahaal
The English officers had regard for me
They confirmed all territories and hereditary estates

810. Vaali ka jo hai kaam karte rahe
Na sultan pesheen aise hue
They discharged the duties of a guardian,
The former kings were not like this

811. Unhi ko sazawaar hai sultanate
Yeh karte hain har shakhs ki manzilat
Only they deserve the empire
They honour every person

812. Na agle salateen ne aisa kiya
Balke uske baraks unse hua
The previous rulers did not do so
But in fact the antithesis of this transpired through them

813. Kiya qatal Sarmad-o-Mansur ko
Kaha khaal Tabrez mein bhuns bharo
Assassinated Sarmad and Mansur
Ordered that the skin of Tabrez be filled with straw

814. Jo darwesh aamil-o-kamil hue
Khususan unhi ke woh qatil hue
The saints who were spiritual and learned
They unequivocally became their murderers

815. Yehi qadar-e-darwesh karte rahe
Faqiron ki iza pe marte rahe
This is the value that they gave to the pious ones
They sweated and toiled for the affliction of mendicants

816. Mohammad Hasan mard misl-e-Shimar
Usi zulm par usne bandhi kamar
Mohammad Hasan was a man like Shimar
He steeled himself for the same kind of brutality

817. Tasheea par tha naaz apne use
Main Shia hoon apni zabaan se kahe
He took pride in his profession of Shiite faith
"I am a Shiah" he professed with his tongue

818. Azakhana ka maal lutwa liya
Magar Shimar-o-mardaan ka ustad tha
Got the property of the mourning house plundered
Perhaps he was the master of inhuman men like Shimar

819. Yeh kaisa aqeeda tha Hasnain se
Azakhana ke log bechain the
What kind of fidelity was this for Hasnain?
The people of the mourning house were agitated

820. Pas az qatal Ibn-e-Ali Shamiyan
Liya loot ahle Haram ka makaan
After assassination of the son of Ali, Shamiyan
Looted the houses of the citizens of Mecca

821. Usi khandaan mein yeh tha naabkaar
Na ki qadr matamsaraa zeenahaar
This sinner was from that family
On no account did he value the mourning house

822. Paka tha jo khana niyaaz-e-Imam
Moharram ke woh bad hota mudaam
The food which had been cooked for offering to the Imam
It always was subsequent to Moharram

823. Woh taqseem basti mein hota raha
Faqir aur fuqra ko milta raha
It used to be distributed in the township
Destitutes and beggars used to get it

824. Paka khana deghon mein sab rah gaya
Jo na pukhta tha us pe pahra hua
All the cooked food was left in the cauldrons
That which was uncooked was put in custody

825. Rahe muhtamin jo woh baahar hue
Aqidat nishaan darr se chup rah gaye
Those who were the managers were turned out
The marked devotees kept quiet due to fear

826. Yehi hubb-e-Hasnain dil mein rahe
Zara ghaur se esko dekho sabhi
This was the affection for Hasnain in their hearts
Everyone should witness it judiciously

827. Woh zalim jo zahir mein Shia bana
Tasheea par apne woh maghroor tha
That brute who apparently became a Shiah
He was proud of his Shiism

828. Tasheea chadha tha use es qadar
Woh sunnat se Sunni ki karta hazar
He was so very fanatically Shiite
That he abstained from the practices of the Sunnis

829. Jo pucho kisi se toh kahta yehi
Namaaz usko padhte na dekha kabhi
Inquire from anyone, they used to say the same thing
Have not seen him offering Namaaz ever

830. Hue jama yahaan aise aise sab aa
Kiya shahar ko bas tabaah-o-siyaah
All of such kind collected here
They simply squandered and blackened the town

831. Abbasi ke firqah mein hain sab ke sab
Bahut jald ghaarat tu kar unko Rabb
They all belong to the sect of Abbasi
O God! You destroy them very soon

832. Jo hai zad boom unka howe tabaah
Maa khanma howen khaak-e-siyaah
May their birth place be destroyed
With their households they may be reduced to black dust

833. Woh khaana kharaab ang bain ki namat
Jahan se miten misl-e-haraf-e-ghalat
Those wretched ones like the body of lamentation
May be erased from the world like a wrong letter

834. Tu kar mukhtasar raavi yeh daastaan
Riwaayat jo hai zahan mein kar ayaan
O narrator! Shorten this tale
Reveal the narrative which is in your mind.

Riwaayat Mushtamil Ba Kaifiyat

Report comprising details

835. Yeh hai daastaan qabil-e-yaadgir
Sune gosh-e-dil se saghir-o-kabir
This tale is worth remembering
All big and small should listen to it from the core of their heart

836. Riwaayat buzurgon se aisi suni
Nahin farq esmen hai asla zari
Had heard such a legend from elders
In fact there is no change in this at all

837. Qayaamat talak sultanate liswi
Rahegi karenge yeh amr-o-nahy
Right upto the doomsday, the Christian empire
Will remain, they shall issue commandments

838. Che Rome wa che Sham wa che Iran zamin
Sab aajayengee unke zeer-e-nageen
Be it Rome, be it Syria or be it the territories of Iran
All will come under their control

839. Yeh hain sherq se gherb tak baadshah
Jo inse ladega woh hoga tabaah
They are the Emperors from the East to the West
Whoever fights with them will be destroyed

840. Na mulla na ulema ko kuch hai khabar
Na duniya ki ghairat na uqba ka darr
Neither the priests nor the learned have knowledge
Neither modesty of the world nor fear of hereafter

841. Nahin hai kitaabon par inka amal
Woh maani ko karte hain radd-o-badal
They do not act according to the scriptures
They modify and refashion the meanings

842. Jo kahte hain hum ahle Islam hain
Woh Islam ko karte badnaam hain
Those who say that we are the followers of Islam
They vilify Islam

843. Kitaabon se raavi ne paya khabar
Ke karta hai tehreer use bekhatar
The narrator has come to know from books
So he writes it undaunted

844. Hain sab ahle Hindustan chashm koor
Banate hain apne liye aap goor
That all the people of Hindustan are blind
They dig graves for themselves

845. Agar hashrnama hua motamad
Toh Iisi ki hai sultanate taa abad
If record of the day of resurrection happens to be infallible
Then the Christian empire would last upto eternity

846. Qalamroo ka inko kiya baadshah
Risala qayaamat ka kar tu nigaah
They have been made emperors of dominions
Look at the tract of doomsday

847. Ke Rome aur Sham unko Haq ne diya
Shahanshah mulkon ka inko kiya
That Rome and Syria have been given to them by God
They have been made emperors of countries

848. Yehi amr Tauret mein hai likha
Taamul se dekh usko pehle vila
The same matter is written in the Tauret also
First deliberate over it carefully

849. Likha hai yehi amr Injeel mein
Mili khabar Quran se bhi humen
Synonymous point is written in the Injeel
I received information from the Quran also

850. Ke lisi ki hai sultanate lazawaal
Nigahban hai Khaliq-e-Zuljalaal
The empire of Christians is indestructible
The Glorious Creator is their custodian

851. Riaayat murawwat hai in mein azeem
Nahin Hindiyon mein yeh faiz-e-amim
They have great kindness and benevolence
The Hindis do not have this all-comprehensive bounty

852. Riyaasat gayee Hindiyon se nikal
Kisi ka nahin khair par hai amal
Hindis have lost the empire
No one practices good deeds

853. Tahe tegh Mansur-o-Sarmad hua
Tab hi se yeh hukkaam ko hai mila
Mansur and Sarmad were put to death
Since then the rulers have obtained it

854. Liya sultanate cheen ta dukh saheyn
Diya Ahkamal-Haakimeen ne unhen
Empire was snatched so that they may bear sorrows
Which the Strongest-Sovereign gave them

855. Tawareekh-e-pesheen dekha nahin
Buzurgon ne likhkha so seekha nahin
Did not look at the former history
Did not learn from the scriptures of ancestors

856. Hai naaraaz Khaliq mera Hind se
Yakayak sab aafat mein az khud phanse
My Creator is angry with Hind
Impetuously all are entangled in calamity by themselves

857. Kitaaboon pe gar sabka hota amal
Toh raahat mein asla na aata khalal
If everyone had adhered to the books
Then no interruption at all would have come in pleasure

858. Zara Hindiyon ko jahan kuch hua
Kitaabon ko juzdaan mein dhar diya
Whenever anything at all happened to the Hindis
They kept the books aside in embellished binders

859. Farasat ko rakh kar ke baalaa-e-taaq
Lage kaam-e-bad karne andar rawaaq
Isolating sagacity in the topmost shelf
Started doing evil deeds inside canopies

860. Kafan ke silaane ka armaan hai
Lahad ke khudaane ka saamaan hai
They desire the stitching of their shrouds
This is the preparation for digging of grave

861. Padenge yeh ek rooz sakaraat mein
Giraftaar honge yeh aafaat mein
One day they will fall in the agony of death
They will be arrested by catastrophes

862. Yeh zahir ko lete hain batin ke koor
Ab es waqt apni banate hain goor
They are absolutely blind towards the obvious
Now at this time they are digging their graves

863. Na aage na peeche ka hai kuch khayaal
Hai ab zindgi apni sabko wabaal
They have no concern for the past or future
Now everyone's life is a vexation for them

864. Hain Abbasiyon ki yeh aulaad mein
Hain mashhoor-o-maaruf bedaad mein
They are among the descendents of the Abbasis
They are famous and well known for tyranny

865. Sitam in ke mazhab mein jaiz rawa
Abayee tariqa ko choden bhala
Cruelty is acceptable and practiced in their faith
Would they ever leave their traditional ways?

866. Agar beza zaaq zulmat sarisht
Nahin zeer-e-taaus baagh-e-bahisht
Never will the nature of a crow's egg change
Even if it is put under the peacock of the heaven

867. Bahangaam in beza parwar danash
Za Injeer jannat dahi arz nash
At the time when this egg is hatched
Even the Injeer of heaven will have no value for the crow

868. Dahi aabash az chashma-e-Salsabeel
Biran baiza gardum damad Jibraeel
If it is given water of the stream of Salsabeel
Even if the shadow of Gabriel's glazed wings falls upon it

869. Bood aaqibat bacchcha zaaq zaaq
Bard ranj baiho dah taaus baagh
In the end the baby of a crow shall remain a crow
It is fruitless bearing pains to nurture him like the peacock of the garden

870. Na hoga kalaam-e-buzurgaan khilaaf
Kitaaboon mein hain likh gaye saaf saaf
There shall be no misrepresentation by pen of the elders
They have written very clearly in the books

871. Agar tifl ho usko dekha karo
Kitaabon ki baaton ko seekha karo
If you are a child then refer to them
Learn from sermons in the books

872. Naseehat jo likha hai attaar ne
Kiya usko maqbool sutaar ne
The precept which has been written by the druid
Has been acknowledged by time

873. Qalamrau se mit jayen baaghi tamaam
Hain badkhah sarkaar-e-aali maqaam
May all rebels be erased from the dominions
Who are evil wishers of the highly-placed government

874. Baqahar-e-Khuda jald howen tabaah
Maa khaanumaan howen khaak-e-siyaah
May they soon be destroyed by the wrath of God
With their households they may be reduced to dark dust.

Hikayat-e-mutzaman Bidat-e-ghaaratgaraan

Report inclusive of heresy of plunderers

875. Raqam kar kuch asbaab ka mere haal
Musibat pe meri tu kuch kar khayaal
Write some account of my properties
Contemplate a little about my misfortunes

876. Azeeyat se meri ghadi sab kati
Woh kya thi jo mujh par na sakhti hui
All my time passed under great torment
Which authoritarian rigour was not exercised over me!

877. Koi aap se jaan marta nahin
Hilaak aap ko koi karta nahin
No one wishes death for oneself
Nobody destroys his own self

878. Va lekin main jeene se bezaar hoon
Fana hone par apne taiyyaar hoon
But nevertheless I am disgusted with living
I am myself ready to die

879. Kiya yeh bhi tadbeer ta hoon fana
Na dekhon rukh-e-Nazim-e-behaya
Devised such contrivance also, that I may meet death
I need not see the face of the shameless Nazim

880. Va lekin jo likha hai taqdeer ka
Woh mazmoon ayaan hoga tehreer ka
But whatever is written by providential fate
That content of the script of destiny shall become manifest

881. Khuda ki hai khwahish sabhon par buland
Har ek par uska hai hukm arjmand
God's will dominates over everyone
His orders are applicable for everyone

882. Likhi thi azeeyat yeh taqdeer mein
Kisi ki nahi chalti tehreer mein
This sorrow was written in my fortune
No one can exert any power over written destiny

883. The pachpan baras ahad-e-hukkaam mein
Rahe khush bahut aish-o-aaraam mein
For fifty-five years I was in the reign of the rulers
Remained very happy, in ease and luxury

884. Kisi tarha ki kuch na takleef thi
Bahut sahibon ne bhi tauqeer ki
There was no discomfort of any kind
The officers also venerated me

885. Governor ne bhi meri izzat kiya
Session Judge Magister ne rafat diya
The Governor also respected me
Session Judge and Magistrate bestowed exaltation

886. Kiya Laat ne bhi bahut ehtaraam
Unhi ko rakhe Khaliq-e-Zulkaraam
The Laat also was extremely respectful
May the Noble Creator sustain him

887. Lute ek zalim ke hum ahad mein
Ke juz-us-tahaqquq bhi kya kahen
I was looted by the government of a tyrant
What can I say with exception of its ascertainment?

888. Esi nasl mein sahibon tha Yazid
Hue yeh sazawaar halmin mazeed
Sahibs, Yazid was in this very race
These people deserve more, still more criticism

889. Na thi us ko jab hubbe-e-Aale abaa
Toh Saiyyed ka kab paas karta bhala
When he had no love for the immediate family of the Prophet,
So would he ever have any regard for ordinary descendents of the Prophet?

890. Liya usne ek-ek asbaab sab
Diye mujh ko laakhon hi ranj-o-taab
He took each and every possession
Gave me lakhs of sorrows and debility

891. Gorakhpur mein jo luta baar-baar
Hui us ki meezaan chauntees hazaar
When I was looted in Gorakhpur repeatedly
The total count of losses amounted to thirty-four thousand

892. Chale jab ke hukkaam es shahar se
Yahaan aan kar humse youn kah gaye
When the rulers were leaving this town
Came here and said this to me

893. Ke teen maah tak sab karen intizaar
Taab se adu ke na hon dil-figaar
That for three months all should wait
They should not be broken-hearted by the endeavours of the enemy

894. Toh teen maah ke baad aawenge hum
Mita denge har ek ka ranj-o-sitam
So after three months we shall return
Will erase everyone's grief and affliction

895. Kiya kitnon ne kuch na uska khayaal
Mulazim hue kitne bas haal-haal

Very many did not pay any attention to this
So many of them immediately became attendants

896. Kiya khub sa mujh ko zaar-o-nizaar
Jahan tak ke unka chala ikhtiyaar
Made me drastically weak and helpless
To the utmost of their capacity

897. Koi kahta tha bhej do Lucknow
Koi kahta tha qatal ho du-ba-du
Someone said that he may be sent to Lucknow
Someone commented that he should be assassinated in public

898. Yahaan maaro inko ke dil shaad ho
Yeh dushman hai ghar eska barbaad ho
Liquidate him here so that the heart may be delighted
He is an enemy, his house should be ruined

899. Jo kuch maal tha woh toh jaa hi chuka
Faqat jaan jane ka ek rog tha
Whatever goods I had were already lost
The only impending danger was of losing my life

900. Kiya maal-o-asbaab ghaarat mera
Hazaaron hi sadma bhi dil par dhara
Plundered my property and belongings
My heart was overburdened by a thousand tribulations

901. Kahan tak likhe un ki bidat ka haal
Likhe sab jo raavi ihaanat kamaal
How much can one chronicle the condition of their heresy?
If the chronicler writes all, it would cause extreme defamation

902. Karun kya bayaan apna haal-e-kharaab
Na zindah na murda raha yeh hisaab
What should I relate about my miserably poor state?
Neither alive nor dead such was my fettle,

903. Nahin mujh ko malum main kaun hoon
Pada hon kidhar khwaar-o-zaar-o-zabun

I have lost consciousness of self-identity
Where do I exist, humiliated, wounded and helpless?

904. Khud apne ko ab main nahin jaanta
Na apne ko main aap pahchaanta
Now I do not know myself
Neither do I recognize my selfhood

905. Ye taghaiyyur-e-haalat hui doostoon
Ke dushman ke dushman ki aisi na ho
Friends, there was such an alteration in conditions
May even an enemy's enemy never reach this state

906. Amaanat ke hain kaam sab sakht yaar
Chane hain yeh lohe ke aiye hoshiyaar
O friend! All tasks of security are Herculean
O Wise one! They are rigorous like chewing grams of iron

907. Amini bahut kaar-e-dushwaar hai
Har ek shakhs ko espe iqraar hai
Trusteeship is a very difficult assignment
Everyone accepts this fact.

Hikayat Zarbulmisl

Report of Aphorism

908. Likhun ek hikayat main zarbulmisl
Qawaif bhi tehrir ho qul-o-dil
I would write a proverbial report
The details would also be documented with all my heart

909. Tha Abdullah Ibn-e-Saba ek mard
The us waqt mein Imam ahle dard
There was a man Abdullah Ibn-e-Saba
At that time, was an Imam of the afflicted people

910. Raha Jafar-e-Sadiq unka alam
Kaha karte log unko aksar hakam
His banner was Jafar-e-Sadiq
Often people called him the arbitrator

911. Rahe marja-e-khalq jo woh Imam
Unhen jaan kar usne khairul anaam
That Imam who was the resort for asylum of all
Considering him the most virtuous person

912. Kitaab ek usne amaanat rakha
Batarz-e-amaanat use wahaan dhara
He deposited a book for safekeeping
As entrusted property kept it there

913. Imam us ko rakhte the jaan ki tarah
Na dekha kabhi usme radd-o-qadah
The Imam protected it like his life
Never witnessed in it any alteration or expostulation

914. Na khola na dekha kabhi woh kitaab
Na jaana ke kya hai sawaal-o-jawaab
Neither opened nor read that book ever
Was unaware of the questions and answers therein

915. Na tha unko maalum usmen hai kya
Likha kis ne aur us mein hai kya likha
He had no knowledge of its contents
Who has written it and what is written therein

916. Amaanat ko seene par apne rakhe
Woh duniya se darul baqa ko gaye
With the deposit held close to his heart
He left this world for his eternal abode

917. Gharaz us ke kahne se yeh hai meri
Amaanat mere paas sab cheez thi
My motive behind narration of this is
Everything was entrusted to my charge

918. Amaanat tha asbaab-e-aali tabaar
Bhala kyon na ho uske jaane ka khaar
Possessions of persons of noble descent were entrusted property
Wonder why a grudge should not be harboured for its loss?

919. Kahan tak ho tafseel uski raqam
Bayaan kar sake kab zabaan-e-qalam
How much can its intricate details be recounted?
What potency does the pen's tongue have to portray it?

920. Sharahwar likhne se majboor hoon
Bayaan karne se uske maazoor hoon

I am constrained in writing an exhaustive explanation
In giving detailed description, I am helpless

921. Magar khaas jo maal mera gaya
Bahut mukhtasar kar ke usko likha
However some special things which I lost
I have written them with conciseness.

Tashreeh Asbaab

Elucidation of properties

922. Bayaan ab main karta hoon aiye doostoon
Luta maal balwa mein usko suno
O friends! Now here I relate
Listen to the account of property looted in the riots

923. Faqat chand cheezon ko likhta hoon main
Ke taa sab koi yaad usko rakhen
I am writing only about a few things
So that everyone can remember them

924. Raha maal sab waqf-e-nazar-e-Imam
Hifazat kiya haakimon ne dawaam
All the possessions were trust of offerings to the Imam
The rulers protected them perpetually

925. Faqat barah sandooq baaja yahaan
Diya teen sau qeemat us ki ayaan
Exactly twelve boxes of musical instruments were here
Definitely paid three hundred as its price

926. Tha paltan ke Major se maine liya
Hifazat se woh paas mere raha
I had bought it from a Major of the platoon
It was with me very securely

927. Moharram mein woh bhi paye intizaam
Daham aur panjum ko aata tha kaam
In the course of arrangements for Moharram
It was used on the tenth and fifth

928. Tufang usne loota mere shaanzdah
Nikalte the ashrah mein bandhe sipah
He looted sixteen of my guns
On Ashrah, soldiers marched with their interlacement

929. Rahi us ki qeemat bhi yak sad chahal
Use le gaya yahaan se woh pur daghal
Its price was also one hundred and forty
That fraud carried it away from here

930. Tamaashe ka sandooq do chaar tha
Saman teen sau uska aiye yaar tha
There were a few boxes of entertainment shows
O friend! Its price was three hundred

931. Aur ek baks auzaar compass tha
Kharida tha maine use tees ka
And one box of instrument of compass was there
I had bought it for thirty

932. Zarufat chaandi tamaam-o-kamaal
Ke tha ek hazaar aur cheh sai ka maal
Things entirely of silver
So, they were worth one thousand and six hundred

933. Qraabeyn ek panzdah ki rahee
Bahut khub woh khushnuma thi bani
One carbine was for five hundred
Excellent, it was very beautifully made

934. Aur baad uske leen meri shatranjiiyan
Woh ginti mein barah theen aiye doostaan
And after that, took my chequered carpets
O friends! They were twelve in count

935. Rahi qeemat uski bhi sau rupiyah
Utha le gaya usko bahruupiya
Price of that too was a hundred rupees
The street histrionic took that away

936. Liye usne qaleen ikkis adad
Bhav uska tha alif aur paan sad
He took carpets, twenty-one in number
Their cost was one thousand and five hundred

937. Aur thooda sa cheeni ka bartan raha
Saman uska maalik ko nawwe diya
And there were a few utensils of bone-china
Gave a price of ninety to the owner

938. Kayee bakas sheesha ka bartan bhi tha
Ke do sad aur do uski qeemat diya
There were many boxes of glass utensils also
So, paid two hundred and two as price

939. Deewaargeer wa handi bahut khoob thi
Woh qeemat mein do sad aur dus ki rahi
Chandelier and pot were very good
In terms of price it cost two hundred and ten

940. Aur nuh ka do shamiyana raha
Shamul uske deyra pachchasi ka tha
And two canopies were for ninety
Along with that, tent was for eighty-five

941. Aur pashmina cheh sau se afzoon ka tha
Woh mardud khush ho use le gaya
And pashmina was for more than six hundred
That immoral one took it happily

942. Pachattar ki shamsheer meri rahi
Tapancha ki jodi rahi tees ki
My sword was for seventy-five
A pair of revolvers was for thirty

943. Shamadaan chandi ka tha cheh adad
Dhai sau keemat thi aiye nek mard
Silver candle stands were six in number
O virtuous man! Its price was two hundred and fifty

944. Rahi khub kya teen almaariyaan
Woh ek-ek sattar ki theen aiye miyan
How marvelous were the three almirahs
O Mister! Each one of them was for seventy

945. Aur tha ek hazaar do sad naqad bhi
siwa uske theen teen sau asharfi
And there was one thousand and two hundred cash also
Besides that were three hundred gold coins

946. Luta maal aur naqad jo baar-baar
Hui uski meezaan chauntees hazaar
The cash and belongings which were looted repeatedly
Its value was thirty-four thousand

947. Raqam saat sau us pe zaayid dharo
Chhehattar ko bhi uske shamil karo
Keep a sum of rupees seven hundred over that
Also add to it seventy six

948. Ye goya ke sab unke daade ka tha
Ke bekhauf ghar se mere le liya
As if it all belonged to their grandfather
That they fearlessly took it from my house

949. Kahan tak karun ab main tafseel-e-maal
Qalam ko nahin likhne ki hai majaal
How much of an explicit account can I give of the goods?
The pen does not have the courage to write

950. Gharaz maal mera aur hukkaam ka
Liya usne sab kaisi aafat kiya
Therefore belongings, mine and of the rulers
He took it all, what a disaster he executed!

951. Raha ek sipahi Allahdad Khan
Jafa pesha humraah ghaaratgaraan
There was a soldier, called Allahdad Khan
Oppressive, he came along with the plunderers

952. Kaha maine us se yeh shayaan nahin
Bas ab zulm-o-bidat ka payaan nahin
I said to him that this is not proper
That now there is no limit of ruthlessness and heresy

953. Zara lutf ki baat hai Sahibon
Diya kya jawaab usne akhir suno
Sahibs, it is an interesting matter
Just listen to the reply he finally gave me:

954. Agarche woh Saiyyad aur darwesh hain
Sipahi hain pesha ko hum kya karen
Although he is a Saiyyad and a saint
Being a soldier by profession, what can I do?

955. Usi ne diya tala kothri ka tod
Aur zanzeer bhi usne phenka marod
He broke the lock of the room
And he also twisted the chain and flung it

956. Wohi sara tala tutate rahe
Wohi sab qayaamat machate rahe
They kept getting the locks broken
They were the ones who kept raising a tumult

957. Woh sab ghar mein ghus-ghus ke lete the maal
Aur Aali Hasan sab ka karta khayaal
They picked up things from right inside the house
And Aali Hasan used to take care of all

958. Jo cheezen nafees aur undah milin
Woh sab haath mein us ne khadim ke deen
The beautiful and good things that were found
All those he gave in the hands of a servant

959. Aur Sardar Ali Khan ke sab aqriba
Mere maal ka dete the sab pata
And all the allies of Sardar Ali Khan
Used to give all information about my assets

960. Khairati lohaar aur Bishan todte
Woh sanduq ko khol kar dekhte
Ironsmith Khairati and Bishan broke the locks
They opened and checked the boxes

961. Tha Faiz Ali ek mardud jo
Laga kahne looto sab asbaab ko
One Faiz Ali who was an immoral man
Started saying, 'loot all belongings'

962. Kaha usne hukkaam ab hain kahan
Kahan hain Bird aur Chester kahan
He said, where are the rulers now?
Where is Bird and where is Chester?

963. Na jaana ke yeh rashq-e-deo murid
Ke zahir Musalman hain baatin Yazid
Do not know that these, envy of the disciples of Ogre
Are only visibly Muslims; internally they are Yazid

964. Na maane gaye dargaah-e-Husnain ko
Na hargiz sunenge mere bain ko
Did not obey and proceeded to the shrine of Husnain
They would never pay attention to my lamentation

965. Karenge sab asbaab khaak-o-siyaah
Yeh mardood honge ek din tabaah
They would reduce all goods to black dust
One day these wicked ones shall be destroyed

966. Makaan ka nishaan mere pate jahaan
Use loot lete the ghaaratgaraan
Wherever they found a clue of my abode
The plunderers used to loot it

967. Anta ghar mein lattha humara raha
Ganwaaron ne usko bhi sab le liya
My sticks were in the Billiard room
The rustics took all of them as well

968. Hars aur patti churane lage
Sitam pe sitam unke hum ne sahe
Began stealing the plough share and tablets
I endured their brutality after brutality

969. Rahe dus adad lattha woh dar shumaar
Wa fee lattha dus rupiya qeemat thi yaar
Those sticks were ten in numbers
Friend, each of those sticks cost rupees ten

970. Woh bagghi woh ghoodi bhi meri liya
Woh Baker ne mujh ko baqeemat diya
They also took my light carriage and mare
Those Baker had given me for a price

971. Diya teen sau uski qeemat baham
Hua hai yeh mujh par sitam par sitam
I had given altogether three hundred as its price
Upon me have been implemented atrocities over atrocities

972. Jo mehnat mashaqqat se paida kiya
Khareeda banaya wa ghar mein dhara
That which was created with diligence and hard work
Bought, produced and safeguarded in the house

973. Use sarf mein apne laye na hum
Aminon ki manind rakha baham
I did not bring it in my own use
Kept it intact like a trustee

974. Liya zalimon ne kiya kuch na gham
Sitam hai sitam hai sitam hai sitam
The brutes took it, they did not sympathize
This is injustice, this is injustice, this is injustice, injustice!

975. Hawakhah sarkaar ke jo rahe
Wohi haath se zalimon ke lute
Those who were the well-wishers of the government
Were the ones who were looted by the hands of the barbarians

976. Hua ahle amla par ziyaadah sitam
Ke har kas-o-nakas ki hai chashm nam
The people of government establishments were more oppressed
So the eyes of all and sundry are moist

977. Muharrir-o-munish pe yurish kamaal
Karam kar tu aiye Khaliq-e-Zuljalaal
On the clerks and secretaries was excessive aggression
O Splendid Creator! Kindly be merciful

978. Hunudon pe us waqt ziyaadah sitam
Mahajan pe azbas ke ranj-o-alam
At this time, there was more violence against the Hindus
Over the Mahajans came quite a lot of sorrow and torment

979. Musalmanon mein sirf raavi gharib
Bayaan kya kare apni haalat ajeeb
Among Muslims, only the poor chronicler
How should he describe his bizarre condition?

Bayaan ghaaratgari-e-asbaab Pipraich Waghairah

Account of the plundering of properties of Pipraich etcetera

980. Thi taarikh gyarahween aiye azeez
Rabiul-Aakhir ki tu kar le tameez
O Dear! The date was eleventh
Of Rabiul-Aakhir; do listen prudently

981. Ke Gadhwa wa Gaya ka asbaab sab
Hai Pipraich mein sab se ziyaadah ghazab
That all the assets of Gadhwa and Gaya
In Pipraich is the greatest tumult

982. Bandhu Singh ne luta-o-ghaarat kiya
Sab asbaab taaraaj unka hua
Bandhu Singh looted and ravaged
All their goods were plundered

983. Bihari bhi ja kar ke bazoor-o-shoor
Liya naqad zar unse gardan marood
Bihari also proceeded there and forcefully
Twisted necks and took cash and gold from them

984. Yeh zalim ki janib se pahuncha wahaan
Raha yeh to sardaar-e-ghaaratgaraan
He reached there on behalf of the brute
He was the leader of the plunderers

985. Liya maar aur bandh ke haft hazaar
Kiya zulm aur zoor bas beshumaar
By thrashing and trussing up, took seven thousand
Committed unlimited brutalities and atrocities

986. Kisi ne na fariyaad unki suna
Na ahle committee ne pucha zara
No one paid any heed to their plea
Nor did the members of the committee take care

987. Na Raja na Babu madadgaar hain
Ab es waqt azlam ke sab yaar hain
Neither the kings nor the officers are helpful
Now, at this time, all are friends of the most inhuman

988. Mahajan ilaaqah ke mere rahe
Woh becharah na haq pe loote gaye
The Mahajan was from my region
Helpless, he was unjustly looted.

Hikayat Barbaadi-e-Mohiuddinpur

Report of the ruin of Mohiuddinpur

989. Suno yaaro yeh turfa tar maajra
Gharib aur umra ka kab ho bhala
Friends, listen to this strange occurrence
When will the poor and noble be gratified?

990. Kanu joor-e-zalim bahad-e-raseed
Ke eeyn bar shud hukm haaye shadeed
Now the brute's brutality reached such zenith
That this time more severe atrocities were ordered:

991. Ke kothi aur banglon ko mismaar kar
Braabar karo khaak ke sarbasar
Raze to ground the warehouses and bungalows
Reduce them entirely to the state of dust

992. Jo tha ek bangla Mohiuddinpur
Bhala us makaan ne kiya kya qusoor
One bungalow which was at Mohiuddinpur
After all, what crime did that house commit?

993. Makaan se musafir ko aaraam hai
Sirf us se Ahmad ka ek naam hai
Travellers derived comfort from that house
Only the name of Ahmad is attached to it

994. Mera us se ek naam hai doostoon
Zara thoda uska yeh qissa suno
Friends, due to that I have a name
Just listen to this brief anecdote related to it:

995. Mohiuddinpur ki jo surat kiya
Yehi haal Tura ka bhi kar diya
The state that Mohiuddinpur was reduced to
The condition of Tura was also made similar

996. Nahin dekha hum aise ghaaratgaraan
Koi munhadim aisa karta makaan
I had never seen such plunderers
Would anyone have demolished the house in this manner?

997. Kadi khood lete hain afwaaj keyn
Na aisa sitam humne dekha kahin
The rancorous armed forces dug out the chains,
I have never witnessed such violence

998. Mera astabal munhadim kar diya
Kharabi ka din raat bas dhyaan tha
They demolished my stable
Day and night they concentrated only on mischief

999. Hua benishaan bekh-o-bun se makaan
Liya jo tha wahan barmala wa nihaan
The house was wiped out right from foundation
Took from there whatever was exposed or enclosed

1000. Makaan-e-kalan par jo niyat hai bad
Baqahar-e-Khuda unka kat jaye yad
Since they harbour evil intentions for big houses
By God's wrath may their hands be severed

1001. Na kuch khauf-e-haakim na ahle makaan
The sangeen dil zulm ke baniyaan
There is neither any fear of the rulers, nor of the owners of the house
The originators of tyranny were stone-hearted

1002. Kiya jisne jisne makaan munhadim
Khudaya na uske rahe dam-mein-dam
All of those who have demolished the house
O God! May their life-breath become comatose

1003. Shujaat thi un sab ki ghurba ke saath
Hifazat hai es waqt Khaliq ke haath
All of them displayed valour before the poor
At this time only the Creator's hands are powerful enough to protect

1004. Rakhe sab ki izzat Khuda-e-Kareem
Hai bidat gharibon pe es dam azeem
May the kind Almighty safeguard everyone's honour
At this moment there is great oppression of the poor

1005. Hain Haiti ke Rawat ki sarkash sipaah
Woh karte hain raahi ko aksar tabaah
The soldiers of the Rawat of Haiti are rebels
They often devastate the travelers

1006. Taiyyun Mehra ke hain ghaat par
Aur Shahbaaz Ganj ki bhi hain chounki par
They are deputed at the wharf of Mehra
And are also appointed at the check post of Shahbaaz Ganj

1007. Aur Nakaha mein bhi unki chounki hui
Unhi sab ki rasta mein sakhti hui
And their outpost was fixed at Nakaha as well
Along the routes they subjected others to violence

1008. Aur danku ke bhi log rahte rahe
Jafa saath un sab ke karte rahe
Accomplices of the dacoits were also present
Together with them, they too oppressed

1009. Doon Singh tamam leke rahta raha
Giraftaar raahi ko karta raha
Doon Singh used to stay with armed forces
Travellers were captivated by him

1010. Kiya tark khazan ne es shahar ko
Pakad laaye usko yeh sab zasht-e-khu
The treasurer quit this city
He was captured and brought back by these malicious ones

1011. Jo tha naqad aur jins loota tamaam
Hai yeh shahar mein baat mashhoor-o-aam
They looted all the available cash and material
This matter is famous and is commonly known in the town

1012. Hui Ram Nawaaz ki bhi haalat ajeeb
Pakad kar ke raste se aaye gharib
Condition of Ram Nawaaz also became strange
The poor fellow was captured enroute.

Kaifiyat Ittalai; Bakhidmat-e-Hukkaam Aali Shaan

Nature of intimation in the service of the magnificent rulers

1013. Rawaana hua yahaan se Abdur Rahim
Jo lisai mazhab mein hai mustaqim
Abdur Rahim departed from here,
He is steadfast in the Christian faith

1014. Woh hukkaam-e-faiyyaz ke ja ke paas
Zabaani meri youn kiya iltemaas
He appeared before the munificent rulers
Put forth an entreaty in my words

1015. Agar hukm ho aawen hum sab chale
Baiqbaal-e-sarkaar jaan to bache
If it is so ordered, we all shall proceed
By the favoured acknowledgement of the government, at least our life will be saved

1016. Kisi cheez ki ab nahin hai hawas
Bakhubi kiya aish pachpan baras
Now there is no craving for anything at all
Spent fifty-five years in great luxury

1017. Tha sab ke muradon ka roshan chiraagh
Quloob-e-raaya raha baagh-baagh
The lamp of everyone's wishes was brightly lit
Subject's hearts were extremely joyful

1018. Na dil basta tha koi ghuncha misaal
Shagufta tha dil misl-e-gul maah-o-saal
No one was frozen hearted like a bud
Months and years, the heart was happy like a blooming flower

1019. Na tha misl-e-Bulbul koi narahzan
Toh Lala sifat dil mein daag-e-mehan
Like the nightingale no one was crying
And none had the dark scar of suffering in his heart, like the Poppy flower

1020. Yeh naazil hua kaisa naagah ghazab
Phanse ek moozi ke changul mein sab
What kind of an uncalled for calamity has descended?
Every one is trapped in the clutches of a tormentor,

1021. Ladakpan jawani kati jaish mein
Zaifi mein aaya khalal aish mein
Childhood and youth were spent in pleasure
In old age has come an intrusion in ease

1022. Na khauf-e-riyaasat na daulat ka gham
Judaai ki sarkaar ka hai alam
There is no fear of loss of lordship, neither is there sorrow for lost wealth
The pain is of separation from the government

1023. Iraadah hai aa kar ke masroor hoon
Ba majboor-o-maazoor maqsoor hoon
There is an intention to come and be pleased
But I am constrained, helpless and belittled

1024. Woh mardood aamaadah hai ghaat par
Muaiyyan taman hai har ek ghaat par
That reprobate is insistent on slaughter
Armed forces are appointed at every wharf

1025. Kiya usne rasta ko es tarha band
Ke saktah yahaan ke hain sab dardmand

In such a manner has he sealed the route
That all the sympathizers here have fallen into a death-swoon

1026. Yahaan se nikalna hua hai mohaal
Sabhon ke taaluq hain aulaad-o-aal
Evacuation of this place has become impossible
Everyone's concern is their children and family

1027. Taaluq ki hai gardanon mein kamand
Esi shahar mein rah gaye shahar-band
Their necks are in the stranglehold of the lasso of concern
Remained arrested in the town in detention

1028. Hai dariya ke ghaaton pe chauki kamaal
Chale chaal chunti nahin hai majaal
At the wharfs of the rivers are extraordinary guard outposts
Even an ant cannot dare to budge

1029. Na yaara-e-raftan na taab-e-qiyaam
Ajab kashmakash hai ajab izdehaam
Neither is there strength to go, nor the power to stay
It is a strange dilemma, bizarre chaos

1030. Na humdam na moonis na yaawar koi
Bajuz aap ke hai na afsar koi
There is neither a friend, nor companion, nor a collaborator
Except you, there is no other officer

1031. Siwa aapke dard kis se kahein
Jabeen kaun se dar pe apni ghisen
Besides you, to whom shall we report our agony?
At which doorway should we abrade our forehead?

1032. Suno ya karo radd mera iltemaas
Esi dar se taazeest hai mujh ko aas
Pay heed to or reject my entreaty
For entire life I have hope from this gateway

1033. Na taab-e-paridaan, naa hi baal-o-par
Na paidal na aswaar ka hai guzar

Doorway to the tombs of
Roshan Ali Shah and Ahmad Ali Shah

Gold *Tazia* presented by
Nawab Asaf-ud-Daula of Awadh

Modern enclosure over Roshan Ali Shah's *Dhooni*

Scenes of armed confrontation between British and Rebel forces.

Neither the power of flight, nor wings and feathers
Neither for pedestrians nor for riders is ingression and egression

1034. Ab es waqt mein keejiye kuch madad
Bache jaan az fazl-e-Rabb-ul-Samad
Now at this time render some help
By the grace of the Sublime God life may be saved

1035. Bulaao humain ya ke khud aaiye
Ilaaj-e-shifa jald bhijwaiye
Either call me or come yourself
Quickly send the remedy for healing

1036. Us azlam ke haanton se hai jaan-balab
Masihaai ka waqt pahuncha hai ab
Due to that brute I am close to death
Now has come the time to use your power to restore life

1037. Khuda phir na dikhlaye in sab ka ru
Yehi aarzoo hai yehi aarzoo
May God not show their faces to us again
This is my desire, this is my yearning

1038. Yehi hai dil se darkhwast-e-Ahmad Ali
Dua ki shagufta ho ya Rabb kali
This is an appeal from the heart of Ahmad Ali
O God! May the bud of my prayer bloom!

1039. Salamat rahen haakimaan-e-Firang
Bache gar toh dekhenge phir baagh rang
May the European rulers remain safe and sound,
If saved, shall again behold the gardens of merriment

1040. Khuda jald dikhlaye shaadi ka rooz
Yahaan howen hukkaam raunaq furooz
May God show the day of rejoicing soon,
May the rulers grace this place by their benign presence!

1041. Jo irshaad-e-sarkaar ho woh kare
Majholi ke rasta ko raavi dhare
Would follow whatever is ordered by the government
The writer shall proceed on the route to Majholi.

Bayaan Mushtamil Chand Hikayat

Description comprising some reports

42. Bulakar Braj Lal se hum kaha
Azamgarh ka ahwaal humko mila
I called Braj Lal and said that
I have received a report of the conditions in Azamgarh

43. Makaan par tum apne chalo ke rahen
Jagah aman ki tumne payee kahin
You proceed to your house so that we can stay
Have you discovered any peaceful place?

44. Jaunpur mein aapka hai makaan
Aur hukkaam hain wahaan ke sab qadardaan
Your house is at Jaunpur
And all the administrators of that place are patrons

45. Mujhe aap humraah le kar chalen
Waheen kuch dinon ta ke bahum rahen
Take me along with you
For some days we can stay there together,

46. Rahunga main paas unke ezaaz se
Bahut khush-o-khurram rakhenge mujhe
I will reside with them very honourably
They will keep me very happy and cheerful

1047. Hain hukkaam mere woh sab qadardaan
Rahunga wahaan main ba aman-o-amaan
All those rulers value my worth
I will live there in peace and order

1048. Kaha humse Munshi ne aiye Shahji
Koi din yahaan par raho tum abhi
The Munshi said to me, 'O Shahji'
As of now, prolong your stay here for some more days

1049. To kahne se unke raha main yahaan
Nahin to chala jata ab tak kahan
Because of his advice, I dwelt here
Otherwise by now I would have gone heaven knows where

1050. Kiya mutmaeen mujh ko es taur se
Zara khauf rakho na tum aur se
Convinced me in this manner
That you need not be fearful of anyone at all

1051. Ke hukkaam English ke aate hain jald
Jo mufsid yahaan par hain jaate hain jald
That the English rulers will soon arrive
The seditious elements present here shall depart soon

1052. Sanaullah ne humse yeh bhi kaha
Buran Sahib ne maslehat yeh diya
Sanaullah said this also to me
Buran Sahib too gave this reasoning

1053. Musharraf Khan dushman jo hai naabkaar
Yeh kahta hai woh har ghadi baar-baar
Musharraf Khan, who is a notorious enemy
Every moment he repeatedly re-echoes this statement

1054. Likha karte hain Shahji toh hamesh
Araaiz bakhidmat-e-hukkaam khesh
Shahji keeps writing unceasingly
Applications addressed to his own rulers

1055. Jo Nazim unhe Lucknow bhej den
To ahsaan gardan par meri karen
If the Nazim sends him to Lucknow
He would be doing a great favour to me

1056. Yaqinan woh bhijwayega Lucknow
Humen haal malum hai hu-ba-hu
Undoubtedly he shall despatch to Lucknow
The exact situation is known to me

1057. Koi yeh khabar Shahji se kare
Ke dinar-o-zar kuch muhaiyya rahe
Someone should advice this to Shahji
That some Dinars and gold should be readily available

1058. Khabar tum yeh sab jaa ke fauran karo
Yeh sab kaifiyat Shahji se kaho
You go and apprise all this immediately
Communicate all these circumstances to Shahji

1059. Suni kaifiyat humne aiye doostoon
Kaha jo munasib hai usko karo
O friends, I heard the state of affairs
Said that, do whatever is appropriate

1060. Ba waqt-e-talab jaan dewenge hum
Nahin karne paawenge hum par sitam
When the occasion demands I shall lay down my life,
The rebels shall be unable to tyrannize me

1061. Nahin ahle izzat ka hargiz yeh kaam
Sahe zulm-e-zalim ko jo subh-o-shaam
This is not at all the business of honourable persons
To tolerate morning and evening, cruelty of the cruel

1062. Yeh Iblees insaan ki surat mein hain
Inhe chahiye log shaitaan kahen
They are Iblees in the form of human beings
It is suitably apt that people should call them Satan

1063. Laundon ke hote hain hum kab mutih
Khuda ne kiya mera rutba rafi
When have I been obedient towards minions?
God has made my status exalted,

1064. Inaayat se English ke mumtaaz hain
Sghar se haakim ke damsaaz hain
Due to kindness of the English I am honoured
Since childhood am a supporter of the rulers

1065. Bahut qadar-o-ezaaz se mushfaqah
Governor ne humko muaziz kiya
Friendly, with a lot of patronage and esteem
The Governor made me honourable

1066. Raha meri izzat ka haakim ko dhyaan
Kab aise dinon ka tha waham-o-gumaan
The rulers were conscious of my dignity
Who could have anticipated such days in remotest fantasy or imagination?

1067. Magar haq toh yeh hai ke Ahmad Ali
Woh hote toh kyun hoti youn bekali
But O Ahmad Ali! The truth is that
In their presence why should there have been such restlessness?

1068. Bhala kis ka munh tha ke deta woh ranj
Taalli se kyun hote yoon baad-e-sanj
Who had the daring to give distress?
Why would have castles in the air been built by conceit?

1069. Mere saamne es tarha beadab
Kamar bandh kar dete ranj-o-taab
So very disrespectful before me
Gave sorrow and feebleness with absolute resolution

1070. Pale jinki godon mein ladkon ki tarha
Na likhen unhen haal ki apne sharah

Was brought up in whose laps, like sons
Should not write to them an exposition of my situation?

1071. Sharifon se yeh kaam hote nahin
Kabhi haq nemat ko khote nahin
Gentlemen cannot have this kind of a calling
They never lose rightful divine blessings

1072. Ataat se aaqa ke aaraam hai
Bhalai se ab har jagah naam hai
Due to obedience of the Lord there is comfortable reassurance
Now there is eminent fame owing to good virtues

1073. Unhi se mohabbat hai dil mein mere
Mere qadardaan hain woh chote-bade
There is love for them in my heart
They, small or big, are my patrons

1074. Na chodoon ga ifraat-o-tafreet mein
Main hoon doost unka jahan woh rahen
I will not abandon them even in the ultimate extreme circumstance
No matter where they are placed, I am their friend

1075. Saadat samajhta hoon unke nazar
Kisi ko hai es baat ki kya khabar
I consider their glance auspicious
Who knows a thing about this matter

1076. Abbot rahte the aathon pahar
Maa aal-o-atfaal the bekhatar
Abbot used to stay all the time
With his family and children; he was completely safe

1077. Azakhana ke dar pe maujood the
Hamesha woh raavi se khushnood the
He was present at the doorway of the mourning house
He always was happy with the narrator

1078. Barabar madad kharch deta raha
Khabar unki har waqt leta raha
Often helped and advanced money for expenses
Always enquired after him

1079. Puran aur Morris bhi damsaaz the
Yehi log har waqt humraaz the
Puran and Morris were also intimate
These people always were close confidants

1080. Jo kahte the lisai karte the hum
Madad kharch bhi dete the dam-ba-dam
Whatever the Christians said, I did
Also continuously gave them assistance and financial allowances

1081. Shab-o-rooz English ka leta tha naam
Unhi ka duago tha raavi mudaam
Night and day I praised the English
The chronicler was perpetually prayerful for them

1082. Na masnui Nazim se rakhta tha kaam
Tawaqqo thi sarkaar se subh-o-shaam
Did not associate with the fake Nazim
Dawn to dusk, had hopeful trust in the government

1083. Mubarra ataat se sabki raha
Jo kuch haal tha mu-ba-mu likh diya
Remained free from subservience to everyone
Whatever were the conditions; wrote with precision

1084. Kiya laakh surat ka mujh par sitam
Hua haal mera na kuch besh-o-kam
Innumerable atrocities were committed upon me
Neither better nor worse; my state remained unaltered

1085. Raha vaaz par apni sabat qadam
Rahoonga yunhi dam mein jab tak hai dam

Remained firm-footed in my attitude
Till the last moment of life I shall persist in status quo

1086. Maroonga bhi jab main toh ek aan par
Yehi vaaz wajib hai insaan par
Whenever I shall die, it will be with a proud dignity
This style is expedient for human beings

1087. Hua jiska, uska hua jeete dam
Na chode use garche sar ho qalam
The one to whom I belong, will remain committed to him till the last breath
Did not forsake him; despite the probability of being beheaded

1088. Na kuch rishta-e-aal-o-aulaad hai
Ataat mein English ke dil shaad hai
There are no relationships of family and children
My heart is glad being dutiful towards the English.

Kaifiyat amalgaan-wa-rausa-e-shahar

Condition of the workers and nobles of the town

1089. Rahe Jamna Parshad Munshi gharib
Sitam un pe bhi hum ne dekha ajeeb
Jamna Prasad was a poor Munshi
I witnessed astonishing injustice being done to him too

1090. Woh Munshi Niranjan hua hai tabaah
Ghazabnak zalim ki us par nigaah
That Munshi Niranjan has been destroyed
The indignant brute had set his eyes on him

1091. Bechanlal tha Qanoongoh-e-hoshiyaar
Brabar raha raavi ka ghamgusaar
Bechan Lal was a wise Qanoongoh
He was a constant sympathetic friend of the narrator

1092. The diwani ke Munshi jo bavaqaar
Hue dono bhai bahut zer baar
Munshi of the civil court who was dignified
Both the brothers were extremely over-burdened and indebted

1093. Sitam Ganga Parshad par bhi hua
Saubat mein sakhti mein tha mubtala
Ganga Prasad was also oppressed
He was trapped in hardship and harshness

1094. Kiya Bhawani Parshad par bhi sitam
Uthaya bahut usne ranj-o-alam
Did injustice with Bhawani Prasad as well
He suffered a lot of pain and agony

1095. Gaya jis jagah par woh luta gaya
Ajab kashmakash mein har ek ja raha
Wherever he went; he was looted
At every place he stayed in a strange perplexity

1096. Azamgarh ka jis dam iraadah hua
Iswanji mein ja kar ke dera kiya
The moment there was contemplation for Azamgarh
Went and camped at Iswanji

1097. Faraari Tillangon ne narghaa kiya
Tha jo kuch ke paas unke sab le liya
The fugitive soldiers cordoned him
Robbed him of whatever possessions he had

1098. Bechanlal Mukhtaar wa Debi Charan
Rahe ibtida se yeh sab khush magan
Bechanlal Mukhtaar and Debi Charan
From the beginning they all were happy and self-contented,

1099. Na the shahar mein dono yeh hoshmand
Rahenge woh hukkaam ko dil pasand
Both these sensible men were not present in the town
They shall always remain favourites of the rulers

1100. Kanhaiyya Mudarris ka likhta hun haal
Tha English Bahadur ka usko khayaal
I am narrating the condition of Kanhaiyya Mudarris
He was concerned about English Bahadur

1101. Tulsi Ram Aminon mein hoshiyaar tha
Ke yeh mard har waqt bedaar tha
Among the revenue officials Tulsi Ram was clever
For this person was constantly vigilant

1102. Muhalle mein mere rahe Ramnawaaz
Rahe yeh to sab log baimtiyaaz
In my alley was one Ramnawaaz
All these people were distinguished,

1103. Raha paas naqad uske so le liya
Kuch asbaab thoda sa uska gaya
Took whatever cash he had
A few of his things were also gone.

1104. Debi Dutt ke pote bhi hoshiyaar hain
Saubat wa sakhti se bezaar hain
The grandsons of Debi Dutt are also smart
They are disgusted by hardship and severity;

1105. Ahaata ke Pande rahe nek naam
Duago yeh sarkaar ke the mudaam
Pandey of the compound was known for good virtues
He was always praying for the government;

1106. Dhampat Rai ek jo hain Tehsildaar
Woh bidat se zalim ke the beqaraar
Dhampat Rai, who is a Tehsildaar
He was restless due to violence of the brute;

1107. Mohammad Latif sahib-e-zee sho'oor
Rahe ibtida se woh Sadr-us-Sudur
Mohammad Latif was a very sensible person
From the beginning, he was a Sadr-us-Sudur

1108. Maa aal-o-atfaal the yaan muqeem
Gaye paas Nazim ke bakhauf-o-beem
He resided here with his family and children
Went to the Nazim due to fear and terror.

1109. Jo Hadi Ali Khan the Dipty yahaan
Brabar yeh rahte the ghar mein nihaan
Hadi Ali Khan who was a Deputy here
He always remained hidden in the house;

1110. Woh Hafiz bhi bharte the English ka dam
Hamesha raha Haq ka un par karam
That Hafiz also praised the English
The grace of God always remained upon him;

1111. Hidayat Ali bhi rahe bahrawar
Bafazl-e-Khuda woh rahe nek tar
Hidayat Ali was also a fortunate person
By God's mercy he was most virtuous.

1112. The Dipty jo ek Mir Wahid Ali
Tabiyat bahut saaf unki rahi
There was a Deputy, Mir Wahid Ali
He was very clean-hearted,

1113. Na tha dushmanon se unhe ittehaad
Na jana ke hain shahar mein bad nihaad
He had no alliance with the enemies
Did not perceive the existence of evil in town,

1114. Yeh zahir-o-batin mein hain ek rang
Azamgarh mein haazir hue bedirang
Un-hypocritical, he is constant in appearance and actuality
He was present in Azamgarh without hesitation.

1115. Khuda Baksh, Husain Baksh aaqil rahe
Kisi ke na yeh log shaamil rahe
Khuda Baksh and Husain Baksh were intelligent
They were not attached with anyone;

1116. Woh Ahmad Ali poor hain Meher Ali
Rafa unse hoti thi kuch bekali
That Ahmad Ali, the son of Meher Ali
Due to him some anxiety was avoided;

1117. Husain Ali aur Mehboob Ali
Yehi log kahte the bateen bhali
Husain Ali and Mehboob Ali
These people spoke nice things;

1118. Nawaazish Ali sabse achche rahe
Yahaan tak ke moaalij na uske bane
Nawaazish Ali fared the best amongst all
So much so that he did not become his doctor,

1119. Na dekhi kabhi surat-e-pur jafaa
Na jana ke zalim kidhar hai pada
Never beheld the beastly face
Did not bother to know the whereabouts of the barbarian.

1120. Pada shab ko bimaar zalim kamaal
Nawaazish Ali ka tab aaya khayaal
The brute fell seriously ill at night
Then he was in need of Nawaazish Ali.

1121. Gaye paalki leke uske rafiq
Hamesha se bimaar ke ho shafiq
His friends went with a palanquin
Said that you have always been kind and affectionate towards the sick,

1122. Zara chaliye Nazim ki kije dawa
Ke Nazim waba mein hua mubtala
Please come and prescribe some medication to the Nazim
Because the Nazim has fallen prey to pestilence.

1123. Nawaazish Ali ne diya yeh jawaab
Dawa karte hain hum baraah-e-sawaab
Nawaazish Ali answered as follows:
I give medical treatment for the sake of earning merits,

1124. Yeh Nazim ka kuch qarz dharte nahin
Dawaa hum amiron ki karte nahin
I do not owe anything to this Nazim
I do not furnish medicines to the rich,

1125. Karoge jo kad hunga dariya ke paar
Yehi kah do Nazim se ja kar pukaar
I shall cross over the river, if you act importunate
Go and communicate this loud and clear to the Nazim;

1126. Kisi doosre ki karen woh dawaa
Tamanna na rakhen humari zaraa
He should seek medical treatment from someone else
May not at all be desirous of me.

1127. The kuch aur sahib jo baaql-o-faham
Khuda ne kiya haal par unke raham
There were few other, endowed with intelligence and perception
God was kind towards their condition.

1128. Yeh dekha ke ab jaan bachti nahin
Mubaddal hai sab aasmaan-o-zamin
Realized that it is impossible to save one's life,
All skies and lands have metamorphosised transmogrifically.

1129. Kisi ka use paas-e-izzat nahin
Raeeson ko ek laihzah rahat nahin
He does not care for anyone's honour
The noble do not have a moment of relief.

1130. Bache aabroo hai yeh mushkil kamaal
Woh hai kaun jis par na aave zawaal
Safeguarding dignity is a drastic dilemma
Who is it, who does not undergo decline?

1131. Kharabi ke aasaar sab hain badeed
Hua karti hai sab pe aafat shadeed
All signs of ruination are visible,
Everyone suffers extreme hardships,

1132. Kisi tarha bachne ki surat nahin
Bhara shar se hai aasmaan-o-zamin
There is absolutely no way to escape,
All lands and skies are jammed with villainy.

1133. Toh soncha ki kuch dijiye yaan fareb
Bache jaan zalim se bazain-o-raib

Thus planned to act with some secretive design
So that life may be saved from the tyrant with grace and incredulity.

1134. Yahaan hoshiyaari bhi darkaar hai
Bahut zulm ka garam bazaar hai
Cleverness is also required here
Acute tyranny is the order of the day.

1135. Ajab hoshiyaari ki baazon ne waah
Bahut khoob jaldi Khuda hai gawaah
Some people here, acted with great dexterity
Very fine, brisk, God is a witness.

1136. Bilaakhir samajh kar yeh apna naseeb
Hue ek Puran musalman gharib
Ultimately considering it as his fate
One poor Puran became a Muslim,

1137. Musalman ki surat yeh rahne lage
Gham-o-ranj sab dil pe sahne lage
He began living like a Muslim
Quietly suffered loads of pain and misery.

1138. Aur Morris ne bhi aisi hi baat ki
Na kuch milk-o-miraas uski bachi
And Morris also did the same thing
None of his property or hereditary estate remained,

1139. Bazahir matih musalman rahe
Na hargiz khatawaar yeh sab hue
Apparently remained submissive to the Muslims
They did not at all become miscreant culprits;

1140. Kiya jo sukhan maslehat se kiya
Khiradmad ka fel sab se bhala
Whatever they spoke, they spoke with guarded precaution,
Behaviour of the intelligent is the best.

1141. Yeh hi log English ka bharte the dam
Dilon mein sabhon ke tha ranj-o-alam
These were the people who praised the English
Their hearts were full of anguish and agony.

1142. Bachaate the zalim se hurmat ko sab
Raaya ke upar pada tha ghazab
Everyone strived to save their honour from the tyrant
The subjects were besieged by calamity;

1143. Koi pesh-e-zalim gaya shaad-shaad
Koi apne dil mein samajhta fasaad
Some appeared before the tyrant very happily
Some in their hearts felt discordancy.

1144. Dilon se toh khwaahish yehi thi sahi
Musharraf pe aafat ho zalim pe bhi
The truly heartfelt wish was this:
May misfortune befall Musharraf and also the brute!

1145. Tawassul se English ke Ahmad Ali
Kiya karta tha aish bakhushdili
Ahmad Ali, through mediation of the English
Lived in ease and comfort with a happy heart.

1146. Luta maal-o-asbaab mera tamaam
Chuta ghar kiya taal mein jaa qiyaam
All my money and property was looted
Home was forsaken, went and resided near the lake,

1147. Na paya kisi rooz aaraam-o-chain
Taraddud tafakkur se kat ti thi rain
Did not get rest or peace for a single day
The nights passed in anxiety and pensiveness.

1148. Rahe Maan Khan mere mukhtaar-e-kul
Hua yeh toh mukhtaaron mein misl-e-gul
Maan Khan was my agent for everything
Among attorneys he was like a flower,

1149. Yeh darbaar zalim ka dekha nahin
Qadam dar se ghar ke nikala nahin
He did not glance at the court of the cruel
Did not step beyond the doorway of the house.

1150. Rahi uspar hukkaam ki iltifaat
Yeh kaarindon mein hai mere nek zaat
The rulers were courteous towards him
Among my workers he is a virtuous person,

1151. Yeh kahta tha chupke raho Shahji
Rahe ga na yeh zulm inka kabhi
He used to advice: remain quiet, Shahji
This oppression of their's will never last.

1152. Gharaz nek rasta batata raha
Khabar haakimon ki sunata raha
Thus he tried to show the right path
Conveyed information regarding the rulers.

1153. Luti jumla maaliyat-e-Maan Khan
Ghuse ghar mein uske bhi ghaaratgaraan
All the valuables of Maan Khan were looted
The plunderers invaded his house too.

1154. Mulazim humare bahut hoshmand
Agarche unhon ne bhi paya guzand
My employees were very sensible
Even though, they too received injuries.

1155. Brij Lal Munshi bhi sahib-e-sho'oor
Salamat rakhe usko Rabb-e-Ghafur
Brij Lal Munshi is also a man of intellect
May the Forgiving God keep him safe!

1156. Ke Sahibo mard woh benazeer
Khudaya use jald kar de amir
O Sahibs, he is a matchless man
May God bestow riches upon him before long!

1157. Tassalli woh har waqt deta raha
Khabar meri har laihzah leta raha
He always kept consoling me
Every moment, he enquired after me.

1158. Yahya Khan bhi dete the aksar khabar
Ke hukkaam aate hain ab jald tar
Yahya Khan also often reported to me
That now the rulers will arrive very soon.

Arzi Ittalaayi bakhidmat hukkaam wala-shaan

Communication of petition in the service of highly dignified rulers

1159. Azamgarh mein hum ne yeh bheji khabar
Ke bechain hain sab yahaan ke bashar
I dispatched this report to Azamgarh
That all people here are very restless

1160. Jo hain aapke khairkhah es ghadi
Bahut sakht hai unpe aafat padi
Those who are your well-wishers at the moment
Very draconian disaster has befallen them

1161. Pade hain woh sakhti mein es waqt sab
Gorakhpur mein aap aawenge kab
At present they are besieged by merciless rigour
When will you come to Gorakhpur?

1162. Jo ek shahar-e-Machli ka bashinda tha
Humari taraf se khabar le gaya
A person who belonged to the town of Machli
Took the information from my side

1163. Likhe maine arzi mein haalaat sab
Hunudon pe Dajjaal ka hai ghazab
I described all the conditions in the application
The Dajjaal is very wrathful towards the Hindus

1164. Bache hain Musalman bajaan-o-maal
Rahe khush-o-khurram bavila-o-vaal
Muslims are safe; with life and property
Were happy and cheerful with amity and shelter

1165. Duago-e-sarkaar hai yeh faqir
Esi se nazar mein hai sab ke haqir
This mendicant prays for the government
That is why in everyone's eyes he is vile

1166. Yahaan mujh pe rahta hai har rooz shoor
Faraaham hain mardud sab chasham koor
Here, every day there are agitations against me
All blind-eyed, reprobates have gathered

1167. Hai kaarindon pe mere aafat kamaal
Muakkil-o-mukhtaar ka ek haal
My workers are in great difficulty
The condition of defendant and defender is similar

1168. Na hai chain es dam na aaraam hai
Faqat yaad-e-sarkaar se kaam hai
At this moment there is neither peace nor rest
Yearning for the government is the only occupation

1169. Bachi jaan meri bafazl-e-Ilaah
Zara ghaur se keejiye ab nigaah
My life was saved by the mercy of God
Now please pay careful attention to this

1170. Bahut jald tashrif laoo idhar
Zara aake lo ab humari khabar
Please come here at the earliest
Do come now to our aid and rescue

1171. Woh khidmat mein sab Sahibon ke gaya
Aur ahwaal sab yaan ka zahir kiya
He went before all the Sahibs
And revealed all the circumstances of this place

1172. Bird Sahib se arz ki sarbasar
Ke ab aap jald aake leejiye khabar
He communicated everything to Bird Sahib
To come expeditiously now for our help

1173. Hain ab muntazir sab raeesaan-e-shahar
Hua unpe zalim ka bedaad-o-qahar
All noblemen of the city are presently awaiting
They have suffered injustice and fury of the brute

1174. The Judge Sahib us waqt masroof-e-jung
Ke taa baaghiyon pe karen arsah tang
Judge Sahib at that time was busy in warfare
So as to give hell of a time to the rebels

1175. Aur Barackley Sahib aali himam
Shuja-o-diler-o-saraapa karam
And Barackley Sahib, the most brave
Bold, valiant and kindness incarnate

1176. Yeh Sahib Bahadur ne chiththi likha
Jawaab aaya wahaan se ke thahro zara
Sahib Bahadur had written this letter
Reply came from there, to wait for a while

1177. Sahib Judge jab aaye mulaqaat ki
Kaha tha jo humne woh sab baat ki
When Judge Sahib arrived, met him
Conveyed to him whatever I had said

1178. Suna humne yeh mujda vah jaan fiza
Kiya shukr Khaliq ka humne ada
I heard this programme, wonderful, invigorating
I thanked the Almighty Creator

1179. Ke Sahib Bird aate hain jald ab
Ab aata hai in zaalimon par ghazab
That Sahib Bird will be arriving soon
Now fury will engulf these beasts

1180. Inaayat ka ab tukhm boote hain woh
Jafakaaron ko yaan se khote hain woh
Now he would sow the seed of kindness
He would banish the oppressors from here

1181. Karenge unhe jald khaak-o-siyaah
Yeh ek dam mein hojayenge sab tabaah
They would soon be ignominiously ruined
In a startling stroke they shall be destroyed

1182. Yeh jitney hain ek rooz honge faraar
Nahin unko hone ka ek dam qaraar
One day all of them will flee
They will have no rest at all

1183. Governor ne bhi hukm aisa diya
Ke faujon ka har ja se bandh kar para
Governor also gave such an order that
Powerful army troops were drawn up in battle array

1184. Chadhaai kare char su se wahaan
Na rakhe kahin baaghiyon ka nishaan
An attack should be launched from all directions there
No trace of the rebels should remain

1185. Yeh mazmoon phir ishtehaaron mein aaye
Jo baaghi ko pakde woh inaam paye
Then this subject should be advertised
Whoever catches a rebel shall be rewarded

1186. Mohammad Hasan gar giraftaar ho
Toh girandh ka bakht bedaar ho
If Mohammad Hasan is arrested
Then his arrestor shall become fortunate

1187. Milen usko sarkaar se seh hazaar
Karen khairkhahon mein uska shumaar
He should receive three thousand from the government
He should be listed among the well-wishers

1188. Chadhaai bade din ke hovegi baad
Khuda jald dikhlayega yaum-e-saad
Attack will be launched after Christmas
God will soon show that auspicious day

1189. Ye sunkar hui shaadmani do chand
Hawakhah jo the hue shaadmand
On hearing this was doubly pleased
The sympathizers were very happy

1190. Dilon se kiya shukr-e-Parwardigaar
Khushi sab ke chehron se thi aashkaar
Thanked Divine Providence from the core of their hearts
Happiness was evident on everyone's faces

1191. Dua hai ke aiye Khaliq-e-ins-o-jaan
Bahut jald hukkaam ko bhej yahaan
O Creator of human life! It is a humble prayer
Send the rulers here very soon

1192. Ke hum sab hain hammaal-e-ranj-o-bala
Jo hukkaam aawen toh hoga bhala
For we are the porters of sorrow and distress
We shall be benefited when the rulers arrive

1193. Kisi ko nahin ek laihzah bhi chain
Bala se chedo Ali ya Husain
No one has a moment's peace
Even if there is a discourse on Ali or Husain

1194. Na khane na peeyne ki khwahish hai ab
Hamesha dil-o-jaan ko kaahish hai ab
Now there is no desire to eat or drink
The heart and soul is always pining now

1195. Jo chote bade dil se the khairkhah
Karen unpe hukkaam aali nigaah
The small and big who were true well-wishers
May the exalted rulers acknowledge them.

Hikayat Zulm Raja Satasi

Report of tyranny of the King of Satasi

1196. Likha kaifiyat raavi ne sab tamaam
Jo tha zulm Raja Satasi ka aam
The chronicler has written all conditions in totality
That the cruelty of the king of Satasi was rampant

1197. Bayaan uska karna pada es maqaam
Hai ab mukhtasar kaifiyat ikhtitaam
I had to narrate it at this juncture
At the end the circumstances are summarized

1198. Ke Raja Satasi jo badraah hain
Woh masnui Nazim ke dilkhaah hain
The king of Satasi who is wicked
Is covetous of the fake Nazim

1199. Yurish hai jo Raja ki es dam kamaal
Hifazat kar aiye Khaliq-e-Zuljalaal
At the moment, aggression of the king is excessive
O Glorious Creator! Protect us

1200. Kisi ahad mein jisko dekha nahin
Nazar mein kisi ke na aaya kahin
Who was not seen at any time
Who was not noticed by anyone, anywhere

1201. Woh Balwa ka Babu maa ek taman
Har ek mauza us se hua pur mehan
That Babu of Balwa with an army
Caused every village to be engulfed in suffering

1202. Jahan pahuncha laya ek aafat nayee
Kiye usne veeraan mauze kayee
Brought untold miseries to the places he reached
He reduced many villages to desolation

1203. Jahan haathi ghode ko le kar pade
Woh daakuon ki manind ja kar ade
Wherever they arrived with elephants and horses
They acted wayward and obstinate like dacoits

1204. Nazar bhent dus bees lete rahe
Aur dehaat ko khaam karte rahe
Collected ten-twenty (rupees) as an offering-oblation
And reduced the villages to crudity

1205. Bhawapara ka Babu tehsil kar
Rawaana woh karta tha Raja ke ghar
The Babu of Bhawapara after collection
Used to dispatch it to the King's place

1206. Yehi log patra ke maalik bane
Unhi ke sabab tabaah ghaarat hue
These very people became the proprietors of destruction
Because of them there was ruinousness

1207. Himayat se Raja ke sab loot te
Aur qaryah ba qaryah yeh bakte phire
They looted under the patronage of the King
And from village to village they kept babbling

1208. Ke sab milk Raja Satasi ka hai
Kisi ki nahin milk koi kahe
That all properties belong to the King of Satasi
No one should claim the properties to be of anyone

1209. Mangaate hain Patwari ka kaghazaat
Yeh taqreer sab unki thi besabaat
Have summoned papers of the revenue official Patwari
All this oration of theirs was transitory

1210. Aur Patwariyon par bhi yurish hui
Jo the ahle-mulk unpe shorish hui
And the Patwaris were also oppressed
Those who were residents of the region were disturbed

1211. Pe Raja Majholi raha ustuwaar
Aur Nimkohi ka Raja raha hoshiyaar
After all the King of Majholi was strong
The King of Nimkohi was intelligent

1212. Tha Bansi ka Raja bhi sabit qadam
Gopalpur ka Raja bharta tha dam
The King of Bansi was also firm–footed
The King of Gopalpur was full of praises

1213. Jo sab rubkaari pe karte khayaal
Kisi par na phir hota aisa zawaal
Had they all paid attention to the court's order
Then probably none would have suffered such downfall

1214. Yeh Raja bahut ahl-e-maazoor the
Kisi tarha se yeh na majboor the
These kings were very incapable people
They were not under any kind of compulsion

1215. Rahi terahween jo ke maah-e-August
Zila ka banaya unhen sarparast
On the thirteenth of the month of August
They were appointed guardians of the town

1216. Jo taameel karte toh hoshiyaar the
Tab hukkaam English ke woh yaar the
Had they obeyed, they would have been wise
Then they would have been proven comrades of English rulers

1217. Na ki sarparasti na haazir rahe
Na vaali na vaaris zila ke bane
Neither did they undertake guardianship, nor remained present
Became neither protectors nor successors of the town

1218. Jo yeh log karte yahaan intizaam
Toh phir koi leta na azlam ka naam
Had they discharged administrative responsibilities here
Then none could have dared to support the most cruel

1219. Na aata na jaata na karta uboor
Banata kisi ko na ahle-qusoor
Would have neither advanced nor retreated nor crossed over
Would not have made anyone worthy of blame

1220. Na darhum na barhum koi hota ghar
Yeh ahle committee jo lete khabar
No house would have been jumbled or upset
Had these members of the committee taken care

1221. Yahaan ke rausa-e-aali nasab
Saha thoda sa sabne ranj-o-taab
The high-born nobles of this place
Everyone suffered some pain and debility

1222. Badargaah-e-Khaliq ke karte dua
Bahut jald tu bhej aiye Kibriya
Prayed at the royal court of the Creator
Send them at the earliest, O Magnificent One!

1223. Ke jab tak na aawenge hukkaam sab
Mitega kisi ka na ranj-o-taab
That unless and until all the rulers come
No one's sorrow and fatigue would be erased

1224. Sharifon pe aafat hui charkh se
Musibat mein zalim ke har ek phanse
Upon gentlemen befell calamities from heavens
Everyone was entrapped in affliction of the cruel

1225. Likhi kaifiyat humne sab saaf saaf
Ke asla nahin es mein bhi kuch khilaaf
I have written all the conditions clearly
For in it nothing at all is contrary to truth

1226. Gharibon ki taqseer kya hai bhala
Ke khud apni haalat mein the mubtala
After all what is the fault of the poor?
They were entangled in their own problems

1227. Zabardast gar sar pe hota koi
Toh dete shikast usko mil kar sabhi
Had there been any powerful leader at the top
They would have unitedly defeated him

1228. Shujaat ki jauhar ko karte ayaan
Kiya humne upar bakhubi bayaan
Would have exhibited the mettle of bravery
I have earlier described it very well

1229. Jo dekha nahin karte Raja madad
Na masnui Nazim se karte hain kad
When they realized the Kings would not help
They do not endeavour to combat the fake Nazim

1230. Na tha pesh Munshi na amla wahaan
Aur ohdah ko kis tarha karte nihaan
Neither clerks nor staff was present there
And how could they have made their responsibilities latent?

1231. Wa Munshi waghairah rahe dur-dur
Bhala koi vaali se karta qusoor
So the clerks and others remained aloof
Would anyone have dared to commit a fault against the
Governor?

1232. Bilachaare Darogha dete the kaam
Faqat unke ohde ka tha ek naam
The unfortunate Darogha used to assign work
His post was only in name

1233. Woh Naib ke kahne se har ek par
Kaha sab par dastak karo zudtar
He, on instructions from the Naib for everyone
Said: summon everybody expeditiously

1234. Kumak se piyaadon ke aaye pakad
Chupe the gharoon mein na thi kuch khabar
Were summoned with the aid of the infantry
Those who were unwittingly hiding in their houses

1235. Ataat na waise kisi ne kiya
Likha tha jo kismet mein so ho gaya
Although, no one was truly obedient
However, what was destined, happened

1236. Raha sar par un sab ke bedaadgar
Na imaan mein unke aaya zarar
On their head was a tyrranous superior
No detriment came upon their certitude

1237. Hain sarkaar ke taabe yahaan ke raees
Na vaali na sar par hai koi anis
The noblemen of this place are loyal to the government
But neither is there a protector nor a friend

1238. Areeza mein sab haal maine likha
Azamgarh ko fauran rawaana hua
I wrote all the conditions in the letter
Was dispatched immediately to Azamgarh

1239. Phansa jab saoobat mein Shiv Bakhsh Lal
Kaha ja ke kah pesh-e-hukkaam haal
When Shiv Bakhsh Lal was arrested in hardships
Asked him to go before the rulers and convey all the circumstances

1240. Likhi maine arzee ke ja pesh kar
Tu Raja aur Babu ki de sab khabar
I have written an application, go and present it
You convey all news regarding the kings and clerks

1241. Musharrah mufassal bayaan kijiyo
Jo irshaad ho usko likh bhejiyo
Describe intricately, up to the minutest details
Write back to me, the responsive command.

Kaifiyat Khilatposhi

Report of the donning of Robe of Honour

1242. Main yeh kaifiyat taaza karta raqam
Ke mit jaayenge ek din bal qalam
I narrate this report while it's still fresh
Because one day the power of the pen may be erased

1243. Talab kar ke Nazim ne khilat bajabar
Use jailkhane mein pahna bamakr
The Nazim demanded the robe perforce
Wore it in the prison by deceit

1244. Jab pahunche yahaan sezdah thi Safar
Tamaashaaiyoon ko hui jab khabar
When he reached here, it was the thirteenth of Safar
When the spectators heard of this news

1245. Kaha un sabhon ne ke andher hai
Nahin uske jaane mein ab der hai
They commented that it is sheer violence
Now its end is close at hand

1246. Nahusat ka aasaar aaya nazar
Karo log sab mil ke unse hazar
Symptoms of bad presage became apparent
Unitedly, all people should be cautious of them

1247. Na samjha tilismaat hai zoor ka
Mukhil hua Raja Telpur ka
Did not understand that this is a magical spell of power
The King of Telpur became an intermeddler

1248. Phansa Toliya ka Gosain bhi aa
Pahanne mein khilat ke shamil hua
The Gosain of Toliya was also entangled
He was involved in donning the robe of honour

1249. Badhyyapaar ka Raja bhi hai kharaab
Pahan kar woh khillat phansa dar azaab
The King of Badhyyapaar is also bad
For donning the robe of honour he was in trouble

1250. Mukhalla hue hain jo yeh bekhirad
Mudaam unpe hoga azaab-e-ashad
Since these unwise ones have worn the robe of honour
Soon will befall upon them the most violent torture

1251. Woh Raja Satasi bhi baaghi hua
Maa apne aulaad daaghi hua
That King of Satasi also became rebellious
He, together with his descendants, was defiled

1252. Tama mein Satasi ka Raja phansa
Kiya raat bhar jashn usne bada
The King of Satasi was lured by greed
Celebrated pompously the entire night

1253. Likha unko Bansi ke Raja ne khat
Raho muntazir haakimon ke faqat
The King of Bansi wrote a letter to him
Just wait for the rulers

1254. Mulaqaat zalim se rakhna hazar
Rakho meri aamad par tum munhasar
Keep your meeting with the cruel prudent
Keep it dependent upon my arrival

1255. Na tahreer pe ghaur asla kiya
Likha jo ke taqdeer mein tha hua
Paid no attention at all to the writing
Whatever was predestined had to happen

1256. Muqaddar ki tehreer aati hai pesh
Nahin kaam karti hai tadbeer-e-khesh
The script of fate materializes into reality
Devices of people do not work before its finality

1257. Kahan tak likhun haal-e-khusraan-e-maal
Bichaaya tha nahaq ka zalim ne jaal
How much more should I describe the loss of property?
The cruel had unjustly laid a trap

1258. Mashiyyat ko tu dekh Ahmad Ali
Khudawand ko baat kya hai bhali
Ahmad Ali, you look at the will of Providence
What is it that pleases the Lord?

1259. Na aate na lete hain sab ki khabar
Kharaabi raaya ki hai sarbasar
Neither do they come, nor bother to take care of everyone
The subjects are being completely ruined

1260. Karam kar Khudawand Parwardigaar
Raaya hai es shahar ki beqaraar
O Lord of Providence! Be kind
The subjects of this town are restless

1261. Ab English ko la jald Rabb-e-Kareem
Tu rakh khush sabhon ko bafazl-e-Amim
O Kind Lord! Now bring the English soon
All-Comprehensive One! keep everybody happy with your bounty

1262. Bahut jald aawen ke yeh shar mite
Maa fauj zalim ka ab sar kate
May they arrive very soon to erase this turmoil
Now together with the army, the tyrant's head may be severed

63. Yehi apne Khaliq se hai ab dua
Bajuz raham tere nahin aasra
This is now the prayer to my Creator
That except your mercy there is no other hope

64. Karam se nazar kar tu Khaliq mere
Nahin koi vaaris siwa ab tere
O My Creator! View with kindness
Now there is no guardian besides you

65. Esi intizaari mein kat ti hai raat
Gharon mein sabhon ke yeh hoti hai baat
Night passes in this expectant sleeplessness
In everyone's house this is the subject of conversation

66. Ke Sahib Bird le ke aate hain fauj
Rahenge raaya ab sab mauj mauj
That Sahib Bird is coming with an army
Now all the subjects shall be rapturously ecstatic

67. Bird ko yahaan bhej de aiye Kareem
Ke woh aawen yahaan leke fauj-e-azeem
O Kind Lord, send Bird here
May he arrive here with a magnificent army

68. Khudaya teri nazar karta hun main
Yehi vadah bas ab dil mein dharta hoon main
O God, I make an oblation to you
Now in my heart, I make this resolute promise

69. Ke har hafta main rakhunga ek saum
Ke haakim yahaan hon sab lisai qaum
That every week I shall keep one fast
If so happens that rulers here are all Christian people

70. Chohal memberi umr bhar ki karon
Jo zalim ke haanthon se main bach rahoon
All my life I shall be caroling from a rostrum
If saved I am from the clutches of the cruel

1271. Karun kuunda Mushkil-Kusha ka zaroor
Jo dushman ka mere woh toden ghuroor
Definitely I shall give a ritual feast in the name of Mushkil-Kusha
If he destroys my enemy's pride

1272. Ke hoon jaan-o-dil se main umeedwaar
Abhi jald ho hukm English ka yaar
For I am hopeful with all my heart and soul
Friend, that soon now authority of the English be established

1273. Na aawenge jab tak yeh hukkaam sab
Rahega mere dil mein ranj-o-taab
Till the time all these rulers do not arrive
My heart will be full of depression and exhaustion

1274. Mushir unke karte hain yeh abtari
Sikhaate hain zalim ko baaten buri
Their counsellors instigate this mismanagement
They teach bad things to the cruel

1275. Ke jo log hain doost hukkaam ke
Unhe sakht takleef iza mile
That those who are friends of the rulers
They should get harsh torment and distress

1276. Khususan jo hain Shah Ahmad Ali
bahut unko haakim se ulfat rahi
Specially the one, Shah Ahmad Ali
Great attachment he had to the British

1277. Shab-o-rooz hain woh esi fikr mein
Har ek dam woh English ke hain zikr mein
Night and day he is immersed in this very thought
Every moment he remembers the English

1278. Karo unko tang aisa taa yaad ho
Museebat nayee un par eijaad ho
Trouble him so that he may always remember
New vexations should be put on him

279. Jab aaya nazar sab ka yeh dhang-o-taur
Sawaar ho ke kashti pe karta tha ghaur
After I noticed this manner and conduct of all
Sailing on the boat I used to ponder

280. Kiya taal mein ja ke apna qiyaam
Nigahbaan ho Khaliq-e-Zulkaraam
Went and resided near the pond
May the Gentle and Noble Creator be my Protector

281. Karam kar Khudawand Rabb-e-Jahan
Ke haakim hon es shahar par meherbaan
Master, Lord of the world bestow favour upon us
So that the rulers may be kind to this town

282. Gorakhpur mein aawen ab zoodtar
Bahut jald len aake sabki khabar
May now come to Gorakhpur as soon as possible
Should show up very quickly and inquire after everybody's
welfare

283. Abhi tak bachi jaan az fazl-e-Rabb
Agarche luta maal-o-asbaab sab
Till now life has been saved by the mercy of God
Although all cash and property has been looted

284. Magar ab toh bachne ki soorat nahin
Kisi ki madad aur quwat nahin
But now there is no way to saviour
There is no help or empowerment from any quarter

285. Supurdam tabad maye khesh ra
Tu dani hisaab-e-kum-o-besh ra
I have submitted my full fortune to you
Now you keep an account of its highs and lows.

Kaifiyat-e-ghammaazi Sardar Ali Khan

Case of back-biting by Sardar Ali Khan

1286. Bayaan karta hoon ek hikayat ajeeb
Ayaan jis se hota hai mahshar qareeb
I narrate a strange happening
Because of which the day of resurrection appears close

1287. Bada zulm Sardar Ali ne kiya
Mohammad Hasan baaghi se ye kaha
Sardar Ali did great injustice
He said this to Mohammad Hasan, the rebel:

1288. Kiya fitna barpa zireh keejiye
Ke tarik hain salaat ke Shah ji
Raised the devilment that manacle him
Because Shahji is relinquisher of the salaat

1289. Nahin mutlaqa paye bandhe salaat
Kisi ko nahin dete Khams-o-Zakat
He has never ever been found offering salaat
Does not give Khams or Zakat to anyone

1290. Juma ko bhi masjid mein jaate nahin
Raah-e-rasti par woh aate nahin
Does not go to the mosque even on Fridays
He never treads the path of good conduct

1291. Kisi ke nahin saath woh ham taam
Hain hukkaam-e-English ke pairau mudaam
He does not have meals together with anyone
Has always been a disciple of the English rulers

1292. Na Sunni na Shia se raghbat unhe
Umoorat-e-Din se hai nafrat unhe
He is inclined neither towards the Sunnis nor the Shiahs
He hates the matters of religion

1293. Suno Sahibon meri yeh arz ḥai
Namaaz aur Rooza faqat farz hai
Listen Sahibs, this is my entreaty
The Namaaz and Rooza are only obligatory duties

1294. Hamesha main padhta hon ghar mein Namaaz
Na Sunni na Shia ko hai imtiyaaz
I always offer Namaaz at home
There is no discrimination between Sunnis and Shiahs

1295. Khudawand har ja pe moujood hai
Hunood aur Musalman ka Maabud hai
The Lord is omnipresent
He is the God of Hindus and Muslims

1296. Ke Aalim wohi Aalim-ul-Ghaib hai
Khabar sab ki usko toh laaraib hai
He is the only learned one, who knows the invisible
He undoubtedly has knowledge of everyone

1297. Koi mujhsa bandon mein kamtar nahin
Ibadat numaaish ki behtar nahin
Among slaves, none is as humble as me
It is no good to pray for exhibition

1298. Na masjid na butkhane se kaam hai
Parastish se Khaliq ke bas naam hai
Have nothing to do with the mosque or temple
Am renowned only for devoted worship of the Creator

1299. Sambhala hai jis din se maine sho'oor
Hua hai na taqwaa mein mujh se qusoor
From the day I have gained consciousness
There has never been an omission in piety by me

1300. Salaat aur taqwaa bafazl-e-Khuda
Na ab tak hua ibtida se qaza
By God's mercy, in prayer and piety
There never has been a lapse right from the beginning

1301. Karun apne munh se main taareef kya
Namaaz aur Rooza ki tauseef kya
What should I praise by my own mouth?
What is the commendation of Namaaz and Rooza?

1302. Vale chunke the sab ke sab bekhirad
Na es baat ka jante nek-o-bad
But, because all of them were fools
They knew nothing about the ethical or sinful of this matter

1303. Hamesha se mazhab hai Sufi mera
Ke hota hai dil Sufiyon ka safa
My faith has always been Sufi
For the heart of Sufis is pure

1304. Nahin Sufiyon ko kuch unse gharaz
Chon daru-e-talkh ast dafa-e-maraz
The Sufis have altruism in their attitude
Like the bitter medicine which repulses diseases.

Kaifiyat badgumaani Mohammad Hasan Dajjaal

Case of suspicion of Mohammad Hasan Dajjaal

1305. Hikayat main likhta hon ek begazaaf
Yeh hai haal Dajjaal ka saaf-saaf
I write a report free of vanity
This is a clear statement of condition of the Dajjaal

1306. Woh kahta hai Saiyyad hon main beriya
Main Shia hoon Husnain par hoon fida
He says, 'I am a pure Saiyyad
'I am a Shiah and am devoted to Husnain'

1307. Main hairaan hoon esmen aiye doostoon
Ke Saiyyad aur Shia mein yeh baat ho
O friends, in this case I am amazed
That a Saiyyad and Shiah should have such qualities

1308. Imambaade mein jo ki bidat kiya
Batafseel humne usko likha
The heresy which was committed in the mourning house
I have written that in detail

1309. Nahin usmen shubha zara raib ka
Taasub se khali hai qissa mera
In that there is no doubt of hypocrisy at all
My narrative is free of prejudice

1310. Kiya usne ghaarat sab asbaab ko
Liya maal sab mera khushnood ho
He plundered all the possessions
Happily took all my wealth

1311. Zarih ki bhi lene ki tadbeer thi
Magar Shimar ki usmen taaseer thi
There was a ploy to take away the holy sepulchre as well
Perhaps he had the efficacy of inhuman Shimar

1312. Faqat khauf balwa ka karta tha woh
Qadam ko hadiqa mein dharta tha woh
He only had fear of riots
He used to step into the walled garden

1313. Kaha sabse mardood ne barmala
Taasub jo tha uske dil mein bhara
The reprobate said to everyone publicly
Because of the bigotry which was filled in his heart

1314. Ataat mein unke hain yaan ke Hunood
Usi firqah se Shahji ko hai sood
Hindus of this place are obedient towards him
From that very sect (Ahmad Ali) Shahji has gains

1315. Musalman se unko hai ziyaadah nifaaq
Faqat ek firqah se hai ittifaaq
For Muslims he has excessive inward malice
He has concord with only one sect

1316. Yehi unke yaar-o-madadgaar hain
Siwa unke sab unse bezaar hain
They are his friends and helpers
Besides them, all are disgusted with him

1317. Na khaate hain hargiz Musalman ke ghar
Hain yeh raah-e-Islam se bekhabar
Never ever eats in the house of Muslims
He is unaware of the manners of Islam

1318. Hai English se inko mohabbat kamaal
Nahin kuch bhi Islam ka dil mein khayaal
He has great love for the English
In his heart, he has no consideration at all for Islam

1319. Hain Hindu tamaam in ke khidmatguzaar
Musalman ka inko nahin aitbaar
All his devoted servants are Hindus
He does not trust the Muslims

1320. Pakaya hua Hinduon ka tamaam
Hamesha se khaate hain yeh subh-o-shaam
All his food is cooked by the Hindus
That is what he eats morning and evening

1321. Yeh hukkaam-e-English se bas shaad hain
Himayat se unke yeh aabaad hain
He is pleased only with the English rulers
Due to their patronage he is flourishing

1322. Kisi hilah se qatal inko karo
Ke taa shahar mein fitna barpa na ho
Murder him by some kind of trick
So that no disturbance is caused in the city

1323. Dafeena jo ho jaa ke sab khood lo
Zarih ko ba aasaani yahaan bhej do
Go and dig out whatever buried treasure is there
With ease send the holy sepulchre here

1324. Esi fikr mein the woh sab naabkaar
Ke aamad hui fauz ki ek baar
All those wicked ones had these designs
That suddenly the army arrived

1325. Yehi ziyaadah bachne ki surat hui
Ke hukkaam ki unko haibat hui
This became an additional means of saviour
That they dreaded the rulers

1326. Hua rang faq baaghi-e-badgumaan
Ke pahunche Mairwa mein aali-nishaan
The colour of the distrustful rebels turned pale
Because the high-statured reached Mairwa

1327. Rahe jo yahaan log ghaaratgaraan
Mairwa gaye phir na aaye yahaan
Those people who were plunderers here
Went to Mairwa; never again came back here

1328. Musharraf maa fauj apni gaya
Pada phir talaatum mein woh behaya
Musharraf went with his army
Then that shameless one became intertwined in buffeting

1329. Jab aaya Musharraf hue beqaraar
Hue kitne us rooz dariya ke paar
When Musharraf came they became restless
On that day many crossed over the river

1330. Jo reh jaate ek hafta ghaaratgaraan
Nahin shahar ke bachte baashindagaan
Had the plunderers stayed for another week
Residents of the city would not have been saved

1331. Khabar gar na sarkaar leti meri
Zarih ka pata phir na lagta zari
If the government had not inquired after my welfare
Then no trace of the holy sepulchre would ever have been found.

Kaifiyat Ghaaratshudan Mahajanaan wa Raaya Pipraich

Condition of the plundered Mahajans and subjects of Pipraich

1332. Jo pahle Jamadi ki thi chaudahween
Ke aafat yeh naazil hui bar zameen
It was the fourteenth of the first *Jamadi*
When this misfortune descended upon the earth

1333. Diya hukm zalim ne bashadd-o-mad
Ke Jamna ho tehsil par mustaid
The cruel passed this order with force
That Jamna should begin collection with promptitude

1334. Woh lewe raiyyat se phir seh hazaar
Agarche saubat se hain beqaraar
He should again take three thousand (rupees) from the subjects
Even though they are worried by hardships

1335. Ilaaqah pe phir ja ke taalib hua
Raaya ne aakar ke humse kaha
He proceeded to the region and became a seeker
The subjects came and reported this to me:

1336. Hai Jamna ki janib se bidat kamaal
Kisi ki na hurmat ka usko khayaal
There is extreme oppression from the side of Jamna
He does not care for anyone's honour

1337. Asaami luti aapki baar-baar
Jo aata hai karta hai sab maar-maar
Your properties were looted repeatedly
Whoever comes tries to usurp and embezzle everything

1338. Nahin hum ko es waqt vaaris mila
Raaya ka kis tarha hoga bhala
I did not find any master at this time
How will the interest of the subjects be protected?

1339. Kaha humne ab sabr darkaar hai
Siwa uske koi na ab yaar hai
I said that patience is the need of the hour
Besides that there is no other friend

1340. Ek hafte mein hukkaam aate hain sab
Mitega tab hi sab ka ranj-o-taab
All the rulers would come in a week
Only then everyone's sorrow and exertion shall be erased

1341. Jo bhejega English ko Rabb-e-Kareem
Jigar uska us waqt hoga do neem
When the Kind Lord shall send the English
At that time the courage of his heart and soul shall be asunder

1342. Nazar bar Khudawand rakhta hoon main
Shab-o-rooz Khaliq se kahta hoon main
I look up to God with hope
Night and day, I say to the Creator

1343. Adaalat karen aake hukkaam sab
Ki mazloom par hove afzaal-e-Rabb
May all the rulers come and do justice
That, God may bestow favours upon the oppressed

1344. Yeh shahar unke aane se dil shaad ho
Badastur-e-saabiq sab aabaad ho
May this city rejoice upon their arrival
Everyone should flourish in the earlier fashion

1345. Ke zulm-o-sitam saaf mit jaaye yahaan
Bazer-e-zamin hove zalim nihaan
That here injustice and oppression may be absolutely erased
That the cruel may be latent underground

1346. Khabar jald le Paak Parwardigaar
Madad bhej de Shah-e-Duldul Sawaar
O Pure Providence! Take notice of us soon
O King Chevalier; the rider of Duldul, please send help

1347. Karen aake talwaar ko dar niyaam
Ba-aasaani rasta len ghar ka tamaam
Should come and put the sword into scabbard
Everyone may take the route to their homes with ease

1348. Dua meri maqbool ho aashkaar
Karunga tera shukr Parwardigaar
May my prayer be accepted visibly
O Divine Providence! I shall thank you

1349. Magar hai ajab qudrat-e-Zulminan
Ke aasaan hota hai ranj-o-mehan
Perhaps the power of the Bountiful is marvellous
That sorrows and sufferings are removed

1350. Madadgaar ghurba ka haakim hua
Jo hain khairju unka hoga bhala
Rulers became the helpers of the poor
Those who are the seekers of welfare shall receive a good turn

1351. Ke jo log English ke damsaaz hain
Woh aane se English ke mumtaaz hain
For those who are the supporters of the English
They are pleased by arrival of the English

1352. Rahe jaan se apni aabaad sab
Gaya maal hai go ke ranj-o-taab
Everyone was happy that their life was saved
Although there is sadness and trouble over lost goods

1353. Jo hukkaam aaye toh farhat hui
Jo the khairkhah unko sarwat hui
When the rulers came there was euphoria
Those who prospered were their well-wishers

1354. Ba afzaal-e-Khaliq ke payee najaat
Dobarah hui az sare nau-hayaat
By the grace of the Creator received liberation
Once again was granted a new life

1355. Khabar jald mere Khuda ne liya
Raha main ba dastur Nazim gaya
My God took care soon enough
I regained my normal life, the Nazim was gone.

Daastaan Raunaq afrozi-e-Sarkaar Daulat-mudaar bamaqaam Pipraich

Legend of the arrival of the government in charge of the wealth at Pipraich

1356. Suno Sahibo qudrat-e-Zuljalaal
Kisi ka na pahunche hai waham-o-khayaal
O Sahibs, listen about the power of the Glorious One
No one's fantasy or thought can reach there

1357. Satrahween ko afwaaj Nepaliyaan
Do-sham'bah raha rooz aiye doostaan
On the seventeenth arrived the Nepalese armies
O Friends! The day was Monday

1358. Sidhawa mein afwaaj aakar rahi
Ke har kas-o-naakas pe shaadi hui
The armies came and stayed at Sidhawa
Happiness descended upon all and sundry

1359. Pahunch kar Badal Khan ne humse kaha
Rasad ki taiyyaari bakhubi kiya
Upon arrival, Badal Khan said to me
Made good preparation for provisions

1360. Hain Sahib Collector bhi humraah-e-fauj
Zahe shaan-o-shaukat zahe farr-o-auj

Collector Sahib also came along with the army
Excellent glory and splendour, wonderful zenith of humility

1361. Aur Sahib Bird unke humraah hain
Jo khursheed hain woh to ye maah hain
And Bird Sahib is along with him
If that one is the Sun, then this one is the Moon

1362. Aur Sahib Commissioner bhi lashkar ke saath
Nishaan-e-zafar sab ke hai haanthon haath
And Commissioner Sahib is also accompanying the army
Everyone flaunts signs of a speedy victory

1363. Siwa unke paltan ke sab sahibaan
Chale aate hain yahaan ke hamlakunaan
Besides them all the officers of the platoon
Are arriving here for making attacks

1364. Suna maine jab muzhdah-e-jaan fiza
Kiya shukr-e-Haq sidq dil se ada
When I heard the refreshing good news
I sincerely thanked the Almighty

1365. Padhi hum ne fauran do rikat Namaaz
Ba sidq-e-safa-o-baru-e-niyaaz
Immediately I offered two sets of Namaaz
With pure veracity; as a humble oblation

1366. Do-sham'bah se-sham'bah ko sab sahibaan
Maa fauj-e-Gorkhai ba-izz-o-shan
On Monday and Tuesday, all the officers
Escorted by the Gorkha army, with dignity and grandeur

1367. Paye hadm-e-buniyad jour-o-sitam
Baqatl-o-dafaa baaghi-e-badshiyam
In pursuit of razing down the foundation of oppression and tyranny
With assassination and repulsion of the ill-mannered rebels

1368. Sidhawa mein aakar hue khaimazan
Hua wan ka maidaan rashq-e-chaman
Arrived at Sidhawa and encamped
The fields there became the envy of gardens

1369. Woh afwaaj-e-Gorkhai ba-karr-o-far
Ajab ek sama se thi waan jalwagar
Those Gorkha armies with powerful splendour
Were present there in a fantastically ecstatic state

1370. Koi gore-gore koi sabz rang
Kisi mein the mushk-e-Khutan ke se dhang
Some fair and white, some green-colored
Some had the style of the musk of Khutan

1371. Koi surkh wardi se misl-e-Chanaar
Kisi par thi Sosan si udi bahaar
Some with the red uniform were like the Poplar
Some had the purple-blue flourish of Iris

1372. Koi Sarvju-e-chaman koi gul
Koi Bulbul-e-gulshan-e-nasha mul
Some are Cypress of the region of garden; some flowers
Some are like intoxicated nightingales of rose gardens

1373. Bayabaan hua bazm-e-Jamshedwaar
Baje baaje Angreezi basad vaqaar
Wilderness became like the company of Jamshed
English musical instruments were played with much dignity

1374. Mere kaarpardaaz haazir the wahaan
Jamaaya tha humne rasad ka saamaan
My efficient workers were present there
We had collected materials for provisions

1375. Jo kuch chahiye wahaan faraaham tha sab
Muhaiyya thi har cheez az-fazl-e-Rabb
Whatever was required, all was obtainable there
Everything was available by the grace of God

1376. Jise jo kuch hota tha darkaar wahaan
Woh milta tha usko wahaan begumaan
Whoever needed, whatever there
He got it in that place undoubtedly

1377. Kisi cheez ki wahaan shikaayat na thi
Kami ki kisi ko hikaayat na thi
There was no complaint regarding any matter
Nobody had reports of any shortcoming

1378. Agarchee tha main tang us waqt mein
Ke zalim ne ghaarat kiya tha humain
Even though I was constrained at that time
Because the barbarian had plundered me

1379. Va lekin basad jaan fishaani-w-kad
Faraaham ki hum ne tamaami rasad
But however, with much diligence and effort
I managed to supply all the provisions

1380. Rasad ka kiya es tarha intizaam
Hue raazi hukkaam wala maqaam
Made such an arrangement of supplies
That the highly exalted rulers were pleased

1381. Jo raazi hue hum se hukkaam sab
Toh hasil hui mujh ko farhat ajab
When all the rulers were happy with me
Then I derived a quixotic pleasure

1382. Tu goi ke aan rooz bud rooz-e-Eid
Na ba shud az aan rooz rooz-e-sayeed
You can say that the day had become like the day of Eid
Undoubtedly no day is more auspicious than that day

1383. Sada toop ki phir nikalne lagi
Banadeeq ki baadh chalne lagi
Then the sound of cannons started coming
Flood of muskets started flowing

1384. Chali toop-e-Nepaliyan dhaeeyn-dhaeeyn
Aur banduq karne lagi thayeen-thayeen
The cannons of the Nepalese boomed with a great din:
'dhayeen' 'dhayeen'
And the fired shot-guns made a noise of 'thayeen' 'thayeen'

1385. Toh afwaaj-e-adu mein khal-bal machi
Kamar bhaagne par har ek ne kasi
Thus chaos and confusion reigned in the armies of the enemy
Everyone was prepared to flee

1386. Phira jab ke Dehli se woh Har Kishan
Giraftaar-e-iza-o-ranj-o-mehan
When that Har Kishan returned from Delhi
Arrested by affliction, grief and suffering

1387. Lada Raja se su-e-Gopalpur
Gaya pesh jab uska us se na zoor
Fought with the king in the direction of Gopalpur
But when he could not overpower him

1388. Toh bhaaga wahaan se bhi misl-e-shuaal
Sohanpur mein ja lada badkhisaal
Then he fled from there too in a flash
The evil one went and fought at Sohanpur

1389. Kiya qasad ladne ka haakim se jab
Tamaache lage ghaib se munh pe tab
When he pledged to fight against the rulers
He received slaps from the invisible Omniscient

1390. Wahaan se bhi bhaaga hazeemat-kashaan
Kushadah dahaan khaakash andar dahaan
Fled from there too after suffering a defeat
Open-mouthed with thorny brambles inside his mouth

1391. Gorakhpur mein aaya bhaaga hua
Kai rooz tak yahaan pe sakin raha
Fleeing, he came to Gorakhpur
For many days stayed here at rest

1392. Woh masnui Nazim se jaa kar mila
Ladaai ka dil mein iraadah kiya
He went and met the false Nazim
Determined in his heart to fight

1393. Chala ladne English se woh naabkaar
Dil-e-murda ba haal zaar-o-nizaar
That mischievous one proceeded to fight the English
With a dead heart and a weak body

1394. Diya toop zalim ne phir do adad
Gaya ladne haakim se woh bekhirad
Then the barbarian gave him two cannons
That fool went to fight the rulers

1395. Qaza le chali su-e-Shahbaz Ganj
Mila wahaan pe usko har ek tarha ranj
Death carried him towards Shahbaz Ganj
There he received all kinds of torments

1396. Kiya wahaan se bhi aakhir usne faraar
Raha ek dam bhi na usko qaraar
Then finally he fled from there as well
He did not get an iota of peace

1397. Jo bhaaga toh pahuncha woh ja Lucknow
Hua phir na hukkaam se ru-ba-ru
After escaping, he reached Lucknow
Thereafter he never came face to face with the rulers

1398. Jo afwaaj adu ki thi wahaan muqeem
So haibat se unka hua dil do-neem
The armies of the enemies which were stationed there
Due to terror their heart tore into two

1399. Hua fauz-e-ada mein aisa hiraas
Na baaqi rahe unke hosh-o-hawaas
Armies of the opponents were so terror stricken
None of their wits or senses remained

1400. Tillangi faraari faraari hue
Udanchu sab ek baar naari hue
The native soldiers fled helter-skelter
All the condemned ones vanished suddenly

1401. Sawaar-o-piyaada ka kya likhun haal
Sira sima bhaage woh sab badkhisaal
What should I write about the infantry and cavalry?
Those ill-mannered ones fled from one end to another

1402. Kisi ne kaha jaa ke zalim se yaar
Raho Shahji se bahut hoshiyaar
Friend, someone counseled the cruel
That be very cautious of Shahji

1403. Ke shab bhar kiya Shahji ne jashan
Hui inko English ke aane se aman
For Shahji celebrated the whole night
Arrival of the English has brought him peaceful security.

1404. Usi subh hamla ka saamaan tha
Magar mera Khaliq nigahbaan tha
On the same morning were preparations for an attack
But the Creator was my custodian

1405. Talaatum mein masnui Nazim pade
Sitam kya karen khud faraari hue
The fraudulent Nazim was buffeted by the dash of events
What could he oppress? He himself became a fugitive

1406. Jo aawaz toopon ki aane lagi
Hui tab to zalim ko ek bekali
When the sound of cannons started coming
Then the ruthless one became very restless

1407. Misaal-e-nazar fauj pahunchi yahaan
Chali aayi kahti ke baaghi kahaan
Instantenously, like a momentary glance the army reached here
Came bellowing, where are the rebels?

1408. Toh dariya pe jaa ke hue sab baham
Faramosh sab dil se raah-e-sitam
So they all collected near the river
All violent ways discarded by their heart

1409. Bahut log kishti pe hokar sawaar
Lage hone jaldi se dariya ke paar
Many people boarded the boats
Started crossing the river in haste

1410. Ke yakbargi fauz English ki wahaan
Jo pahunchi toh sab ko kiya benishaan
However, unexpectedly the English army came there
And reaching wiped out everyone

1411. Diya taak ke ek goola wahin
Ke lahra ke kashti hui tahnashin
Then and there they aimed and fired a shot from the cannon
Swinging and out of balance, the boat sunk

1412. Jo hone lage pher-e-toop-o-tufang
Hue shaad dariya ke saare nahang
When the exchange of cannons and guns began
All the crocodiles of the river were pleased

1413. Bahut baaghi dariya pe maare gaye
Bahut khud ba khud duub kar ke muye
Many rebels were killed by the river
Many drowned themselves to their death

1414. Mohammad Hasan tha jo ek badkhisaal
Woh bhaaga hai yahaan se ba-misl-e-shaghaal
Mohammad Hasan who was an evil man
Fled from here like a jackal

1415. Sitam aur jaur us ka sab ho gaya
Raaya ko aaraam bas ho gaya
All his tyranny and oppression was over
Finally now the subjects were at rest

1416. Woh Sahib Bird mard chust-o-diler
Ke fauj-e-English mein maanind-e-sher
That Bird Sahib is a smart and brave man
For in the English army he is like a lion

1417. Jawan-mard khush-tabiyat-o-khush-khisaal
Na Rustam tha aisa na tha Saam wa Zaal
Youthful man, good-natured and good-mannered
Neither was Rustam like this, nor Saam, nor Zaal

1418. Adaalat ka unke karun kya bayaan
Ke qaasir hai khud khaamah-e-dozabaan
What description should I compose of his justice?
For the 'double-tongued' pen itself is incapable of writing it

1419. Collector jo aaye hain es shahar mein
Gorakhpur mein ta qayaamat rahein
The Collector who has come to this town
May stay in Gorakhpur till Doomsday

1420. Karun adl aur jood ka kya bayaan
Na Hatim tha aisa na Nausherwan
What should I narrate of his equity and munificence?
Neither was Hatim like this nor Nausherwan

1421. Karun Sahib Judge ki main taarif kya
Likhun main Commissioner ki tauseef kya
How should I eulogize Judge Sahib?
What should I write in commendation of the Commissioner?

1422. Yeh dono khiradmand hain bemisaal
Sikander manish aur Aristu khisaal
They both are incomparably intelligent
With Alexander's temperament and Aristotle's traits of character

1423. Jo paltan mein Captaan Angreez hain
Woh dushman ke kis darja khoonreez hain
The English Captain of the platoon
How very much is he delighted by the enemies' bloodshed!

1424. Kiya unko ek dam mein aisa tabaah
Na sujhi kahin bhaagne ki bhi raah
In a moment destroyed them in such a manner
Could not even contemplate any route of escape

1425. Bahadur hain beshubh yeh sahibaan
Ke upar likha maine jiska bayaan
Undoubtedly these persons are brave
Those, whom I have mentioned above

1426. Shujaat sakhaawat karun kya raqam
Unhi ke hai hisse mein sab yak qalam
What should I write of their generosity and bravery?
All these are exclusively in their share of authority

1427. Na aisa adaalat mein Nausherwan
Aristu se dana hain yeh sahibaan
Nausherwan's sense of justice was not so sharp
These persons are much wiser than Aristotle

1428. Kahan tak likhun unki ab aur madah
Kiya shahar jo aa ke ek dam mein fateh
How much more should I write their eulogy?
They came and conquered the town with lightning speed

1429. Gorakhpur mein aaye sab sahibaan
Chahaar sham'bah tha rooz aiye doostaan
All these persons came to Gorakhpur
O Friends! That day was a Thursday

1430. November mahine se tha intizaar
Rahe intizaari mein sab beqarar
They were expected since the month of November
Everyone was waiting anxiously for them.

Hikayat Zafaryaabi-e-Sarkaar wa Abtari-e-Baaghiyaan

Report of the government's victory and ruin of the rebels

1431. Ba taarikh shashum maah-e-Janwari
Hui fauz-e-ada mein yeh abtari
Dated the sixth in the month of January
There was such destruction of the enemies' armies

1432. Attharah sad-w-hashtam-w-panjah saal
Hui fauz ada ki sab paimaal
The year was eighteen hundred and fifty-eight
All the armies of the enemies were devastated

1433. Thi Awwal Jamadi ki unneesween
Ke bhage yahaan se adu-e-laain
It was the nineteenth of the Awwal Jamadi
When the accursed antagonist fled from here

1434. The barah saye Hijri aur haftaad chaar
Ke bhage yahaan se baghaavat sheaar
It was twelve hundred and seventy-four Hijri
When those distinguished for rebellion fled from here

1435. Banaya jise doost mahjub hain
Sitam mein rahe jo ke mahboob hain
Those who were made friends are bashful
Those who suffered oppression are beloveds

1436. Nigahbaan ho Khaliq-e-Beniyaaz
Tu kar raham ab sab par aiye Kaarsaaz
May the All-Sufficient Creator be the guardian
Bestow your mercy upon all, O Skillful One!

1437. Jo batin mein sab doost-e-English rahe
Zamaana ki gardish mein woh bhi pade
All those who remained friends of the English with heart and soul
They too were entangled in the vicissitudes of times

1438. Jo duniya ka rakhte the sab kaarobaar
Tu mahfooz rakh unko Parwardigaar
Those who were involved in all kinds of wordly business
O Providence! Keep them safe and sound

1439. Tu kar raham ab unpe aiye Kibriya
Woh hukkaam ke jurm se hon reha
O Magnificient One! Be merciful towards them now
May they be acquitted of offences against the rulers.

Hikayat Altaaf-e-Hukkaam Bakawaif-e-deegar

Report of the favours of the rulers; other particulars

1440. Bayaan ab main karta hoon haalaat-e-khesh
Rahe unke altaaf hum par hamesh
Now I narrate the state of my own people
They always bestowed favours upon me

1441. Khabar meri hukkaam lete rahe
Mere ranj ki daad dete rahe
The rulers always enquired after me
They made reparations for my distress

1442. Musibat ko sunte the karte the aah
Mere qadr-o-rutba pe karte nigaah
Used to hear of my misfortunes and sigh
They were the custodians of my honour and status

1443. Sitam se main moozi ke nashaad tha
Sabhi naqd aur jins barbaad tha
I was unhappy due to oppression of the torturer
All cash and kind was ruined

1444. Raha dil mein hukkaam ke yeh khayaal
Ke dushman ko uske karen paimaal
The rulers had this design in their heart
That their enemies should be crushed

1445. Bula kar ke Mukhtaar se yeh kaha
Abhi tak na darkhaast tumne diya
Summoned the attorney and said that
Up till now you have not submitted petition

1446. Azakhane ki sab suni kaifiyat
Lute maal ki kashaf hai mahiyat
Heard all the conditions of the mourning house
Intrinsic value of the looted goods is manifest

1447. Iwaz maal-e-nuqsaan ke hoga bhala
Aur ghaaratgaron ki bhi hogi saza
Loss of goods shall be well recompensated
And the plunderers shall be also punished

1448. Luta jo ke Kosamhi se asbaab-o-maal
Woh ghaaratgaraan honge sab paimaal
Those who looted property and money from Kosamhi
All those plunderers shall be ruined

1449. Kaho Shahji se ke ab jald tar
Woh darkhaast deween ke hon bahrawar
Ask Shahji that now at the earliest
He should give an application, so that he can be compensated

1450. Kiya humne taameel es hukm ki
Ke darkhaast daakhil kiya humne kayee
I obeyed this order
For I submitted many petitions

1451. Collector Commissioner Session Judge ne yaan
Kiya mujh ko mumtaaz ba-izz-o-shaan
The Collector, Commissioner and Session Judge here
Honoured me with respect and dignity

1452. Yehi raat din ghaur mein tha pada
Ke hukkaam-e-aali ko dekhen zara
Night and day I was engulfed in this thought
That I must go and see the exalted rulers once

453. Hui Eid dekha jo hukkaam ko
Mulaqaat ki humse khushnud ho
The day I met the rulers, was like celebrating Eid
They met me with happiness

454. Tashaffi kiya meri hukkaam ne
Kaha kuch na ab ranj dil mein rahe
The rulers gave me consolations
Said no anguish should now remain in my heart

455. Qadardaan na aisa milega kabhi
Barabar nazar lutf hardam rahi
Would never be able to find such patrons
Their benign attitude remained constant forever

456. Karam mujh pe English ka din raat hai
Hamesha se unki inaayaat hai
Day and night, the English are gracious towards me
Their favours have always been bestowed

457. Wa Karnail Captaan ne yeh kaha
Sitam tum pe zalim ka behad hua
'Alas!' said the Colonel and the Captain
The brute inflicted unlimited atrocities on you

458. Hue hum to mumtaaz az Padri
Woh Sahib Bahadur ne ki dilbari
I was honoured by the Priest
Sahib Bahadur treated me like a beloved

459. Barabar rahe dil se jo khairkhah
Unhi par ab altaaf ki hai nigaah
Those who remained perpetual well-wishers
Now a favourable eye is being cast on them

460. Jo the khairkhah ab woh hain beguzand
Khiradmand-o-dana hain aur hoshmand
Those who were the well-wishers are now unharmed
They are intelligent, wise and alert

1461. Ataat mein Dajjaal ke jo rahe
Wohi log duniya se ghaaib hue
Who were in obedient service of the Dajjaal
Those were the people who vanished from the world

1462. Na kuch doosre se kiya intiqaam
Sarasar yeh insaaf ka hai maqaam
Did not take revenge from anyone else
Totally, this is a setting of fair play

1463. Hamesha Khuda unko haakim rakhe
Sada aalam aabaad inse rahe
May God always retain them as rulers
May times always flourish due to them

1464. Karen sultanate haft-e-iqliim ki
Raaya chalen raah tasleem ki
May they rule over the seven climes
And the subjects should accept and salute them

1465. Humare shahar ke jo naadaan the
Woh masnui Nazim se ja kar mile
Those who were the fools of my town
They joined hands with the fake Nazim

1466. Unhi ko ziyaadah mili hai saza
Woh pakde aate hain az ja-ba-ja
They are the ones who have received Draconian punishment
They are being arrested from everywhere

1467. Haqiqat main likhta hun es waaste
Ki aainda koi na aisa kare
I am writing the truth so that
In future no one may act in this manner

1468. Na vaali ka apne khataawaar ho
Baghaavat se jo laaiq-e-daar ho
Should never be a culprit of his guardian
Who would deserve the gibbet due to rebellion

1469. Musharraf Ali dekho khaati raha
Ali Nagar mein usko phaansi diya
Look, Musharraf Ali was guilty
He was hanged in Ali Nagar

1470. Rasool Ali aur Aulaad-e-Ali
Unhe ja ke maqtal mein phaansi hui
Rasool Ali and Aulaad-e-Ali
They were taken to the place of execution and hanged

1471. Tha Navandah Rai unke durbaar mein
Ghanimat ke rahta tha woh kaar mein
Navandah Rai was in their court
It was a blessing that he remained on duty

1472. Nahin naukri uski usne kiya
Badaulat mohabbat ke woh bhi gaya
He did not ever serve him
Because of affection, he too was gone

1473. Musharraf ka dildaar Wahid Ali
Yeh chaaron ko ek rooz phaansi hui
Musharraf's beloved, Wahid Ali
These four were hanged one day

1474. Pashupatnath bhai tha Trilok ka
Musharraf ke humraah woh bhi gaya
Pashupatnath was the brother of Trilok
He also went with Musharraf

1475. Taman ka sipahi raha Lal Khan
Hui usko phaansi gaya az jahan
Lal Khan was a soldier of the army
He was also hanged and left the world

1476. Wohi log duniya se ghaaib hue
Musharraf ke jo log naib hue
Those very people disappeared from the world
Who had become assistants of Musharraf

1477. Rahe ek Khairaat Ali badsiyar
Yeh hukkaam-e-English se the bekhabar
One Khairaat Ali had a bad character
He was unaware of the English rulers

1478. Hue qaid mahbas mein woh dus baras
Hoti thi jinhe lootne ki hawas
For ten years were they jailed in prison
Those who had the lust for plundering

1479. Raha Shaikh Faizu jo mard-e-sakha
Bataarikh doum Rajab ki gaya
Shaikh Faizu, who was a liberal man
Departed on the second day of Rajab

1480. Validaad Khan wa Karimdaad Khan
Rajab ke dahum ko gaye az jahan
Validaad Khan and Karimdaad Khan
Left this world on the tenth of Rajab

1481. Aur Haider Husain ek Tehsildaar
Raha woh bhi Dajjaal ka yaar-e-ghaar
And Haider Husain, a Tehsildaar
He too was an intimate friend of the Dajjaal

1482. Ilaaqah Brajman ka ghaarat kiya
Bainsaaf-e-hukkaam phaansi chadha
Ravaged the region of Brajman
By justice meted out by the rulers, he was hanged.

Hikayat Tashreef Bari Hukkaam-e-Aali Shaan; Maa Lashkar-e-Zafar Paikar Samt Lucknow

Report of the timely departure of the highly grand rulers, with the victorious army in the direction of Lucknow

83. Rahe thode din yahaan pe hukkaam sab
Bakhubi kiya yahaan ka anjaam sab
All the rulers remained here for a few days
Managed the affairs of this place very well

84. Yahaan se fateh kar ke Tanda mein jaa
Diya baaghiyon ko wahaan ke saza
After gaining victory here they left for Tanda
Handed out punishment to the rebels of that place

85. Wahaan se gaye Lucknow sahibaan
Hue khoob taaraaj sab baaghiyaan
From there the gentlemen went to Lucknow
All the rebels were thoroughly devastated

86. Hue jo wahaan jama Abbasiyaan
Woh dushman the sarkaar ke begumaan
The Abbasis who had gathered there
Were undoubtedly enemies of the government

87. Satrahween ko humne suni yeh khabar
Ke hukkaam English ne paayi zafar

On the seventeenth I heard this news
That the English rulers have been victorious

1488. Bafazl-e-Khuda Lucknow ko liya
Ijabat ko pahunchi humari dua
Captured Lucknow by the grace of God
Our prayers had been accepted

1489. Kiya raah-e-Sultanpur se guzar
Usi raah se ja ke paayi zafar
Passed through the roads of Sultanpur
Progressing on that road they gained victory

1490. Hue kushta sab dushman-e-badnihaad
Yeh sun kar mera dil hua shaad-shaad
All the ill-natured enemies were destroyed
On hearing this, my heart was mighty pleased

1491. Karen sultanate ahle English mudaam
Dua hai yehi meri har subh-o-shaam
May the English people always rule
Everyday and night, this is my prayer.

Hikayat Ijlaas Janaab Bird Sahib Bahadur

Report of the session of Janaab Bird Sahib Bahadur

1492. Bird Sahib naamwar khushnihaad
Hue haakim-e-waqt ba-adl-o-daad
Bird Sahib is famous and good-natured
Endowed with justice and equity, he became the ruler of the times

1493. Mohabbat unhe shahar se hai kamaal
Hai madd-e-nazar unko shafqat kamaal
He has extreme love for the town (Gorakhpur)
He keeps in mind the splendour of mercy

1494. Yeh Sahib Bahadur ki hai zaadbum
Riyaasat se unke hai sabko ulum
This is the native land of Sahib Bahadur
Everyone is aware of his princely ways

1495. Pazeera hui baare sabki dua
Yahaan ka Collector Magister kiya
At last everyone's prayer was answered
(He) Was made the Collector Magistrate of this place

1496. Hai umeed tujhse ye aiye Zuljalaal
Dikha khairkhahi ka sabko ma'aal
O Glorious One! I have expectations from you
Show everyone the consequences of approbation

1497. Likhe jaayen daftar mein ab sabke naam
Ke aaindah ho baais-e-ihtiraam
Now everyone's names should be written in an official register
So that from now on it can be the basis of deference

1498. Rajab ki thi teesween begumaan
Inaayat Ali uff sar-e-saalehaan
Undoubtedly it was thirtieth of Rajab
Inaayat Ali, shamelessly rebellious against the righteous,

1499. Jo purtaab tha sab se baaghi sawa
So woh rub-e-ashreen ko makhfi hua
Who was powerful, most terrific amongst all mutineers
Thus he was camouflaged in some quarter of the empyrean

1500. Rafiq uske dono madadgaar the
Yehi fauz-e-baaghi ke sardaar the
Both his friends were helpful
They were the leaders of the army of rebels

1501. Sazawaar yeh mard tha daar ka
Nateeja yehi tha ke phaansi chadha
This man deserved the gibbet
The culmination was that he was hanged

1502. Ke taarikh dusween thi Shabaan ki
Hui jaan qalib se dus ke thi
For it was the tenth of *Shabaan*
On that day ten persons lost their lives

1503. Sitaram Zamindaar-e-Mansurganj
Taman ke sipahi se hai sab ko ranj
Sitaram, Zamindaar of Mansurganj
Everyone is distressed by the soldier of the army

1504. Gaye bast dus youm ko daarul baqa
Hue sadma-e-phaansi se dono fana
Left on the tenth day, bound for their eternal abode
Both died from the shock of hanging

1505. Chahaarum rahi maah-e-Ramzaan ki
Ke Ramzaan Ali Khan ko phaansi hui
It was the fourth of the month of Ramzaan
When Ramzaan Ali Khan was hanged

1506. Ke haftam ko nau aadmi mit gaye
Woh baaghi the baaghi mein jaa kar mile
On the seventh, nine persons were annihilated
They were mutineers, so they joined other mutineers

1507. Rudhauli ka Babu raha Shiv Ghulaam
Hua ab jahannum mein uska maqaam
Shiv Ghulaam was the Babu of Rudhauli
Now his dwelling was situated in hell

1508. Va maara use fauj-e-sarkaar ne
Aur ghaarat kiya usko idbaar ne
Friday, he was killed by the army of the government
Indeed he was ravaged by misfortune

1509. Haider Khan Umar Khan ke chele rahe
Khataawaar ho kar ke phaansi chadhe
Haider Khan was a follower of Umar Khan
On being found guilty, he was hanged

1510. Thi taareekh untees Shabaan ki
Ke maqsoom se unko phaansi hui
The date was twenty-ninth of Shabaan
As per destiny, he was hanged

1511. Kahan tak likhun ab main yeh maajra
Jo likhna tha mujh ko woh sab likh chuka
Now how much can I write regarding this affair?
I have written whatever I had to write

1512. Karam kar Khudawand Rabb-e-Jaleel
Dua maangta hai yeh banda zaleel
O Lord! Glorious God! Be merciful
This contemptible servant prays to you.

Bayaan Qism-e-Baaghiyaan

Narration of the types of rebels

1513. Qism chaar dekha hai hum baaghiyaan
Ke aage main likhta hun uska bayaan
I have witnessed four kinds of mutineers
In the following verses, I write their description

1514. Woh hai asl baaghi jo tha peshwa
Duuvam baaghi woh jo ke naukar hua
The real rebel is the one who was a leader
Second is the rebel who was a servant

1515. Sawaaron mein jo log naukar hue
Woh sarkaar ke khaas baaghi bane
Among the cavalry, people who became servants
They became notable rebels against the government

1516. Sivuum Raja Babu jo haazir rahe
Maa log apne madadgaar the
Thirdly, kings and clerks who were present for service
Together with their people, were helpful

1517. Bad amli ka aaghaaz jisne kiya
Kalan baaghiyon mein woh baaghi hua
Whoever initiated the bad operations
Among rebels, he was the greatest rebel

1518. Karen unko hukkaam khaarij balaad
Jo aisa karen phir na hoga fasaad
May the rulers banish them from the country
If they do so then there would be no sedition

1519. Hunudon se yahaan balwa mashhoor hai
Bayaan uska har ja pe mastoor hai
Tumultuousness of the Hindus here is well-known
Its description is written everywhere.

Kaifiyat Jaunpur Wa Balwa

Conditions of Jaunpur and Balwa

1520. Suni terahween ko yeh taazi khabar
Rahi maah April ki sun basar
Heard this fresh news on the thirteenth
It was of the month of April, listen readily

1521. Sun attharah sau par athathawan rahi
Khabar raavi deta hai sun Isvi
The year was eighteen hundred and fifty-eight
The narrator is referring to the Isvi dates

1522. Sahib Judge Bahadur ne dilshaad ki
Woh kaarinda mere se irshaad ki
Judge Sahib Bahadur conveyed cheerfulness
Stated to one of my workers

1523. Jaunpur se aaj aayi madad
Maa gore gorkhai chaalees sad
Today help came from Jaunpur
Englishmen, together with Gorkhas, numbering forty hundred

1524. Woh taintees zarb toop humraah le
Ke hukkaam sab leke wahaan se chale
They have with them thirty-three pieces of cannons
After acquiring everything, the rulers proceeded from there

1525. Azamgarh mein dakhil hue honge aaj
Ke hovega barbaad baaghi ka raj
They must have entered Azamgarh today
So the reign of the rebels will be ruined

1526. Ke jurrat shujaat ke yeh shah hain
Udavenge unko jo badraah hain
For they are the kings of daring and bravery
They would exterminate those who are wicked

1527. Jama hain jo baaghi so honge kharaab
Paden ge maa khaanumaan dar azaab
The mutineers who have collected shall be devastated
Together with their households they shall be trapped in torment

1528. Woh Balwa ke bhi baaghi maare gaye
Rahe jo wahaan woh toh saare gaye
Those rebels of Balwa were also killed
All those who were found there were annihilated

1529. Liya toop baaghi ko sarkaar ne
Woh maare gaye baaghi bhi aath saiye
Government seized the cannons of the rebels
Some eight hundred of those mutineers were also killed

1530. Haqiqat mein mardood-o-gumraah the
Gaye maare woh sab jo badraah the
In reality they were reprobates and unrighteous
All those who were evil were put to death

1531. Mohammad Hasan jab giraftaar ho
Esi shahar mein ab usse daar ho
When Mohammad Hasan is arrested
May he be hanged in this very town

1532. Kiya usne taaraaj har ek ko
Na choda hai usne kisi nek ko

He has plundered everyone
He has not spared any virtuous person

1533. Lute khaas sarkaar ke khairkhah
Hua maal-o-asbaab unka tabaah
All the prominent well-wishers of the government were looted
Their wealth and properties were destroyed.

Firozi-yaaftan Sarkaar az Azla

Victorious government of the districts

1534. Hai taarikh aththaarhween ki khabar
Mai ke mahine mein paayi zafar
This is the news of the eighteenth day
The British were triumphant in the month of May

1535. Commissioner Bahadur ne humko likha
Zila paanch baaghi se khaali hua
Commissioner Bahadur wrote to me
Five towns have been relieved of mutineers

1536. Hua Shahjahanpur azbas kharaab
Jo baaghi hue the pade dar azaab
Shahjahanpur had become much corrupted
Those who had rebelled were caught in torment

1537. Moradabad aur Badayun ko jaan
Mite baaghiyaan wahaan ke ba khaanumaan
Came to know of Moradabad and Badayun
The rebels there were wiped out with their households

1538. Woh Bijnaur ke baaghi maare gaye
Musalman jo daaghi the saare gaye
The mutineers of Bijnaur were killed
All the Muslims who had betrayed were finished

1539. Jo the tang balwaeeyoon se Hunood
Woh hain chaiyen se ab ba Rabb-e-Vadood
The Hindus who were distressed by the rioters
They now are at peace, by the grace of Loving God

1540. Jo dekha padha hum ne khushnood ho
Zafar paya sarkaar ne shukr uu
What I saw and read with happiness
Oh! Thankfully the government had been victorious

1541. Khuda unka qaayam rakhe jaah-o-farr
Kaha sunke raavi ne haal-e-zafar
May God sustain their grandeur and splendour
The narrator said on hearing the news of victory

1542. Rahe mulk aabaad sarkaar ka
Mile baaghiyon ko bakhubi saza
May the dominions of the government flourish
The rebels should be accordingly punished.

Hikayat

Report

1543. Rahe Bensh Sahib jo Dipty yahaan
Bairshaad Sahib kiya hum bayaan
Bensh Sahib was a Deputy here
On Sahib's behest I give the description

1544. Hua saaneha jo bazulm-o-sitam
Raha tahalka hashr se kuch na kum
The accident which occurred due to oppression and violence
The panic was no less than the day of resurrection

1545. Bache apni tadbeer se sab yahaan
Lute khairkhahi mein hum begumaan
Everyone here was saved by their own effort
Undoubtedly I was looted because of approbation

1546. Khalish se Musharraf ke Nazir lute
Diya maal-o-zar ko toh jaan se chute
Nazir was looted due to apprehensiveness of Musharraf
Only when he gave money and gold, was his life spared

1547. Mahajan se zar naqad usne liya
Sitam mein woh zalim ke the mubtala
He hauled gold and cash from the Mahajan
He was trapped in oppression of the ruthless

1548. Raaya ki har tarha thi abtari
Na tha zulm se uske koi bari
The subjects were ruined in everyway
No one was spared from his tyranny

1549. Hain Captaan Sahib bahut basifat
Kahi unse raawi ne sab kaifiyat
Captain Sahib has many good attributes
The narrator informed him of all the circumstances

1550. Hai azla mein goron ka rahna zaroor
Karega na phir koi aisa qusoor
Posting whites in the districts is essential
Then no one would dare commit such a crime

1551. Jo sarkaar mein fauj-e-habshi rahe
Yaqeen hai ke woh jaan-nisaari kare
If the government employs army of Africans
It is believed that they would be devoted

1552. Yeh irshaad-e-Captaan Sahib hua
Ke sarkaar ne habshiyon ko rakha
Captain Sahib said this:
That the government has employed Africans

1553. Woh gore bhi sarkaar mein kum nahin
Zara fauj ka humko ab gham nahin
The whites in the government are no less in number
I am not at all worried about the army now.

Hikayat Fatah-w-Firoz-e-Sarkaar Daulat Mudaar az Lucknow wa Rukhsatyaaftan Fauz-e-Nepaliyaan

Report of the victory of the government in charge of the riches at Lucknow and departure of the Nepalese army

1554. Rahi baaqi thoodi si yeh guftagu
Ke likhta hai raawi use du-ba-du
A little bit of this conversation that remains untold
The narrator writes it here as it is

1555. Hai pachchees Aprail ka sar guzasht
San-e-Hijda bud panjah-o-hasht
This is the account of twenty-fifth April
The year being eighteen fifty-eight

1556. Ke az Lucknow fauz-e-Nepaliyaan
Muzaffar–w-mansur aayi yahaan
That from Lucknow the Nepalese army
Came here triumphantly

1557. Aur Sarkaar-e-Aali se rukhsat hui
Badafaat Nepal ko sab gayee
And it took leave from the eminent government
With time, all of them went back to Nepal

1558. Aur afwaaj goron ki aayi yahaan
Basad farr-o-shaukat basad izz-o-shaan

And the armies of whites came here
With much splendour and magnificence and much esteem and glory

1559. Likhun kya main unki shujaat ka haal
Ke Rustam bhi hai saamne unke zaal
What should I write about their bravery?
That Rustam also is antiquated before them

1560. Che Saam wa Nariman che Asfandyaar
Che Sohrab wa Barzu-e-aali tabaar
Be it Saam or Nariman or Asfandyaar
Be it Sohrab or Barzu of high ranks

1561. Hain sab saamne unke misl-e-shaghaal
Kare saamnaa unka kis ki majaal
In comparison to them, all are like jackals
Who can dare to face them?

1562. Karun kya main baaje ka unke bayaan
Sab israar-e-pinhaan hain us se ayaan
What description should I give of their musical instruments?
All mysterious secrets become apparent by it,

1563. Bawaqt-e-vaghaa sur-e-yaum-un-nushoor
Bahungaame ishrat saraapaa suroor
At the time of war they create the sound of the day of resurrection
In the uproar of gaiety they become the very manifestation of pleasure

1564. Likhe kya qalam unka husn-o-jamaal
Hai nazzarah ko usse hairat kamaal
What can the pen write about their beauty and elegance?
Sight is extremely mystified by that

1565. Woh rangat gulaabi woh wardi ghazab
Ajab hai ajab hai ajab hai ajab

That pink complexion and that extraordinary uniform
It is wonderful, it is amazing, it is marvelous, incredible!

1566. Karen toop-o-bandooq ki jab ke pher
Ho surat se saiyyaaron ka haal ghair
When they circulate their cannons and guns
The condition of the planets becomes bizarre due to their swiftness!

1567. Bas aiye raawi likh ab tu aage ka haal
Nahin vasf ki unke mujh ko majaal
Sufficient, O Narrator! Now you write the subsequent circumstances
I do not have ample ability to eulogize them

1568. Jo hain shahar mein bhattiyan maiye ki sab
Kiya band hukkaam ne unko ab
All the furnaces of alcoholic liquor which are in the town
Now the rulers have shut them off

1569. Woh taadi bhi mauquoof hai yak-qalam
Raaya ki takleef ka hai alam
That Toddy is also entirely banned
They are aggrieved by the subjects' suffering

1570. Hai manzoor gore shahar mein na aayen
Aur andar shahar ke na peewen na khaayen
It is sanctioned that the whites should not go in the town
And they should neither drink nor eat in the town

1571. Hifazat bhala aisi karta hai kaun
Raiyyat ka gham dil mein dharta hai kaun
Who protects in such a manner?
Who has such heartfelt concern for the subjects?

1572. Bhala dekho nukhsaan kaisa hua
Hua es mein sarkaar ka kya bhala
Well, see what losses were incurred
How was it to the good of the government?

1573. Faqat hifz-o-hurmat raaya tamaam
Hai manzoor-e-hukkaam wala maqaam
Just the protection of honour of all subjects
Is intended by the eminently placed rulers

1574. Likhun vasf unka toh ho ek kitaab
Hain haakim humare bas aali janaab
If I write their praises it would become a voluminous book
All that can be said is that our rulers are most honourable

1575. Aur daaku jo aaye the yaan badkhisaal
Rahi unse takleef sabko kamaal
And the evil dacoits who had come here
Everyone suffered extremely because of them

1576. Kisi ke na qalb mein baaqi tha dam
Sitam tha sitam tha sitam tha sitam
Nobody's soul had any strength left in it
It was tyranny, it was oppression, it was injustice, violence!

1577. Ijaabat ko pahunchi har ek ki dua
Jo baaghi tha ek-ek ghaarat hua
Everyone's prayer was accepted
Each and every rebel was ravaged

1578. Hue raunaq afrooz hukkaam yahaan
Hua unse aabaad saaraa jahaan
The rulers graced this place with their presence
The whole world blossomed due to them

1579. Bhala aise aaqa se phirta koi
Ke aakhir ko phir kaam aaye woh hi
Well, who could ever turn his back on such masters?
After all, finally it was they who came to the rescue,

1580. Tarahhum karam unka din raat hai
Siwa munsifi ke na kuch baat hai
Their compassion and favour is bestowed day and night
Except justice there is no other etiquette for them.

Hikayat Jurrat-o-Shujaat Wa Husn-e-Intizaami Janaab Sahib Commissioner Bahadur

Report of the bravery and excellent management of Janaab Commissioner Sahib Bahadur

1581. Yahaan ke Commissioner ki hai yeh sifat
Zara dil laga kar suno kaifiyat
These are the attributes of the Commissioner here
Listen to the particulars carefully:

1582. Commissioner Bahadur hain kaise raheem
Hamesha rakhe khush Khuda-e-Kareem
The Commissioner Bahadur is so very kind
May the benevolent God always keep him happy

1583. Hain ausaaf unke likhoon kya bhala
Qalam ko kahaan aisa rutba mila
Well, what should I write about his qualities?
When did the pen have such a powerful status?

1584. Falak rutbah Jam-jaah aali tabaar
Sher-e-barziyaan beshkaar zaar
Sky-statured, glorious like Jamshed, of noble descent,
Like a ferocious lion in the battlefield

1585. Mudabbir khiradmand bedaar maghz
Nizam-ul-mumaalik baguftaar naghz

Statesman, intelligent, enlightened
Administrator of countries, exquisite in conversation

1586. Adaalat mein Kisra hai uska laqab
Sahib-e-karam hai to barq-e-ghazab
In equity Kisra is his title
As he is the master of kindness, so is he full of lightning wrath

1587. Shujaat mein kis se main tashbeeh doon
Majaaz aur haqiqat ko yak saan karun
In bravery with whom should I make a comparison?
So that by the simile, may I make metaphor and reality similar?

1588. Likhun razm ka gar main Balwa ke haal
Zamin-e-sukhan ho abhi khun se laal
If I write an account of the battle at Balwa
The ground of speech would immediately become red with blood

1589. Ho daawaat se josh dariya-e-khun
Qalam se ho fawwaara-e-khun birun
From the ink pot will emerge a boiling river of blood
From the pen will come out a fountain of blood

1590. Lageyn shaakh-e-ashaar mein ser ke phal
Yeh turfa shigoofa ho zarbulmisl
The stem of verses shall bear satiated fruits
This strange bud shall be a proverb

1591. Woh afwaaj-e-baaghi bhi taiyyaar ho
Har ek tarha se chust-o-hoshiyaar ho
That army of rebels was also prepared
Became active and attentive in everyway

1592. Yamin-o-yasar apna kar ke durust
Jab hote the paikaar par tang-o-chust
Positioned the right and left wings of their army appropriately
When they prepared with agility for the war

1593. Jo yakbargi misl-e-zarghaam nar
Hazaaroon mein karte the seena sipar
Then suddenly, men like ravenous lions
In thousands, took the brunt of assault boldly

1594. Na bachta kisi ka sar-o-dast-o-paa
Na rahta kabhi hosh-e-dushman bajaa
No one's head, hands or feet were saved
The enemies' senses never remained intact

1595. Na laataa koi taab paikaar ki
Faraari sabhi hote yakbargi
No one had the power to face the onslaught
Everyone would flee on impulse

1596. Esi tarha atraaf mein ja-ba-ja
Jo baaghi the unko bhi ghaarat kiya
In the same manner, in different places, here and there
Those who were mutineers, were also crushed

1597. Mitaaya gharaz baaghiyon ko tamaam
Nahin kuch humare sukhan mein kalaam
Therefore all rebels were erased
In my poetry there is no apology of doubt

1598. Sakhaawat ka unke likhun gar main haal
Toh Hatim ka aajiz ho vaham-o-khayaal
If I happen to write about his attitude of generosity
Then the imagination and thought of Hatim would be humbled

1599. Nahin jhoot esme kuch aiye batameez
Sakhaawat hai unke ek adna kaneez
O Judicious one! There are no lies in this account
Munificence is like his trifling maidservant

1600. Za dariya-e-jodash namee yak namee
Zomaan-e-karmash che goyam hamee
The stream of his enthusiasm is so full of moisture
To describe his deeds by conjecture, I would say,

1601. Che goyam Kaik Khusroe naamdaar
Che Jamshed-o-Khaqaan-e-Cheen bavaqaar
Would call him Kaik Khusroe of these times
And the dignified Jamshed or Emperor of China

1602. Che aan Kaiqubaad saraapa nizaam
Hama pesh mamduh man tifl-e-khaam
And he is Kaiqubaad, the personification of order
All are immature children before my patron

1603. Kahan intizaam aisa paawe koi
Siyaasat madan aisi kis ko hui
Where would one find such management?
Who has such love for good governance of towns?

1604. Kiya kisne es taur ka intizaam
Hua kis se es tarha par ehtimaam
Who made arrangements of this kind?
Who has been able to be diligent in this style?

1605. Raaya tamaam unse aabaad hain
Sagheer-o-kabeer unse dilshaad hain
All subjects are prospering due to him
Dignitaries and the ordinary are pleased with him

1606. Sukhan sanj yakta-e-aafaaq hain
Raaya nawaaz wa khushakhlaaq hain
In intelligence he is unique in the universe
Cherishes his subjects and has a happy disposition

1607. Woh mardum shanaas aur hain qadardaan
Shuja-o-sakhi wa diler-o-jawaan
He has the knowledge of judging men and is a patron
Brave and generous and daring and youthful

1608. Faheem-o-aleem-o-hakeem-o-dabeer
Raheem-o-kareem-o-haleem-o-ameer
Intelligent and wise, philosopher and writer
Kind and merciful, serene and princely

1609. Hain mehr-e-darakshaan siphar vaqaar
Muazzaz moaqqar governor ke yaar
Is the brilliant sun; the shield of dignity
Honourable, esteemed; a friend of the Governor

1610. Shahar ke raeeson pe altaaf hai
Yeh hukkaam-e-aali ka ausaaf hai
He is favourable towards the magnates of the town
These are the charecteristics of the exalted ruler

1611. Nahin lutf ka unke hadd-o-hisaab
Raeeson se mujh ko kiya intikhaab
There is no limit or account of his benignity
Selected me among the rich

1612. Report likhee meri jagir ki
Har ek tarha se meri tauqir ki
Wrote a report, recommending land grant for me
Venerated me in everyway

1613. Likhi apni tajviz se aath hazaar
Salamat rakhe inko Parwardigaar
Through his proposal recommended eight thousand (rupees)
May Providence keep him safe!

1614. Gharib aur amir unke daaye tamaam
Raiyyat nawaazi ka karte hain kaam
All, poor and rich are his crusaders
He works for the protection of his subjects

1615. Hue shahar mein jab se raunaq feza
Gharon mein hai shaadi ba-fazl-e-Khuda
Ever since he has re-inforced the splendour of the town
Households are mirthful by the grace of God

1616. Adu ke hain dushman raiyyat ke yaar
Governor kare unko Parwardigaar
He is an enemy of enemy and a friend of his subjects
May Providence make him a Governor!

1617. Yeh Effil Sahib ka ausaaf hai
Karam unka har samt-o-atraaf hai
These are the virtues of Effil Sahib
His benevolence extends in all directions

1618. Raheem-o-kareem-o-sakhi-o-ameer
Duago hain inke sagheer-o-kabeer
Beneficent and bountiful, magnanimous and noble
Small and big, all pray for him

1619. Sulh ka kiya khubtar nazm-o-nasq
Hai maddah-o-khushnud sab yaan ke khalq
Enforced such exhaustive discipline for peace
That all the people of this place are panegyrist and happy

1620. Duago se jo khairkhahi hui
Ayaan maah se taab mahi hui
Whatever solicitousness was done by this well-wisher
Was like manifestation of the luminousness of fish by moon

1621. Hai mumkin sana ki ho qaaim bina
Kahenge magar log hai khud-sita
Even though eulogy may be based on solid facts
Yet people might say, he is an egotist

1622. Hai kaar-e-niko to shaih-e-aaqibat
Sifat jo kare ghair woh hai sifat
Good deeds are an incitement for hereafter
That praise is true praise, which comes from an outsider

1623. Commissioner ne jo hai report kiya
Hai kaafi mere vaaste woh sana
Whatever the Commissioner has reported
That much praise is enough for me

1624. Mataalib report ka ab hai yahaan
Zara gosh-e-dil se suno doostaan
Now here are the objectives of the report
Friends, listen from the depth of your hearts.

Tarjuma report Janaab Sahib Commissioner Bahadur

Translation of the report of Janaab Commissioner Sahib Bahadur

1625. Hai es shahar mein ek musalman faqir
Hai qabze mein uske maeeshat kaseer
In this town lives a muslim mendicant
In his possession are abundant means of livelihood

1626. Hai dil se hawakhah woh nek khu
Azakhana mein jaaye di mem ko
That good-natured man is a true well-wisher
Gave shelter to ladies in the mourning house

1627. Bataarikh haftam za maah-e-August
Baghaavat ki bu se hue log mast
On the seventh day of the month of August
When people had become intoxicated by the odour of rebellion

1628. Rahe chain se uske ghar sahibaan
Maa aal-o-atfaal aur bibiyaan
The officers stayed in his house peacefully
With their children and ladies

1629. Siwa es ke asbaab ahle Firang
Amaanat rakha apne ghar bedirang
Besides this, belongings of the European people
Were entrusted to him and kept in his house without any hesitation

1630. Ruju su-e-Nazim na asla hua
Esi se kayee baar loota gaya
He was never at all inclined towards the Nazim
That is why he was looted many times

1631. Luta khairkhahi mein sarkaar ke
Woh hai mad mein daakhil wafaadaar ke
He was looted for being an approbatory of the government
He is very much included under the head of loyal ones

1632. Samajhte hain nek usko hukkaam sab
Vale hai hawakhah woh khush-laqab
All officers consider him as virtuous
But of course that one of pleasing appellation is a sympathizer

1633. Hua zulm Nazim ka uspar sawa
Ziyaadah luta sab se woh bawafaa
Nazim's oppression was most prolonged upon him
That loyal man was looted the most

1634. Iwaz uske jagir usko mile
Ba aish-o-tarab zindagaani kate
He may be given a land grant in lieu of that
So that he may live in luxury and merriment

1635. Ilaaqah mile laaiq-e-hasht hazaar
Magar haft se kum na ho zeenahaar
A region worth eight thousand may be granted
But it should not at all be less than seven

1636. Sana-e-duago suna sahibo
Zara ghaur ab dil mein apne karo
Sahibs, you heard the eulogy of the well-wisher,
Now do deliberate over it in your heart

1637. Kuja rutba-e-haakimaan-e-Firang
Kuja main duago-e-aajiz wa lang
Where is the status of the European rulers?
(And) Where am I, a powerless, lame, well-wisher?

1638. Bhala zarra mein kab hai taab-o-tuvaan
Muqaabil mein khur ke jo khoole zubaan
How can a particle have such power and strength
That it would open its tongue before the sun?

1639. Main qatra woh hain baihr jud-o-sakha
Woh aaqa main hoon khaadim-e-beriya
I am a drop and they are the ocean of munificence and generosity
They are the masters and I am an unpretentious servant

1640. Na taaqat na jurrat na himmat woh hai
Modi ho khidmat na taaqat woh hai
Neither is there that strength nor daring nor courage
Do not have the capacity to have served as a steward

1641. Yeh sab hai inaayaat hukkaam ki
Nahin meri khidmat kisi kaam ki
All these are favours of the rulers
My services are of no use

1642. Mere haq mein hukkaam hain keemiyaan
Inaayat se mis ko kiya hai tillaah
In my favor, the rulers are alchemists
Through kindness they have converted copper into gold thread

1643. Hamesha gada par hai altaaf-e-shah
Khuda khush rakhe unko sham-o-pagah
The king is always benign towards the beggar
May God keep them happy, dusk and dawn!

1644. Yeh hai aarzoo Shah Ahmad Ali
Rahen haft-e-iqliim ke yeh vaali
This is the entreaty of Shah Ahmad Ali
May they be the owners of the seven worlds!

1645. Hai jab tak falak par darakshinda maah
Rahe sultanate Malika-e-Aalijaah
Till the time the moon is luminous in the sky
May the empire of the High-ranking Queen last!

Bayaan Husn-e-Intizaami Janaab Lawrence Sahib Bahadur Haakim-e-Punjab

Description of the managerial efficiency of Janaab Lawrence Sahib Bahadur, the Administrator of Punjab

1646. Jo Vaali-e-Punjab hain Lawrence
Woh hain laaiq-e-mulkgiri-o-bas
Lawrence, who is the ruler of Punjab
Is worthy of territorial consolidation and authority

1647. Hai sakna-e-Punjab gustaakh dast
Kiya wan ke haakim ne yeh bandobast
The residents of Punjab being audacious
The administrator of that place made this arrangement

1648. Raaya-e-Punjab ko yaar kar
Rawaana kiya su-e-Dehli nagar
Controlled the people of Punjab
Dispatched them towards the city of Delhi

1649. Dikhayee wahaan khub mardaangi
Hue baaghiyan sair az zindagi
Displayed a lot of manliness there
The rebels became fed up with their lives

1650. Bahut unme bejaan-o-naari hue
Jo baqi bache woh faraari hue

Many of them became lifeless and condemned
The rest of them became fugitives

651. Agarche nahin Laat ka hai khitaab
Wale hain Governorgi ke laaiq Janaab
Although he does not have the title of Laat
However, the gentleman is worthy of Governorship

652. Agar hon Governor sazawaar hain
Ba dil yeh hawakhah-e-sarkaar hain
If he becomes a Governor, it is well deserved
He is a supporter of the government with all his heart

653. Dua hai yeh Ahmad ki har raah-o-baat
Karen Malika-e-Aaliya unko Laat
This is Ahmad's prayer, that by all ways and means
May the High-exalted Queen make him a Laat.

Kaifiyat Shah-e-Dehli wa Altaaf-e-Sarkaar

Condition of the King of Delhi and kindness of the government

1654. Rahi terahween maah Ziqaad ki
Aur chabbeesween June ki thi padi
It was the thirteenth of the month of Ziqaad
And was the twenty-sixth of June

1655. Sun alif asneen-o-haftaad-o-chaar
Za Hijri bud w Isvi dar shumaar
The year was one thousand two hundred and seventy four
This is Hijri, the Isvi year is also computed;

1656. Sane hijdah sad ba panja ho hasht
Ke dar sam-e-rawi ba sahat-e-guzasht
The year was eighteen hundred and fifty eight
This the narrator has heard very accurately

1657. Kiya Shah-e-Dehli ne aisa fasaad
Rahegi qayaamat talak jiski yaad
The King of Delhi committed such a rebellion
That will be remembered till Doomsday

1658. Hua sara Hindustan par tar ghadar
Kisi ki na baqi rahi kuch qadar
Entire Hindustan was engulfed in mutiny
No dignity of any one remained

1659. Kiya kaisa barbaad har ek ko
Rahe aap achche yeh turfa suno
How each and everyone was destroyed,
Himself remained good; listen to this astonishing news:

1660. Saza jurm ki kuch na unke hui
Jagah ek jazeerah mein unko mili
He was not punished for his crime
He was given a place on an island

1661. Mile ga unhen naan-o-nafqah wahaan
Rahenge wahaan jaise rahte the yahaan
There, he will be given a maintenance allowance
He will live there, just as he lived here

1662. Yeh English Bahadur ka ausaaf hai
Ke es jurm par bhi yeh altaaf hai
These are the manners of the English Bahadur
That despite such a crime, these are the favours

1663. Karen shukr Khaliq ka dil se ada
Duago hon sarkaar ke ab sada
He should thank the Creator from the core of his heart
Now he should always be a well-wisher of the government.

Kaifiyat Ghazipur waaqiya maah-e-June

Condition of Ghazipur; incident of the month of June

1664. Ghazipur ab tak bahut saaf tha
Ke hai tazkirah uska upar likha
Up till now Ghazipur was very clean
In fact its account has been written above

1665. Vale June mein woh bhi baaghi hua
Amar Singh ke haanth daaghi hua
But in June it also became mutinous
It was soiled by the hands of Amar Singh

1666. Jo aaya woh mardak mile wahaan ke log
Kam aqlee se apne kharida yeh rog
When that mean fellow came, the people of that place joined him
By their foolishness, they bought and nursed this illness

1667. Bahut Hindu us ja ke baaghi hue
Musalman baare ke daaghi hue
Many Hindus of that place became mutineers
At length Muslims were tarnished

1668. Sada Singh Zamindaar Ballia suna
Bada naamwar aur purzoor tha
Heard of Sada Singh, the Zamindaar of Ballia
Was very well-renowned and powerful

669. Makar Singh bhi ek tha bavaqaar
Hue baaghi yeh dono bhi naabkaar
One Makar Singh too was dignified
Both these malicious ones also became rebels

670. Rahe kaise sab log aaraam se
Na baaqi rahe koi ab kaam ke
With what ease and comfort everyone lived
Now they have become good-for-nothing

671. Bhala yaaron sarkaar ne kya kiya
Hunood aur Musalman ko rutba diya.
Friends, after all what had the government done?
Gave distinction to Hindus and Muslims

672. Jo laaiq na tha usko laaiq kiya
Riyaasat sharafat ilaaqah diya
Those who were not worthy, were made worthy
Gave land grants, civility and estates

673. Salaf mein na hargiz tha yeh intizaam
Kiye aglee logon ne aise na kaam
In the past, definitely no such arrangement existed
The predecessors never undertook this kind of work

674. Raha kaisa aaraam har ek ko
Dua unko deta hai khushnud ho
What contentment did everyone have!
Blessed them with happiness

675. Jo vaali ke apne rahe khairkhah
Mila unko hukkaam se izz-o-jah
Those who remained faithful to their guardian
They received honour and status from the rulers

676. Nazar mein jo vaali ke the arjmand
Hua unka es waqt paya buland
Those who were worthy in the estimation of the benefactor
At this time they were highly ranked.

Kaifiyat Madadgaaraan-e-sarkaar

Particulars of confederates of the government

1677. Nahin kizb ka es mein kuch inzamaam
Suno mujh se ab khairkhahon ka naam
There is no assembling of lies in here
Listen now to the names of the well-wishers from me

1678. Ataat mein tha vaali-e-Rampur
Madad us ne sarkaar ko di zaroor
The ruler of Rampur was reverent
He definitely helped the government

1679. Aur Nawab bhi Haidrabad ka
Badil humdam-o-yaar-e-sarkaar tha
And also the Nawab of Hyderabad
Was a compassionate friend and comrade of the government

1680. Kiya saaf usne Dakhan ko tamaam
Liya baaghiyon se bahut intiqaam
He sterilized the whole of Deccan
He took a lot of retribution from the mutineers

1681. Hunoodon mein vaali-e-Jamboor raha
Madadgaar Raja-e-Patiala tha
Among Hindus was the ruler of Jamboor
The King of Patiala was an assistant

1682. Hawakhah-e-sarkaar-e-aali tabaar
Raha khairju vaali-e-Gawaliyaar
Sympathizer of the government of noble descent
The ruler of Gwalior was a well-wisher

1683. Aur Kabul ka vaali madadgaar tha
Aur Nabahiye ka Raja bhi ghamkhaar tha
And the ruler of Kabul was helpful
And the King of Nabahiye was also a sympathizer

1684. Tha Raja Faridkot ka khairkhah
Woh haazir raha le ke apni sipah
The King of Faridkot was a well-wisher
He was present for service along with his army

1685. Raha khairkhah Raja-e-Bharatpur
Dholpur-o-Jaipur ahle sho'oor
A well-wisher was the King of Bharatpur
Of Dholpur and Jaipur, masters of intellect

1686. Wazir Singh Sarodhi ka le kar sipah
Bakhubi kiya baaghiyon ko tabaah
Wazir Singh of Sarodhi, with his army
Crushed the mutineers very thoroughly

1687. Raha Raja Bundi ka bas khairkhah
Jarauti ke Raja ki thi nek raah
The King of Bundi was also supportive
The King of Jarauti was on a noble path

1688. Surat Singh haazir tha manjeythiyah
Tha Bal Singh sardaar Jorkaliya
Surat Singh was present in the great crisis
Bal Singh, the commander of Jorkaliya, was present

1689. Teja Singh Raja tha Losadwa shahar
Hua khairkhahi mein mashoor tar
Teja Singh was the King of Losadwa town
He became very famous for his supportiveness

1690. Muawin tha Shahzada Jamboor ka
Fateh Khan tuvana bhi shahzoor tha
The Prince of Jamboor was an assistant
Robust Fateh Khan was also powerful

1691. Raha Mir Jafar bhi Peshwar ka
Muawin Imamuddin ka poor tha
Also was Mir Jafar of Peshwar
Son of Imamuddin was a tributary

1692. Fateh Khan bhi Kabsa ka haazir raha
Nihal Singh Jhajhi ka maujood tha
Fateh Khan of Kabsa was in attendance
Nihal Singh of Jhajhi was present

1693. Qila Anmb ke jo Jahandaar Khan
Yeh Nawab haazir the ba maal-o-jaan
Jahandaar Khan who is from Qila Anmb
This Nawab was present in service with money and life

1694. Hayat Khan bhi jo ek sardaar tha
Woh sarkaar ka bas tarafdaar tha
Also, Hayat Khan, who was a commander
He was just a partisan of the government

1695. Kalebagh ke jo rahe ek Nawab
Rahi raae unki bahut basawaab
A Nawab who was from Kalebagh
His opinion was full of rectitude

1696. Malik Fateh Khan jo ke sardaar the
Badil woh hawakhah-e-sarkaar the
Malik Fateh Khan, who was a chieftan
He was a hearty well-wisher of the government

1697. Raha khairkhah Tonk ka bhi Nawab
Hamesha se hain woh toh aali-khitaab
The Nawab of Tonk was also a supporter
He always had an exalted title

1698. The humraah Mirza Ali Khanpur
Tha in sab pe afzaal-e-Rabb-e-Ghafur
Also included was Mirza Ali of Khanpur
On all of them was favour of the Forgiving God

1699. Rahe log Punjab ke nek zaat
Kahan tak likhe in ki raavi sifaat
The people of Punjab were noble entities
How much can the narrator write about their attributes?

1700. Rizamand tha inse Parwardigaar
Ke vaali ke apne rahe ghamgusaar
Providence was condescending towards them
Because they were sympathizers of their guardian

1701. Rahe pusht par unke hukkaam sab
Esi se hua kaam anjaam sab
All the rulers were backing them
Due to this, all tasks were accomplished

1702. Woh baqi Hunood aur Musalman bahut
Rahe khairkhahi mein aamaadah chust
The rest of the Hindus and many Muslims
Remained ready and active in support

1703. Rahe jo ke badbakht khaati hue
Batarghib-e-Shaitaan daaghi hue
Those who were malicious, became wrong-doers
They were spoiled by the inducement of the Satan.

Khulaasa Kitaabat

Abstract of Representation

1704. Khulaasa kitaabat ka karta hun main
Mufassal ko mujmal banata hun main
I am summarizing the representation
I am condensing the comprehensive report

1705. Rausa koi yahaan ke baaghi nahin
Bafazl-e-Khuda koi daaghi nahin
None of the nobles of this place are mutineers
By the grace of God none is spoiled

1706. Ataat mein sab haakimaan-e-firang
Rahe ibtida se woh sab ek rang
Everyone in the service of European rulers
They all remained steadfast right from the beginning

1707. Musalmanon mein jo ke baaghi bana
Shareef aur najeeb us mein koi na tha
Those who became mutineers among the Muslims
None among them were of noble birth or courteous

1708. Hunoodon mein bhi aisa hi haal tha
Jo kam zarf tha woh bad-aamaal tha
Same was the case with the Hindus
Those who were ignoble were the evil-doers

1709. Rausa es shahar ke hain gharib
Sayeed-o-hameed-o-shareef-o-najeeb
The elite of this town are indigent
Fortunate, laudable, polite and of noble birth

1710. Areeza Session Judge ko likhte rahe
Dua haq mein English ke karte rahe
Persistently wrote applications to the Session Judge
Kept praying in favour of the English

1711. Jo Hindu hain yahaan ke bahut saaf hain
Bafazl-e-Khuda nek ausaaf hain
The Hindus of this place are very clean
By God's grace they have noble virtues

1712. Diwani ke amla the sab nek tar
Woh amla police bhi rahe khush siyar
All the staff of courts was most virtuous
The staff of police was also good-natured

1713. Woh Raja-e-Bansi rahe khairju
Nahin unke saani koi nek khoo
That King of Bansi was a well-wisher
None is as well-mannered as him

1714. Agarche rahe shahar se bekhabar
Mitaate the buniyaad-e-baaghi magar
Although he was not well-posted about the town
Yet he was erasing the very foundation of the rebels

1715. Nimkohi ke Raja rahe hoshiyaar
Usi ja pe karte the sab kaarobaar
The King of Nimkohi was clever
He used to conduct all business in that place

1716. Yehi haal Raja-e-Gopalpur
Salimpur ke Raja bhi zeesho'oor
Condition of the King of Gopalpur was the same
The King of Salimpur was also a sensible one

1717. Muhaafiz raaya ke apne hue
Usi raj mein kaam karte rahe
Became the protector of his subjects
Kept working in the same state

1718. Jo Babu rahe ahle-maqdoor sab
Wohi ban gaye yaaron mashrur sab
All the Lords who were powerful people
Friends, they all became legitimate

1719. Unhi ki rahi usko taaqat kamaal
Esi se gharibon pe aaya zawaal
He derived great strength from them
That is why the poor became degenerated

1720. Magar yeh rahe Babuaan hoshmand
Pegoli wa Rampur ke arjmand
But these Lords were sensible
The honourable of Pegoli and Rampur

1721. Bishanpur ka Babu tha zeekhirad
Bakhubi samajhta tha woh nek-o-bad
The Lord of Bishanpur was wise
He understood good and bad very well

1722. Yeh kahte the sarkaar aawenge kab
Mohabbat ka dam bharte hain rooz-o-shab
They said when will the government come?
We take pledge of love, day and night

1723. Iisai Musai pe afzaal-e-Rabb
Rahe jo yahaan unke saai the sab
On Christians and Jews is God's mercy
Those who were here, paid their devoirs to them

1724. Kisi tarha unpar na aaya guzand
Madad kharch de dete sab arjmand
No harm came upon them in any way
Fortunately everyone gave them help and allowance

1725. Madadgaar Loren ke Himmat Ali
Bahut unse sahib ko raahat mili
Himmat Ali was the helper of Loren
Sahib derived a lot of courage from him

1726. Bachaaya qawaneen-o-daftar nazeer
Hifazat ke fan mein woh the benazeer
Saved the statutes and registers of precedents
In the art of safe-keeping he is unsurpassed

1727. Woh sarkaar ka dil se hai khairkhah
Esi se nahin dekha rooz-e-siyaah
He is a true well-wisher of the government
That is why he did not witness the black day

1728. Abbot Sahib ka raavi warris bana
Dileri wa jurrat se ghar me rakha
The writer became the protector of Abbot Sahib
Kept him at home with courage and daring

1729. Maa aal-o-atfaal the sahibaan
Hifazat ki humne unho ki bajaan
The gentlemen were with their family and children
I protected them with all my heart and soul

1730. Boran ko zaroorat jo humse hui
Woh unki haajat rafa humne ki
Whatever Boran required from me
I fulfilled that need of his

1731. Hain yahaan jo lisai Abdul Raheem
Rahe unke atfaal yahaan par muqeem
Here is a Christian, called Abdul Raheem
His children were stationed here

1732. Tha lisaiyoon ka madadgaar main
Raha es se unka talabgaar main
I was the helpmate of Christians
That is why they were desirous of me

1733. Barabar unhe kharch deta raha
Khabar unki har waqt leta raha
Gave allowances to them regularly
Inquired after their welfare continuously

1734. Hui jis ko jis cheez ki aarzoo
Kiya usko anjaam bas du-ba-du
Whatever thing was desired by anybody
It was accomplished immediately

1735. Mere paas sab log aate rahe
Kawaif mufassal sunate rahe
Everyone kept coming to me
Kept on narrating precise details

1736. Vazeetor bhi aa kar ke dete khabar
Mere paas aate the sab khush siyar
Visitors also came and gave information
All the good-natured ones came to me

1737. Kanhaiyya Muddaris bhi school ke
Jo kahte the humse woh karte rahe
Kanhaiyya, the school teacher also
Did whatever he said to me

1738. Jo the khairkhah unse tha mujh ko rabt
Woh mujh se bhi rakhte the sab rabt-o-zabt
I had connections with those who were the well-wishers
All of them were also intimate with me

1739. Na tha koi lisaiyon ka rafeeq
Faqat ek raavi tha unka shafeeq
No one was a confederate of the Christians
Only the narrator was their affectionate friend

1740. Bhala kyon na rakta saron par main haath
Hamesha se hai chooli-daaman ka saath
After all why should I not have patronized?
There always had existed an indissoluble link with them

1741. Areeza ba khidmat-e-hukkaam-e-khesh
Kiya karta tha main rawaana hamesh
Applications addressed to the close officers
Were dispatched by me unfailingly

1742. Kiya khairkhahon ko hum intikhaab
Jo batin mein behtar rahe aan janaab
I selected the well-wishers
Dignified and honourable, who were superior from within

1743. Rahe mujraee garche we log sab
Yehi soche hurmat bachane ka dhab
Although, they all were servants
Probably they thought of this as a means of saving their honour

1744. Musalman ko tha paas-e-izzat kamaal
Esi se nahin unpe aaya zawaal
Muslims had intense considerations for esteem
That was why decay did not befall them

1745. Woh faham-o-firasat se apne bache
Har ek makr-o-hilah se milte rahe
They were saved by their intelligence and discernment
They faced all kinds of deceit and trickery

1746. Mahina kata chaar aur bees rooz
Musibat ke humraah aiye dil furooz
Four months and twenty days passed
With great difficulty, O' heart-inflammatory!

1747. Hui jis qadar sab ki haalat tabaah
Nahin uski hukkaam ko intibaah
The extent to which everyone's state was ruined
The rulers have no circumspection of it

1748. Agar kàash sunte musibat ka haal
Toh hukkaam ko sakht hota malaal
If only they heard a report of the disasters
Then the rulers would have felt deeply dejected

1749. The majboor jo nazd azlam gaye
Yeh sach hai ke beyaar-o-haakim rahe
Those who were helpless, went near the most cruel
It is true that they were without any friend or commander

1750. Gaye par woh majboor ho kar gaye
Nahin naukri ki tammaa par gaye
Went, but they went only under compulsion
Did not go due to avariciousness for a service

1751. Rahe aafiyatkhaah har aan mein
Na aaya khalal unke imaan mein
They wished peace at all times
No unsoundness had come in their integrity

1752. Rahe es dua mein woh ratb-ul-lisaan
Ke maalik mere jald aayen yahaan
They were facile in this prayer
That may my masters come here soon

1753. Sitam deedgaan ki khabar jald leyn
Museebat-zadon ki woh hi daad deyn
May they come to rescue from violence, which is worth-watching
They must do justice to the afflicted ones

1754. Kisi ki na ki naukri bedhadak
Woh haazir hain sarkaar mein aaj tak
They did not become anyone's employee readily
They are present in the government till today

1755. Baummid sarkaar jaate rahe
Buraee ke din apne kata kiye
They withdrew with trust in the government
They simply passed off their bad days

1756. Khataa maaf hukkaam-e-aali karen
Ke aaraam se sab raaya rahen
May the exalted rulers forgive their mistakes
So that all subjects can live in peace

1757. Jo baaghi hain asli woh paawen saza
Jo haibat se bhage chupe ja-ba-ja
Those real mutineers should be punished
Who have fled due to fear and hidden here and there

1758. Rahe dil se sarkaar ke khairkhah
Hui sab pe sarkaar ki ab nigaah
Those who were true well-wishers of the government
Now the government paid kind attention to all of them

1759. Ba dastur woh log howen bahaal
Mite ab toh un sab ka ranj-o-malaal
They may be reinstated as usual
At least now their agony and grief should be erased

1760. Na tha jab ke vaali toh hurmat bachi
Bade makr-o-heelah se izzat rahi
Honour was saved even though there was no protector
Only with great pretence and strategy was esteem preserved

1761. Gunaahon se koi bhala saaf hai
Kare raham jo unka ausaaf hai
Is any one at all, pure from sins?
Whoever does kindness that is his virtue,

1762. Kahin chashm-poshi kahin pur-ghazab
Kahin daar-o-giir aur kahin pur-taab
Somewhere forgivingly overlooking, somewhere full of wrath
Somewhere indiscriminate arrests and somewhere langorously

1763. Kahin rahm-o-shafqat kahin par ho zulm
Kahin par ho ujlat kahin par hulm
Somewhere is kindness and affection, somewhere may be cruelty
Somewhere may be haste and somewhere serenity

1764. Kahin afv taqseer ka hai zuroor
Ke ta ho ke mamnoon ahle qusoor
Somewhere, definitely is forgiveness for mistakes
In order that the culprits may be obliged

1765. Badil khairkhahi mein masroof hoon
Paye jaan nisaari woh mashghoof hoon
Should be heartily engaged in solicitousness
May be diligent in pursuit of devotion

1766. Na hoga koi jab ke taqseerwaar
To phir hoga kis tarha afv aashkaar
In case if there would be no sinner
Then how would the magnanimity of forgiveness become manifest?

1767. Yeh sab vasf shayaan-e-sultan hain
Ke yeh naib-e-Haq-o-Rehmaan hain
All these are virtues suitable for the rulers
For they are the vicegerents of the Beneficent God

1768. Commissioner-w-Judge mein yeh ausaaf hai
Sarasar nazar mehr-o-altaaf hai
The Commissioner and Judge have these attributes
Their attitude is of total kindness and favour

1769. Hai manzoor in sab ko ab munsifi
Kisi ko na unse azeeyat mili
Now all of them approve of justice
No one received torment from them

1770. Jo hukm-e-Governor hai aiye sahibo
Wohi amr karte hain aiye doostoon
O Gentlemen! Whatever is ordered by the Governor
O Friends! That is precisely what they command

1771. Mitadenge buniyaad-e-baaghi tamaam
Unhi se razaamand hain khaas-o-aam
They will totally erase all foundations of the mutineers
All the people are in accord with them

1772. Commissioner Bahadur hain munsif kamaal
Collector Bahadur adeemul misaal
Commissioner Bahadur is extremely just
Collector Bahadur is unparalleled

1773. Hain insaaf se unke masroor sab
Rahen khush-o-khurram ba afzaal-e-Rabb
Everyone is delighted with their justice
May they remain happy and cheerful, by the grace of God

1774. Woh karte hain kis tarha ki justaju
Hai insaaf ki dhoom har chaar su
What kind of investigations do they make?
That there is parade of justice in all four directions

1775. Yeh hain waqiful haal raaz-e-nihaan
Rakhe unko aabaad Rabb-e-Jahan
They are well aware of the state of hidden secrets
May the Lord of the world keep them happy and prosperous

1776. Jo khaati hain hoti hai unki saza
Jo phanste hain na haq mein hote reha
Those who are the culprits are punished
Those who are falsely implicated are exculpated

1777. Yeh haakim hain munsif aur ghurba nawaaz
Sada inpe hai saaya-e-Beniyaaz
These rulers are just and gracious towards the poor
Forever on them, is the protective shadow of the Independent One!

1778. Hue sakinaan-e-Bharatpur saaf
Kiye sab qusooraat haakim ne maaf
The residents of Bharatpur were cleared
All offences were forgiven by the rulers

1779. Zila Maghrabi ke rausa tamaam
Hain haakim se khushnood har khaas-o-aam
All the nobles of the Western district,
All elite and commoners are happy with the rulers

1780. Junubi zila ki hai qismat badi
Hai fikr afv-e-khataa har ghadi
Fortune of the Southern district is great
Every moment there is concern over forgiveness of faults

1781. Hain hukkaam masroof dar intizaam
Dua haq mein karte hain sab subh-o-shaam
The rulers are busy in making arrangements
Morning and evening, everyone prays for their well-being

1782. Bandhu Singh baaghi ka sar jab kate
Toh yahaan se bhi gard-e-baghaavat mite
When the rebel Bandhu Singh's head is severed
Then the dust of mutiny shall be expunged from here too

1783. Hai hukkaam ko fikr eski badi
Hai baaqi safai mein sa'aat ghadi
The rulers are very concerned about this
In cleansing remains a duration of time

1784. Baghaavat jo haakim se apne kiya
Paye qatal-e-hukkaam naukar hua
That those who rebelled against the rulers
Became servants in pursuit of assassination of the rulers

1785. Gopalpur Mairwa mein jakar lade
Abas woh baghaavat ki dahan mein pade
Went to Gopalpur Mairwa and fought
Uselessly they fell into the mouth of the mutiny

1786. Sazawaar woh log hain daar ke
Wohi log zalim ke bas yaar the
Those are the people who deserve the gibbet
Certainly those people were friends of the cruel

1787. Diya maalkhana ki jisne kaleed
Hua woh toh vaali se apne baeid
The one who gave the key of the treasure house
He definitely became distant from his guardian

1788. Mulazim woh sarkaar ka ab na ho
Nahin usko darbaar ka kaam do
Now he should not be a servant of the government
Do not assign work of the court to him

1789. Jo ahle qalam unka naukar hua
Woh darbaar-e-Dajjaal mein ja phansa
The men of letters who became their servants
Were entrapped in the court of the Dajjaal

1790. Nahin es mein kuch unki aisi khataa
Woh hain sab ke sab mustahiq-e-ataa
No fault of theirs is in this
All of them are entitled to the bounty

1791. Muhaafiz jo izzat ke apne hue
Ba dil khairkhah woh toh sarkaar the
Those who guarded their own honour
They actually were hearty well-wishers of the government

1792. August ke maheene mein tha shoor-o-shar
Sawaar aur tillangon ka tha bas khatar
In the month of August there was tumult
There was great danger from cavalry and native soldiers

1793. Raaya thi sarkaar par jaan nisaar
Patterson Bahadur pe hai aashkaar
The subjects were devoted to the government
It is known to Patterson Bahadur

1794. Sirif ek Sahib Bird the yahaan
Muti unke sab yahaan ke khurd-o-kalan
Only Bird Sahib was here
Here everyone, small or big was obedient to him

1795. Jahan par gaye sab ne khidmat kiya
Badil sab ne unki ataat kiya
Wherever he went, everybody served him
Everyone was reverent towards him with all their heart

1796. Ke es shahar se leke Mabya talak
Kiya sabne unki bakhubi kumak
So from this town up till Mabya
Everyone succoured him very well

1797. Hain woh log ab mustahiq-e-ataa
Agarche bazahir mein ho kuch khataa
Now those people deserve forgiveness
Even though apparently there might have been some fault

1798. Badil woh hawakhah-e-sarkaar the
Khudawand nemat ke sab yaar the
Deep in their heart they were well-wishers of the government
They all were friends of the beneficent master

1799. Hui baaghiyon ki jo kasrat tamaam
The majboor laachaar sab khaas-o-aam
When the mutineers were in abundance everywhere
All the general public were constrained and helpless

1800. Shareefon se koi na naukar hua
Faqat haazri se woh abtar hua
No one among the gentlemen became a servant
Merely by presence, he was ruined

1801. Hai umeed-e-insaaf hukkaam se
Ke es jurm se hai rehaaii kise
There is hope of justice from the rulers
For who has acquittal from this offence

1802. Agar sab ke aamaal par hai khayaal
Hunood aur Musalmaan ka tha ek haal
If the concern is over everyone's deeds
Then the condition of Muslims and Hindus was the same

1803. Aqeel aur dana hain haakim tamaam
Ke hai zulm-e-Dajjaal mashhoor-o-aam
All the rulers are intelligent and wise
That cruelty of the Dajjaal is well-known and rampant

1804. Karenge jo dariyaaft raaz-e-nihaan
Toh ho jaayegi sabki khud woh amaan
When they will enquire of concealed secrets
Then that itself will become everyone's immunity

1805. Jo zaahir-o-batin mein the khairkhah
Nahin unme se koi hoga tabaah
Those who were well-wishers in appearance and reality
None of them would be destroyed

1806. Ke munsif hain adil hain haakim tamaam
Humen aish-o-ishrat hai unse mudaam
Because all the rulers are fair and just
We have always had pleasure and gaiety due to them

1807. Khuda haft-e-iqliim ka badshah
Kare unko laaiq hain beishtabah
Emperor of the seven worlds; may God
Make them, without doubt they are worthy

1808. Na lewe koi naam inke siwa
Na sultan aisa jahan mein hua
Except them, no one else's name may be recalled
No king like them has ever been in the world

1809. Unhi se mujhe jaa-e-umeed hai
Shahanshahi ta hashr qayam rahe
From them, I have hope
May their emperorship remain stable until the last day

1810. Inhi ki dua par kitaabat tamaam
Kiya humne ba-raasti ikhtataam
All the transcription due to their benediction
I have concluded with veracity

1811. Yeh zahir hai bar sahibaan-e-sukhan
Ke rakhta hai kis darja diqqat yeh fan
It is obvious to the men of letters
How very difficult is this art

1812. Khususan tawarikh kul waqiyaat
Kahan se ho mauzoon sukhan mein yeh baat
Specially the historical narrative of all events
How can this account be narrated in metrical poetry?

1813. Yeh umeed hai naazreen se humain
Talaffuz pe mere na hargiz hasen
I have this hope from the spectators
That they would not at all ridicule my pronounciation,

1814. Takalluf nahin maine kuch bhi kiya
Jo lahja hai mera usi ko likha
I have not indulged in any formality
I have written exactly what my tone is

1815. Reaayat radeef-ul-qavaafi mein gar
Koi lafz makruh aawe nazar
Remit, if in post-rhyme words or rhymes
Any word appears to be odious

1816. Toh uspar na kuch khurdbini karen
Karam kar ke ahsaan mujh par dharen
Then do not conduct any microscopic deliberation over it
With kind generosity grant me a favour

1817. Thi baeesween maah Ziqaad ki
Ke anjaam payee meri masnavi
It was twenty-second of the month of Ziqaad
When my verse genre was completed

1818. Za Hijri san-e-yak hazaar aur do sad
Ba haftaad-o-chaar ast be radd-o-kad
The Hijri year was one thousand two hundred and
seventy four
Without any expostulation.

Tarjuma Ishtehaar Malika Muazzama Mushtamil Afv taqseer-e-Baaghiyaan

Translation of notification of the exalted Queen, including forgiveness of the transgressions of mutineers

1819. Nahin ek tariqah pe lailo naahaar
Kahin sulha hai aur kahin kaarzaar
Day and night are not on the same course
Somewhere reigns peace and somewhere rages war

1820. Bahungaame sakhti masho naumeed
Ke abr-e-siyaah baro aab-e-safed
In times of hardship, do not abandon hope
The black clouds bring white water

1821. Na shaadi ki shaadi na gham ka alam
Ke duniya mein toh aam hai shaadi-o-gham
No ecstasy of happiness; no agony of pain
For in the world happiness and pain are routine

1822. Use fazl karte nahin lagti baar
Na maayus ho usse umeedwaar
He takes no time to be merciful
Hopeful one, do not be disappointed with Him

1823. Rahi jiske sar par museebat azeem
Hua uspe fazl-e-Khuda-e-Kareem

Those, on whose heads were great troubles
They received bounty from the Merciful God

1824. Kiya Hindiyon ne agarche sitam
Magar dekho English ka lutf-o-karam
Although the Hindustanis had done violence
But look at the favour and kindness of the British

1825. Bajaaye ghazab raham ne dakhal ki
Judaai ki ja aai shab wasl ki
Instead of wrath, mercy had access
Instead of separation came the night of union

1826. Karo dhyan berahmi-e-baaghiyaan
Woh qatal-e-zan-o-tifl aur sahibaan
Do recall the ruthlessness of the mutineers
Those murderers of women, children and gentlemen

1827. Khazana liya loot har shahar ka
Na dhayaan aaya Allah ke qahar ka
Looted the treasure of every town
Did not ever remember God's wrath

1828. Jalaaya dafatar-e-qavaaneen ko
Giraaya imaaraat-e-sangeen ko
Burnt records of laws
Razed to the ground buildings of stone

1829. Magar marhaba aafreen marhaba
Iwaz ka nahin dhyan hai mutlaqa
Indeed, well-done! Bravo! Well-done!
There is absolutely no cogitation of recompensation

1830. Hua munkashif jo sadr mein likha
Kiya Haq ne maqbool meri dua
Whatever was written in the Head Office was revealed
God accepted my prayers

1831. Zireh karam Malika-e-Bavaqaar
Kiya afv taqseer taqseerwaar

Armour of kindness, the dignified Queen
Forgave the crimes of the criminals

1832. Kiya Malika ne jurm sabka maaf
Hua jism gard-e-baghaavat se saaf
The Queen condoned everyone's offences
The body was cleaned of the dust of mutiny

1833. Yeh hai Malika-e-Aaliya ki ataa
Sijil kar di jo baaghiyon ki khataa
This is the endowment of the magnificent Queen
That she has made the punishment of rebels precise

1834. Governor ne sab par kiya aashkaar
Yeh Malika ne bheja hai ab ishtehaar
Governor has made it known to everyone
That now the Queen has sent this notification

1835. Ke jo log hain qatilaan-e-Firang
Panah unko jis ne diya bedirang
That people who are assassins of the Europeans
Those who unhesitatingly gave asylum to them

1836. Soum jo ke the afsar-e-baaghiyaan
Chahaarum jo the baani uske miyan
Third, those who were the officers of the mutineers
Fourth, those men who were the founders of rebellion

1837. Jo hain qism-e-awwal ke taqseerwaar
Nahin laaiq-e-raham woh zeenehaar
Those who are criminals of the first type
By no means do they deserve any mercy

1838. Doum aur soum aur chahaarum ke log
Nahin jaan jane ka kuch unko rog
People of the second, third and the fourth category
They have no fear of losing their lives

1839. Munaqqah hua hai saza mein yeh taur
Ke aamaal par pahle howega ghaur

In punishments, this mode has been elucidated
That primarily actions will be taken into consideration

1840. November ki pahli ko aiye yaar phir
Hua mamlukat Hind mein mushtahar
O Friend! Then on the first of November
It was made public in the country of Hind

1841. Bashaarat jo yeh pahunchi nazdeek-o-dur
Hua baaghiyon ko nihaayat suroor
When this good news reached far and wide
The mutineers were extremely pleased

1842. Khushi ke din aaye musibat gayee
Goya jism-e-bejaan mein jaan aa gayee
Calamities vanished and days of happiness came
As if life re-entered in a dead body

1843. November ki pahli ko humgaam shab
Raaya ne ki khub aish-o-tarab
On the night of the first of November
People had a lot of enjoyment and merriment

1844. Hui shahar mein roshni es qadar
Guman saaf tha rooz ka raat par
There was so much of illumination in the town
The night clearly seemed like day

1845. Chiraaghoon mein thi noor ki yeh chamak
Falak tha zameen aur zameen thi falak
Lamps had such brilliance of light
The sky was earth and the earth was sky

1846. Har ek khaana pur-noor tha waah waah
Bana khaana-e-shahar yaan burj maah
Each and every corner was brilliantly illuminated; excellent!
Corners of the town here became bastions of the moon

1847. Safa kahkashan se sawa thi sadak
Gulistaan ke har kuche mein thi mahak

The road was much better than the immaculate milky way
Every alley of the garden was fragrant

1848. Yeh kasrat hui noor ki barmala
Tamaashaaiyoon ko chaka-chaundh tha
There was such conspicuous abundance of light
The onlookers were dazed effulgently

1849. Taraqqi hui aisi tanveer ko
Ke chyunti nazar aati thi pir ko
Refulgence was advanced in such style
That even an old man could see an ant

1850. Khijil us se shab-baraat thi lataad
Diwali ke tha dil mein daagh-e-hasad
It had put innumerable Shab-baraat to shame
In Diwali's heart was the burn of jealousy

1851. Zamin se falak tak lagi aag thi
Ke deewar-o-dar se sada raag thi
On fire was the sphere from the earth to the sky
Sounds of musical modes were emitted from every nook and corner.

Khabar Gawaliyaar

News of Gwalior

1852. Chaththi thi Sitambar ki aiye hoshiyaar
Suno dil se akhbaar-e-Gawaliyaar
O Sensible one! It was the sixth of September
Listen carefully to the news of Gwalior

1853. Taaqub mein baaghi ke sardaar-e-jaish
Raha dil sargarm ba ghaiz-o-taish
In pursuit of rebels, leader of the army
Was heartily zealous with anger and rage

1854. Faraaham hui fauj az chand ja
Magar thode thode woh hain jaan fida
Army was collected from a few places
However, only few of them are pledged devotees

1855. Yehi haal tha janib-e-baaghiyaan
Jama the faraari sipahi wahaan
On the rebels' side the condition was similar
Fugitive soldiers had collected there

1856. Sipahi maa afsaraan-e-diler
Liya baaghiyon ko bas ek baar gher
Soldiers along with brave officers
Encompassed the mutineers all of a sudden

1857. Hui Bijapur mein ladaai azeem
Madadgaar sarkaar ka tha Kareem
There was a massive combat in Bijapur
Bountiful-God was helper of the government

1858. Lade baaghiyaan dil se do ghanta tak
Phir aakhir gaye sab ladaai mein thak
The mutineers fought heartily for two hours
Then ultimately all were exhausted in warfare

1859. Sar-o-pa ki asla na thi kuch khabar
Nikal bhaage ghodoon ko bhi chood kar
There was no cognizance of head or foot at all
They even left behind their horses and fled

1860. Jo thi khet mein nash-e-na-haq shanaas
Woh ginti mein the chaar sau aur pachaas
The vain, unidentified corpses which lay in the field
Those were four hundred and fifty in number

1861. Hue jo ke sarkaar par jaan-nisaar
Sipahi the chaar aur ek Subedaar
Those who laid their life for the government
Were four soldiers and one Subedaar

1862. Faqat ek Sahib jahaan se gaya
Aur gora bhi ek apni jaan se gaya
Only one Sahib departed from this world
And one white man also lost his life

1863. Siwa eske zakhmi hue gore saat
Hue chaar Sahib bhi zakhmi bazaat
Besides this seven white men were hurt
Four Sahibs were seriously injured

1864. Sawaaron mein ghaayal hue seh sawaar
Aur zakhmi hue pandrah raahwaar
Among cavalrymen, three cavaliers were injured
And fifteen horses were wounded

1865. Hui fauz ada ki sab muntashir
Hawakhah-e-Malika ne payi zafar
All the armies of the enemies were dispersed
The well-wishers of the Queen were victorious.

Khabar Maan Singh

News of Maan Singh

1866. Badil Maan Singh sakht nakaaraa hai
Maa apne humraahi awaaraa hai
Maan Singh is very hearty and easy going
He, along with his accomplices, is dissolute

1867. Woh jungle meiṇ ab Shahabad ke
Zabun haal hai khana barbaad ke
Now in the jungle of Shahabad, he
Is in a disgraceful state of ruination

1868. Jo hain Sindhia Raja ke ahlekaar
Pakadte hain un sabko woh zeevaqaar
Those who are the workers of the Sindhia King
Endowed with dignity, they apprehend all of them.

Khabar Jalon

News of Jalon

1869. Yeh hai mukhtasar Jalon ki khabar
Hai afwaaj-e-sarkaar bas naamwar
This is a brief news of Jalon
Armies of the government are simply famous

1870. Jawanmardi se chaapa ek maar kar
Adu ko bhagaya basad karr-o-far
On conducting a raid with bravery
Drove off the enemy with many attacks and strategic retreats

1871. Jo maare gaye hain yeh unke adad
Woh ginti mein the laash-e-bejaan do sad
These are the numbers of those who have been killed
On counting those dead bodies numbered two hundred.

Darbayaan Inaayaat Sahib Commissioner Bahadur

Description of the kindness of Sahib Commissioner Bahadur

1872. December ki taarikh thi bist-o-do
Ilaaqah mila Dai-ilal-khair ko
It was the twenty-second of December
One who makes a call for a noble cause, received a territory

1873. Commissioner Bahadur ne Gahgsa diya
Ilaaqah woh aabaad hai dil feza
Commissioner Bahadur gave Gahgsa
That region is heartily flourishing

1874. Kare jald unko Governor Khuda
Salamat rakhe Khaliq-e-Kibriya
May God make him a Governor soon
May the Magnificent Creator keep him alive and well.

Khabar Raja Gonda

News of the King of Gonda

1875. December ki chaubeesween ki khabar
Commissioner Bahadur ne ki mushtahir
News of the twenty-fourth of December
Commissioner Bahadur made it publicly known

1876. Hain waise jari sahibaan-e-Firang
Ude aur kate baaghiyaan jyon patang
The European gentlemen are so very valiant
The mutineers flew and were cut like kites

1877. Diya Raja Gonda ko bas inhizaam
Liya cheen aalaat-e-jungi tamaam
Gave a sustaining defeat to the King of Gonda
Seized all the weapons of war

1878. Khabar doosri ab suno sahibon
Rifaqat ka sarkaar ke dam bharo
O Gentlemen, now listen to another news
Praise the comradeship of the government.

Bayaan Rutba-e-yaaftan Mahpat Singh

Description of the rank received by Mahpat Singh

1879. December ki pachcheesween ko suna
Mahpat Singh Babu ko rutba mila
Heard on the twenty-fifth of December
That Mahpat Singh Babu has received a rank

1880. Nagar ka woh saakin hai dar–khur aab
Mila hai Bahadur ka usko khitaab
A resident of the town, he is fit for the honour
He has received the title of Bahadur

1881. Diya Laat Sahib ne bartar khitaab
Rahi raae balwa mein uski sawaab
Laat Sahib has given an excellent title
During riots his view was righteous.

Khabar Hazeemat Baaghiyaan-e-Tulsipur

News of the defeat of mutineers of Tulsipur

1882. Attharah sau unsath maah-e-Janwari
Khabar humko aiye sahibon yeh mili
Eighteen hundred and fifty nine, month of January
O Gentlemen, I received this news

1883. Tulsipur mein jo rahe baaghiyaan
Hazeemat hui unko aiye doostaan
The rebels who were at Tulsipur
O Friends, they were routed

1884. Liya pandrah toop sarkaar ne
Yeh zillat diya unko Ghaffaar ne
The government seized fifteen cannons
The Forgiving God gave them this dishonor

1885. Mohammad Hasan aur Bala Rai
Siwa unke sab chal diye zaar-e-jaye
Mohammad Hasan and Bala Rai
Except them, everyone went in a state of affliction

1886. Luta maal-o-asbaab unka tamaam
Hui fateh sarkaar-e-aali maqaam
All their money and property was looted
The high-ranking government was victorious

1887. Khuda ke ghazab mein phanse baaghiyaan
Jamiyyat ki surat na jaa-e-amaan
The mutineers were trapped in God's wrath
With no means of peace and no place of security.

Bayaan rehaaii-e-baaghiyaan

Description of the release of mutineers

1888. Magister Bahadur bade naamwar
Gunahgaar par raham ki hai nazar
Magistrate Bahadur is very renowned
Takes a kind view of the sinners

1889. Khataa hoti hai ab barabar maaf
Reha hote hain baaghiyaan saaf saaf
Faults are now recurrently forgiven
Mutineers are released untouched

1890. Jo haazir hua bas hua woh reha
Sila es ka de Khaliq-e-Kibriya
Whoever presented himself was simply exculpated
May the Magnificent Creator give recompensation for this

1891. Raaya hon sarkaar par sab fida
Aur hukkaam hon unke sar ki rida
May all the subjects be devoted to the government
And may the rulers be a protective stole over their head

1892. Faiz Baksh Subedaar haazir hua
Khataawaar yeh sab se ziyaadah raha
Subedaar Faiz Baksh presented himself in attendance
He was the most guilty of all

1893. Baghaavat se woh bhi hua aaj saaf
Kiya hai Magister ne usko maaf
Today he too was pardoned for mutiny
The Magistrate has forgiven him

1894. Wazir Ali Khan jo ke baaghi rahe
Jab aaye toh woh bhi reha ho gaye
Wazir Ali Khan who was a mutineer
Was also exculpated when he arrived

1895. Woh Sardar Ali Khan ke sab aqriba
Bane the jo baaghi hue woh reha
All those relatives of Sardar Ali Khan
Who had become mutineers were released

1896. Baghaavat na Sardar Ali ki chuti
Shararat na ab tak unhun ki miti
Sardar Ali never forsook rebelliousness
His mischief has not been eradicated yet

1897. Siwa unke sab log haazir hue
Khataa maaf haakim ne sabki kiye
Except him, everybody reported in attendance
The rulers forgave everyone's offences.

Dar Bayaan Silah

Account of the implements of war

1898. Sadar se yeh ab hukm saadir hua
Munaadi hui shahar mein ja-ba-ja
This order was now issued by the headquarters
A public announcement was made everywhere in the town

1899. Ke sab koi hathiyaar daakhil karen
Ba miyaad dus rooz la kar ke den
That everyone should deposit weapons
Within a time limit of ten days they should surrender it

1900. Raaya ne tasleem esko kiya
Ke dete hain hathiyaar ghar se woh la
The subjects have accepted this
So they are bringing weapons from home and depositing them

1901. Raaya ka haakim madadgaar hai
Toh phir rakhna hathiyaar bekaar hai
When the rulers are helpful towards their subjects
Then keeping weapons is in fact useless.

Bayaan Altaaf Sahib Collector Bahadur

Description of the favours of Sahib Collector Bahadur

1902. Ba-taarikh farrukh nahum Janwary
Attharah sau unsath san-e-Isvi
On the auspicious day, ninth of January
In the Isvi year eighteen hundred and fifty nine

1903. Collector Bird ka yeh ausaaf hai
Duago pe bas meher-o-altaaf hai
Such is the virtue of Collector Bird
There is only affection and favour for the prayerful

1904. Yeh farmaya sahib ne Mukhtaar se
Kaee mauze dete hain hum laad se
Sahib said this to the attorney
That I grant many villages for affection

1905. Aur im gola mein denge mauze zaroor
Hai Kothan mein jo mauze Islampur
And will definitely give a village in this part of the road
The village of Islampur which is in Kothan

1906. Mohalla milega tumhen Muftipur
Kachahri mein yeh hukm hoga sudur
You shall get the lane-area of Muftipur
This order will be issued in the court

1907. Humein es khabar se musarrat hui
Mubaddal yeh mehnat ba rahat hui
This news made me happy
Thus hard work was exchanged for comfort

1908. Hai hukkaam ki zaat ba sad safa
Kiya hai jo wada karenge wafaa
Temperament of the rulers is with much impeccability
They shall surely fulfill the promise they have made

1909. Pachattar hai asna ashr bar ziyaad
Yehi sun hai Hijri karo dil mein yaad
Seventy-five were exceeding over twelve hundred (twelve hundred and seventy-five)
This is the Hijri year, recall in your heart

1910. Mahina Rajab aur Shabaan ka tha
Mere haal par fazl Yazdaan ka tha
The months were of Rajab and Shabaan
God was merciful towards my state

1911. Na dekhenge Kosamhi ka phir munh kabhi
Yehi ahad tha aur paimaan yehi
Would never see the face of Kosamhi again
This was the determination and this was the promise

1912. Yehi amr har waqt tha dil nasheen
Ke jaayenge ta uud haakim nahin
This very matter was impressed upon the mind perpetually
That would not go (to Kosamhi) until the ruler's return

1913. Na aayenge jab tak na jaayenge hum
Bajaaye gheza ghum ko khaayenge hum
Until they come I shall not go
Instead of nourishment I shall consume grief

1914. Tamanna yehi dil mein mere rahi
Ke ki jald maqsoom ne rahbari
This was my heartfelt desire
That soon enough destiny guided me

915. Hui baarey meri dua mustajaab
Ke jald aaye hukkaam aali janaab
At last my prayer was accepted
Because the high ranking rulers came very soon

916. Session Judge ko le sath Kosamhi gaye
Sab hukkaam wahaan raunaq afzaan hue
Took along the Session Judge and went to Kosamhi
All the rulers graced the scene with their presence

917. The paltan ke afsar shareek-o-saheem
Rahe ja ke Kosamhi mein ek din muqeem
Officers of the platoon were accomplices and peers
They stayed over for a day in Kosamhi

918. Hui lutf-e-hukkaam se humko Eid
Hai ab mera har rooz yaum-e-sayeed
Due to favours of the rulers it was Eid for me
Now everyday of mine is an auspicious day

919. Barabar ab hukkaam ka hai nuzool
Saadat jahan ki hai mujh ko husool
Now the rulers sojourn here often
All the felicity of the world is my acquisition.

Bayaan Janaab Sahib Commissioner Bahadur

Description of Janaab Sahib Commissioner Bahadur

1920. Commissioner Bahadur se quwat rahi
Ke har kas-o-naakas ko taaqat rahi
Due to Commissioner Bahadur there was strength
For each and everyone there was vigour

1921. Ke tareekh dusween rahi Farwari
Mili Lucknow ki unhe sarwari
The date was tenth of February
That he gained victory over Lucknow

1922. Rahe sarparast yeh to sabke mudaam
Rakhe khush unhe Khaliq-e-Zulkaraam
He always was everyone's guardian
May the Kind God keep him happy

1923. Zila ke jo baaghi the sab mit gaye
Session Judge Bahadur Commissioner hue
All the mutineers of the town were expunged
Session Judge Bahadur became Commissioner

1924. Paye sood-e-aalam woh sote nahin
Vela aise hukkaam hote nahin
In the interest of the people he does not sleep
Nowadays such rulers hardly exist.

Kaifiyat Baaghiyaan wa Khairkhahi Dipty Collector Bahadur

Condition of mutineers and benevolence of Deputy Collector Bahadur

1925. Bane the jo Dajjaal ke peshwa
Bafazl-e-Khuda sabne payee saza
Those who had become the guides of the Dajjaal
By God's grace they all received punishment

1926. Hue Fateh Ali qaid Mirza ke poor
Nagar ka jo Raja raha pur ghuroor
Son of Mirza, Fateh Ali was arrested
King of the town, who was full of conceit

1927. Satasi ka Raja muquaiyyad hua
Yehi uske aamaal ki thi saza
The King of Satasi was imprisoned
This was the punishment for his deeds

1928. Rahi teeswin maah-e-Shabaan ki
Pachattar sun Hijri barah rahi
It was the thirtieth of the month of Shabaan
The Hijri year was twelve hundred and seventy-five

1929. Ke mahbas mein Raja Nagar mar gaya
Woh de jaan apni jahannum gaya
That the king of Nagar died in prison
He gave up his life and went to hell

1930. Mohammad Hasan jo ke baaghi raha
Use Dipty Sahib ne haazir kiya
Mohammad Hasan who was a rebel
He was summoned by Deputy Sahib

1931. Abhi tak na tajweez hai aashkaar
Kiya zulm usne bahut beshumaar
Till now no plan is evident
He has committed extremely unlimited atrocities

1932. Rahe baaghiyaan jo ke daaman-e-koh
Hui unko zillat jo the bashukoh
The mutineers who once were high foothills
Those were disgraced who were once majestic

1933. Thi English Baahadur ki meher-o-nigaah
Badaamaal se apne khud hain tabaah
The English Bahadur had a kind view point
They (the rebels) are ruined due to their own ill deeds

1934. Shujaat jo Khairuddin Khan ne kiya
Kahan aisa Dipty bahadur hua
Khairuddin Khan acted with such exemplary bravery
Where has ever been such a brave Deputy?

1935. Mohammad Hasan ko giraftaar kar
Kiya us ko haazir basad karr-o-farr
He arrested Mohammad Hasan
And presented him with great pomp and splendor

1936. Barabar yeh baaghi se ladte rahe
Giraftaar un sab ko karte rahe
He fought with the rebels ceaselessly
Constantly brought them all under arrest

1937. Batao bhala kis ne jurrat kiya
Jo Dipty Bahadur ne himmat kiya
Say who has ever been so very courageous
To show the kind of enterprise that Deputy Bahadur exhibited

1938. Jahan woh gaye sur ladaai hui
Mukhaalif ke haq mein buraai hui
Wherever he went warfare ensued
Bad times befell the opponents

1939. Ghazipur Ballia ke baaghi tamaam
Hui raah par hai yeh khush intizaam
All the rebels of Ghazipur and Ballia
Have been set right by good management

1940. Kamar basta rahte the aathon pahar
Na tha dil mein ada ka khauf-o-khatar
Remained in a state of readiness day and night
In his heart was no fear or danger of enemies

1941. Woh goloon ko samjha kiye misl-e-goo
Unhen gooliyaan baais-e-aabroo
He considered cannon balls like playing balls
For him bullets were a matter of honour

1942. Milaai sada aankh zarghaam se
Hamesha use kaam tha naam se
Always looked eye to eye at a lion
He was perpetually concerned about good reputation

1943. Shujaat ke dariya ka ghavvaaz hai
Dileron mein woh banda-e-khaas hai
He is the pearl diver of the sea of bravery
Among the valiant he is a very special man

1944. Woh sarkaar ka hai dili-khairkhah
Rahe hifz-e-Khaliq mein shaam-o-pagah
He is a hearty well-wisher of the government
Dawn and dusk he is busy remembering the Creator

1945. Dilaawar na dekha na aisa suna
Hazaar aafreen marhaba marhaba
Have never seen or heard of such a brave man
Thousand praises, bravo! Well done!

Bayaan Janaab Sahib Collector Bahadur Jaunpur

Description of Janaab Sahib Collector Bahadur of Jaunpur

1946. Bayaan ab main karta hun yeh kaifiyat
Collector Magister ki hai yeh sifat
Now I will describe this case
This is the praise of Collector Magistrate

1947. Patterson Magister hain munsif kamaal
Raeeson ki hai parwarish ka khayaal
Magistrate Patterson is extremely just
He is concerned about the patronage of noblemen

1948. Na aisa dilaawar Collector hua
Aur rutba shanaas aisa kamtar hua
Never has there been such a brave collector
And seldom do people have such knowledge of status

1949. Bula kar ke dete hain ohdaa kalan
Woh haakim hain munsif hain aur aali shaan
Summons and grants big posts
He is a commander, fair-minded and magnificent

1950. Collector Magister Jaunpur ke
Rahe woh to haakim Gorakhpur ke
Collector Magistrate of Jaunpur
He was the Commander of Gorakhpur

1951. Jawan-o-jawanmard aur hoshmand
Raheem-o-kareem aur hain dardmand
Young, bold and wise
He is kind, merciful and compassionate

1952. Zile ka bakhubi kiya intizaam
Ke raazi hain Sahib se har khaas-o-aam
Managed the town very well
Because all, elite and ordinary are happy with Sahib

1953. Nahin aisa koi hua nek naam
Razamand ho jis se khilqat tamaam
No one has been so well reputed
With whom all the people would be pleased

1954. Khudaya tu Sahib ka dil shaad rakh
Qayaamat talak unko aabaad rakh
O God! You keep Sahib's heart full of happiness
Let him flourish till the last day

1955. Kiya hai Husain Baksh ko Tehsildaar
Bhatija Darogha ka sar rishtedaar
Has appointed Husain Baksh as Tehsildaar
Nephew of the Darogha, Magistrate's Reader

1956. Zahoor Ashraf aage Darogha jo the
Darogha woh mahbas-e-Jaunpur hue
Zahoor Ashraf, who was the Darogha earlier
Has become the Darogha of the prison of Jaunpur

1957. Raeeson mein yeh bhi rahe naamwar
Jaunpur mein ja hue baihravar
Among noblemen he too was well-reputed
On going to Jaunpur he flourished.

Bayaan shujaat sahibaan walashaan fauj

Description of the bravery of officers of the grand army

1958. Yeh hai daastaan bostaan doostoon
Sifat sahibaan-e-asaa ki suno
Friends, this is the tale of the orchard
Listen to the attributes of the army officers

1959. Jawanmard barkat dabraa Rowcroft
Kiya khub baaghi ke maidaan ko saaf
Rowcroft is brave and a pool of auspiciousness
Marvelously he vanquished the rebels

1960. Tawaana qawi barkat hain maarjin
Woh Major hain baawar karo yeh sukhan
Is powerful, strong, fortunate and relentless
He is a Major, trust this information

1961. Bahadur bade Lord hain Mark Kerr
Woh hain yaaron Kernail fauj-e-zafar
Lord Mark Kerr is very brave
Friends, he is a colonel of the victorious army

1962. Sikander manish aur Aristu khisaal
Na Rustam tha aisa na Barzu na Zaal
With qualities of Alexander and attributes of Aristotle
Neither was Rustam like him, nor Barzu, nor Zaal

1963. Jawanmard azbas hain Kernail King
Saff-e-jung mein hain woh manind-e-sang
Colonel King is very brave
In the ranks of war he is like a rock

1964. Hain Jailor Bahadur bhi Rustam khisaal
Woh lashkar ke Major hain farkhanda faal
Jailor Bahadur is also like Rustam
He is a Major of the army, like an auspicious omen

1965. Bahadur dilawar hain Captaan John
Aur Captaan-e-saani hain Baro Brown
Captain John is brave and daring
And Baro Brown is the Second Captain

1966. Aqeel-o-bahadur hain Captaan Peel
Shuja-aan-e-lashkar mein hain woh jaleel
Captain Peel is wise and brave
Among the dauntless of the army, he is great

1967. Degar King Sahib bhi Captaan hain
Boyed bhi Captaan zeeshaan hain
Other King Sahib is also a Captain
Boyed is also a dignified Captain

1968. Hain Captaan wala hummam Tubenam
Jawanmard aisa hua koi kum
Tubenam is a Captain with great courage
There hardly have been such brave men

1969. Hain Captaan Rawli rafi-ul-makaan
Ejiton Draumer hain sher-e-zhiyaan
Captain Rawli is very highly placed
Ejiton Draumer is a truculent tiger

1970. Ejiton Pollen Sahib hain bas diler
Bahadur hain beshubha manind-e-sher
Ejiton Pollen Sahib is simply daring
He is undoubtedly brave like a lion

1971. Bahut Megnatan bhi hain neknaam
Hain lashkar mein Bakhshi ka Sahib ko kaam
Megnatan is also very well-reputed
Sahib works as a Bakhshi in the army

1972. Rafi-ul-makaan jo ke Captaan Laam
Hindustani paltan mein wala maqaam
Captain Laam who is highly placed
Holds a position of great dignity in the Hindustani platoon

1973. Digar Sam Sahib bhi Captaan hain
Jawanmard dana wa zeeshaan hain
Other Sam Sahib is also a Captain
He is brave, wise and dignified

1974. Hain Captaan Sahib bade maaltin
Qadardaan aisa bhi hota kahin
Captain Sahib is a great disperser of wealth
Could there have been such a patron?

1975. Zabardast azbas Ajeton hain niyat
Gaye baaghiyaan unki haibat se lait
Ajeton's determination is mighty strong
The rebels lay down due to his fear

1976. Muzaffar dilaawar hain Lieutinant Jame
Rakhe unko zinda Khuda-e-Kareem
Lieutenant Jame is successful and brave
May the kind God give him a long life

1977. Sifat Aibart ki mahalaat hai
Woh Captaan kaafi mahummaat hai
Aibart's praise is impossible to note
That Captain is quite expeditious

1978. Karun ab Corfield ki tauseef ko
Nihaayat woh aaqil hain aur nek khu
Now I shall eulogize Corfield
He is very intelligent and good-natured

1979. Hain Wroughton jari jo ke Laftain hain
Raaya ko unse mila chain hai
Wroughton, who is a Lieutenant, is valiant
People have got peace from him

1980. Hain Laftain Rick bhi bade arjmand
Bahut unse ada ko pahuncha guzand
Lieutenant Rick is also very honorable
Enemies suffered great losses due to him

1981. Hain Laftain Rustam sifat Gilbert
Gaye baaghiyaan unki haibat se hat
Lieutenant Gilbert has the qualities of Rustam
The rebels retreated due to his fear

1982. Hain William Bahadur bade tez dast
Karen koh ko ek sa'aat mein past
William Bahadur is very clever
He would reduce a mountain low in a moment

1983. Zabardast Laftain hain Shangrif
Na hote hain ada se woh munharif
Shangrif is a very powerful lieutenant
He is never deflected by the enemies

1984. Hain Laftain Potter bade shokh dast
Jarad bhi hain Laftain chun pil mast
Lieutenant Potter is very daring
Lieutenant Jarad is also like an intoxicated elephant

1985. Sebtory Gailat har do Laftain hain
Wajood-e-raaya ke woh ain hain
Sebtory and Gailat both are Lieutenants
They are intrinsic to the existence of the subjects

1986. Hain junggaah mein Jung Sahib diler
Hain Laftain Saunder bhi darinda sher
Jung Sahib is brave in martial arts
Lieutenant Saunder is also like a ferocious lion

1987. Hobin Master Coat hain khush-khisaal
Rahen gardish-e-charkh se bezawaal
Hobin Master Coat is well-bred
May he remain unspoilt by the vicissitudes of fortune

1988. Hain in men dil ke quawi Barney
Muzaffar woh hain aur dil ke ghani
Among them Barney is strong-hearted
He is noble and rich-hearted

1989. Hai aur Jarad hain az bas faheem
Wa insabin hain yaaron har do hakeem
Hai and Jarad are very intelligent
Friends, both those physicians know the roots of veins

1990. Cross aur Jigs bahut khub hain
Woh hain doctor aur khush asloob hain
Cross and Jigs are very good
They are doctors and are elegant

1991. Hain dana bade doctor Longherst
Nahin rahta unse mareezon ka kasht
Doctor Longherst is very intelligent
Due to him patient's pain does not persist

1992. Jawanmard Laftain hain Powell
Likhun unki kya vasf dariyadili
Lieutenant Powell is brave
What praise should I write of his generosity?

1993. Woh hain Master Nick Sahib azeez
Khiradmand dana wa ahle tameez
That Master Nick Sahib is respected
Wise, intelligent and well-mannered

1994. Hain Jigson Sani bhi aali maqaam
Sifat Sahibon ki hui ikhtitaam
Jigson, the second, is also well-placed
Praise of the Sahibs' is concluded

1995. Jari hain bade aur shujaat sheaar
Qulub-e-raaya ko bakhsha qaraar
Are very courageous and brave in mannerisms
Granted tranquility to the souls of their subjects

1996. Kiya mundafa Hind se zulm-o-shar
Khudaya tu in sab ka dil shaad kar
Fully banished tyranny and evil from Hindustan
O God! Give happiness to their hearts

1997. Rahe Malika-e-Aaliya ka amal
Na aaye kabhi Hind mein phir khalal
May the sway of the exalted Queen remain
May no disorder come over Hind ever again

1998. Yeh hai Shah Ahmad Ali ki dua
Rakhe shaad sab Sahibon ko Khuda
This is the prayer of Shah Ahmad Ali
May God keep all the Sahibs happy!

Sifat Janaab Padri Sahib Bahadur

Praise of Padri Sahib Bahadur

1999. Sifat yahaan tu kar Padri ki bayaan
Yeh Sahib toh hain vaaqif az har zabaan
Here you describe the attributes of the Padri
This Sahib is conversant in every language

2000. Yeh hain shuturang Padri khush khisaal
Hai taskheer ka ilm unko kamaal
This Padri is tall-statured and good-natured
He has great knowledge of spiritualism

2001. Hai altaaf Sahib ka mashhoor tar
Hain khurd-o-kalan unse masroor tar
Sahib's courtesy is very well-known
All, small and big are pleased with him

2002. Hai Sahib Bahadur ka bas faiz aam
Rausa-e-shahri hain raazi tamaam
Sahib Bahadur's beneficence is quite renowned
All the nobles of the town are pleased

2003. Hai Sahib se khalq-e-Khuda shaadmand
Woh azbas raheem aur hain dardmand
People of God are happy with Sahib
He is very kind and empathetic

2004. Balaaghat naseehat mein bas taaq hain
Jo aaqil hain sahib ke mushtaaq hain
He is simply an expert in rhetoric and counselling
The wise are wistful of Sahib

2005. Yeh sahib bahadur hain khush mudaam
Ba fazl-e-Khuda woh rahen shaad–kaam
This Sahib Bahadur is always happy
By God's grace may he always remain delighted and successful

2006. Muddarris hain school ke nek tar
Hue unse tulabaa har ek bahrawar
Teacher of the school is very noble
All students became fortunate due to him

2007. Mohabbat murawwat ke woh kaan hain
Uluv qadr barutba zeeshaan hain
He is a mine of affection and kindness
He is highly honoured, eminent and dignified

2008. Bayaan-e-sifat mein hai qaasir zabaan
Rahe hafiz unka Khuda-e-Jahaan
The tongue falls short in describing his attributes
May the Lord of the World remain his protector!

Sifat Hukkaam Walashaan

Attributes of the grand rulers

2009. Khaaliq ko yeh dastaan hai pasand
Ke esme hai ausaaf-e-hukkaam chand
People like this legend
Because it has some eulogy of the rulers

2010. Sonneton Sahib Session Judge yahaan
Kahan tak likhun unki main khubiyaan
Sonneton Sahib is a Session Judge here
How much can I write of his qualities?

2011. Raheem-o-kareem-o-raees-o-ameer
Faheem-o-khaleeq-o-aqeel-o-dabeer
Kind-hearted, benevolent, rich and noble
Intelligent, creative, wise, a writer

2012. Riyaasat adaalat tabiyat mein hai
Sharafat murawwat bhi khilqat mein hai
Princeliness and equity are in his temperament
Nobility and sympathy are also in his nature

2013. Har ek mauqa par rahm-o-insaaf hai
Kudoorat nahin seena bas saaf hai
On every occasion there is mercy and justice
There is no ill-will, the heart is absolutely pure

2014. Kisi shai ki unko nahin hai niyaaz
Sakhee aur nihaayat hain ghurba nawaaz
He has no need for anything
Generous, and extremely favourable towards the poor

2015. Patterson jo Sahib Collector the yahaan
Karon unki khubi ka kya main bayaan
Patterson Sahib, who was the Collector here
What should I speak of his attributes?

2016. Tahammul tajammul ke yeh kaan the
Sakhaawat shujaat mein zeeshaan the
He was a mine of toleration and magnificence
Was splendid in generosity and bravery

2017. Raaya tamaam unse raazi rahi
Hai afsos Sahib jahan se gaye
All the people were pleased with him
It is a pity that Sahib left this world

2018. Zile ke Collector hain Sahib Bird
Diya tabqah-e-baaghiyon ko ulat
Sahib Bird is the Collector of the district
Gave reversal to the class of rebels

2019. Nihaayat aqeel-o-jawanmard hain
Hukumat ke aain mein fard hain
He is extremely wise and brave
In manners of administration he is incomparable

2020. Mite haath se unke badkhah chand
Mila unko apne kiye ka guzand
Some ill-wishers were obliterated by his hands
They received the injury of their deeds

2021. Adu par bhi raham apna zahir kiya
Jo haazir hua woh reha ho gaya
He showed kindness towards the enemy also
Whoever presented himself was pardoned

2022. Razamand Sahib se har khaas-o-aam
Ye karte hain sab sarparasti ka kaam
All elite and commoners are agreeable with Sahib
He undertakes all works of patronage

2023. Sonneton Sahib jo hain gent yahaan
Raaya pe hain shahar ke meherbaan
Sonneton Sahib who is a gentleman here
Is kind towards the people of the town

2024. Hain aali tabiyat woh mard-e-Khuda
Collector Magister kare Kibriya
That man of God is of noble disposition
May the Magnificent Lord make him Collector Magistrate!

2025. Qadardaan haakim na aisa mila
Na mardum shanaas aisa koi hua
Never known of such a patron ruler
None has had such knowledge of men

2026. Mudabbir khiradmand hain Hem Sen
Woh hain gent khalqat ko unse hai chaiyn
Hem Sen is a wise statesman
He is a gentleman, people have peace due to him

2027. Raaya ki hai parwarish ka khayaal
Unhe khush rakhe Khaliq-e-Zuljalaal
He is concerned about the protection of people
May the Glorious Lord keep him happy

2028. Aqalmand hoshiyaar kahte hain mard
Woh ausaaf karte hain ahle khirad
People call him intelligent and bright
Those who are sagacious people have this praise

2029. Ke hain Watt Sahib bhi Dipty jaleel
Khiradmand daana wa sahib aqeel
Watt Sahib is also a brave Deputy
Intelligent, wise and a sagacious gentleman

2030. Nihaayat bahadur jawanmard hain
Yeh hai sheriyat sahib-e-dard hain
Is an extremely brave and valiant man
It is bravery to be so sympathetic

2031. Hain Khairuddin Khan Dipty ek naamwar
Hai lipty rikaabon se unki zafar
Khairuddin Khan is a famous Deputy
Victory is coiled around his stirrups

2032. Agar ghaiz mein aawe woh nek khu
Abhi pher de panja-e-sher ko
If that good-natured one is enraged
Can overpower the claws of a lion in a moment

2033. Hain Dipty Bihari bhi az bas aqeel
Hukumat ke fan mein woh hain beadeel
Deputy Bihari is also very intelligent
In the art of governance he is peerless

2034. Hain Abdullah yahaan ke jo Sadr-us-Sudur
Khiradmand hain aur nihaayat ghuyur
Abdullah, who is the Sadr-us-Sudur of this place
Is intelligent and extremely self-respecting

2035. Bahut paak aur saaf hain adl mein
Woh hain naamwar raham aur fazl mein
Is very pure and immaculate in justice
He is famous for kindness and graciousness

2036. Bade moaamlah-faihm hain Sadr-e-Amin
Sanakhwaan hain unke har ahle zameen
The Sadr-e-Amin is very shrewd
All people of the world are his eulogists

2037. Woh hain haq parast aur khajista khisaal
Hai mashhoor naam unka Debi Dayal
He is faithful and propitious natured
His name is well-known, Debi Dayal

2038. Khiradmand munsif hain Hafiz Raheem
Rahe meherbaan unpe Rabb-e-Kareem
Hafiz Raheem is intelligent and just
May the Kind Lord be benevolent towards him!

2039. The faazil-o-aalim Mohammad Umar
Rahe ek baras Munsifi shahar par
Mohammed Umar was scholarly and learned
For an year he was posted as à sub-judge of the town

2040. Sabab kuch na zahir hua mar gaye
Sahi-ul-badan the qaza kar gaye
No cause was known, he died
Was able-bodied; somehow, passed away

2041. Ab aaye hain us jaa Mohammad Husain
Rakhe Khaliq unko ba aaraam-o-chaiyn
Now Mohammad Husain has come in that place
May the Creator keep him in comfort and peace!

2042. Mere shahar mein ab woh Munsif hue
Har ek unse woh sabse vaaqif hue
He has now become a Judge in my town
Everyone with him, he with everyone; became acquainted

2043. Jo hai Shehnah es shahar ka Shiv Sahay
Rahe ye to mahfooz az har balae
Shiv Sahay who is the *Shehnah* of this town
May he remain safe from every calamity

2044. Raha tha yeh thana pe sabit qadam
Uthaya bahut usne ranj-o-alam
He had stayed steadfast at the police station
He suffered a lot of sorrow and pain

2045. Khazana bacha uske baais tamaam
Taraqqi karen uski aali maqaam
All the treasure was saved because of him
May the highly designated ones promote him

2046. Maqaam apna Betiya mein ja kar liya
Ke rasta woh hi haakimon ka raha
Went and stationed himself at Betiya
Because that was the route of the rulers

2047. Jo haakim gaya uski khidmat kiya
Muhaafiz yeh English Bahadur raha
Served, whichever officer went there
He remained a protector of English Bahadur

2048. Uthaye tha sab kaam bar dosh-e-khesh
Azamgarh mein akhbaar karta tha pesh
Had taken all responsibilies upon himself
Used to present the newspaper report in Azamgarh

2049. Barabar khabar yan ki leta raha
Woh akhbaar ka kaam karta raha
Constantly inquired about this place
He performed the work of an informer

2050. Jab hukkaam aaye hua Kotwaal
Ke hai khairkhahon mein yeh bemisaal
When the rulers came, he became Kotwaal
Among well-wishers, he is matchless

2051. Rasad ka kiya khub anjaam kaar
Ke raazi hain khushnood aalivaqaar
Made excellent arrangement for supplies
So that the highly dignified ones are happily agreeable

2052. Bahut khub hai aur bahut khub hai
Sabhon ke dilon mein yeh marghub hai
He is excellent, he is excellent
He is the beloved of everyone's heart

2053. Sadanand kya khub Tehsildaar
Ke hai kaar-e-sarkaar mein hoshiyaar
What a fine Tehsildaar is Sadananda
For he is efficient in the works of administration

2054. Hawa-o-hawas se bahut paak hai
Bahut kaar-e-sarkaar mein chaak hai
He is very pure from lust and greed
Is very clever in the works of administration

2055. Qadardaan haakim hain Sahib Bird
Bahut khub hain vaaqif-e-nek-o-bad
Sahib Bird is a patron ruler
He is very well aware of good and bad

2056. Na zahir ke aamaal par hai khayaal
Jo batin mein Nazim se the pur malaal
Is not concerned about the apparent behaviour
Of those who were sorrowful of the Nazim from within

2057. Woh hi log es waqt mumtaaz hain
Woh ahl-e-qadar sahib ezaaz hain
Those are the people who are venerated at this time
They deserve credit and are honourable

2058. Unhi se hai raazi Khuda-e-Jahaan
Woh hukkaam bhi unpar hain meherbaan
Lord of the world is pleased with them
Those rulers also are benevolent towards them.

Hikayat

Report

2059. Gaye shahar se jab ke Sahib Bird
Tha Hitti Bahadur bahut zeekhirad
When Sahib Bird left the town
Hitti Bahadur was very wise

2060. Rahe ek shab unke dehaat par
Rifaqat mein haazir raha woh bashar
Stayed for a night in his village
That man was present in comradeship

2061. Wahaan se Pedrona mein Sahib gaye
Ataat mein Hafiz Tehsildaar the
From there Sahib went to Pedrona
Where with reverence Hafiz Tehsildaar was present

2062. Taman le ke wahaan pahuncha Fazle Ali
Khabar uski Sahib ko unse mili
Fazle Ali reached there with an army
Sahib received his information from him

2063. Bahut khair-o-khubi se Sahib gaye
Ataat se Hafiz ke khurram hue
Sahib left with a lot of ease and pleasantness
Was delighted with the obedience of Hafiz

2064. Hai ek mauze Mathiya nihaayat basa
Ilaaqah woh hai yaaron Pedrona ka
One village Mathiya is very well-populated
Friends, that is the region of Pedrona

2065. Qadam wahaan pe Sahib ka jis dam gaya
Gosain Bandhal aa ke haazir hua
The moment Sahib reached that place
Gosain Bandhal came to present himself

2066. Ataat mein bandhi kamar usne chust
Qadam rakha raah-e-wafaa mein durust
He made a brisk and firm resolve for obedience
He promised to remain steadfast in the path of loyalty

2067. Gaya sath Sahib ke woh chand kos
Phira raah se woh pas az paaye-bos
He went with Sahib for a few miles
Returned from that route only after making obeisance

2068. Esi tarha har ek ne khidmat kiya
Ba maqdoor apne ataat kiya
In this manner each and everyone served
Assisted according to their own resources

2069. Rahe chand ashkhaas sabit qadam
Mohabbat ka har ek bharta tha dam
Some people remained steadfast in their steps
Each one professed love with their breath.

Hikayat Khairkhahaan-e-Aalimiqdaar

Report of the well-wishers of high magnitude

070. Sifat Raja Bansi ki mashhoor hai
Shujaat ka ab unke mazkoor hai
Qualities of the King of Bansi are famous
Now his bravery is being related

071. Musharraf gaya yan se le kar sipah
Na jana ke aaya kidhar rusiyah
Musharraf went from here with soldiers
Did not care to know where the criminal had come

072. Kiya sab khub khairkhahi ka kaam
Yeh Raja to Rajon mein hai nek naam
Accomplished well, all undertaking of friendship
Among kings, this king has a noble name

073. Jo thi ibtida hai woh hi inteha
Hamesha chalan uska hai ek sa
What was initiation, the same is culmination
His behaviour is constantly the same

074. Sifat jo likhun sab sazawaar hai
Belashak yeh Rajon mein sardaar hai
Whatever praise I may write is well-deserved
Undoubtedly among kings he is the leader

2075. Bade khairkhah Raja Balrampur
Mufakhkhar wa mumtaaz hain dar huzoor
Raja Balrampur is a great well-wisher
Is esteemed and venerated in his honour's court

2076. Khabar yeh to har ek ko maalum hai
Meri khairkhahi ki ek dhoom hai
This information is well-known to everyone
There is great fame of my friendship

2077. Hai hukkaam par haal sab aashkaar
Rakhe shaad-o-khurram unhe Kirdgaar
All circumstances are well-known to the rulers
May God keep them happy and pleased!

2078. Report meri khairkhahi ki ki
Zaraah-e-karam mujh ko jagir di
Reported my supportive assistance
By way of beneficence granted a fief to me

2079. Governor ne manzoor usko kiya
Zila ke Collector ko aisa likha
The Governor approved of that
Wrote this to the Collector of the district

2080. Ke phir uski tajweez-e-saani karo
Commissioner Bahadur ki bhi raae lo
That prepare this proposal again
Also take the opinion of Commissioner Bahadur

2081. Collector ki ab raae hai yeh qawi
Ilaaqah Pedrona ka len Shahji
Now this is a strong view of the Collector
That Shahji should take the region of Pedrona

2082. Jo Sahib Bahadur ne aisa likha
Sarasar yeh hai bakhshish-e-Kibriya
The fact that Sahib Bahadur wrote as such
This is totally due to the beneficence of the Creator

2083. Nahin aisa haakim yahaan ab koi
Shareefon ki kya kya na tauqeer ki
Now here, there is no ruler of this kind
Did every possible thing to honour the virtuous

2084. Zamaana mein apne yeh Hatim hua
Ilaaqah bahut khub humko diya
He was the Hatim of his times
Granted a very big territory to me

2085. Kiya lutf-o-ashfaaq hum par kamaal
Rakhe shaad-o-khurram unhe Zuljalaal
Was extremely favourable and compassionate towards me
May the Glorious One keep him happy and pleased!

2086. Ke Sahib Bahadur ka hai faiz aam
Duago rahunga main unka mudaam
For Sahib Bahadur's bounty is well-known
I shall always be praying for him

2087. Vila kaun aisa hua badshah
Ke dil se hua ho raiyyat panah
When in the past has a king been so very exalted?
Who would be a heart-felt protector of subjects?

2088. Sada baagh-o-bakri mein hai ittehaad
Raaya bhi apne gharoon mein hai shaad
There always is amity between the strong and the weak
The subjects also are happy in their homes

2089. Kisi ko sataaye koi kya majaal
Ab insaaf-e-Kisra hai khwaab-o-khayaal
How can anyone dare to harras anybody?
Now the justice of Kisra has become a dream and illusion

2090. Bade qadardaan hain sab ahle Firang
Zaviul haq ko diye hain sila bedirang
All the European people are great patrons
To the rightfully deserving they give rewards without delay

2091. Luta khairkhahi mein jo baar baar
Mila mujh ko sarkaar se paanch hazaar
Since I was looted repeatedly for my loyalty
I received five thousand (rupees) from the government

2092. Ewaz khairkhahi ke sarkaar se
Mili milk bhi nek kirdaar se
From the government, in return for assistance
Received property as well due to noble character

2093. Raaya ko har tarha aaraam hai
Ab Hatim zamaane mein gumnaam hai
Subjects have all kinds of comfort
Now Hatim is unknown in the world

2094. Kitaabon mein Hatim ka mazkoor hai
Magar chashm-e-aalam se mastoor hai
Hatim is mentioned in books
But is veiled from the eyes of the people

2095. Sakhaawat hai English ki sab par ayaan
Hai roshan taraz aftaab-e-jahaan
Generosity of the English is apparent to everyone
Is more evident than the Sun of the universe!

2096. Zara jisne bhi khairkhahi kiya
Hua usko jagir-o-mansab ataa
Whoever gave a little assistance
He was granted estate and post

2097. Raqam vasf-e-English mein jurrat nahin
Qalam ko duago ke taqat nahin
Do not have the courage to write eulogies of the English
The prayerful's pen is not powerful enough

2098. Kiya maine jo khairkhahi ka kaam
Na hoga koi es tarha nek naam
The kind of supportive work that I did
No one will be reputable in this manner

2099. Rakha maine hukkaam ko apne ghar
Sada tha main balwa mein seena sipar
I kept the rulers in my house
I had always put up a bold front during the riots

2100. Rakha maal hukkaam ka bekhatar
Luta us ke baais se main sarbasar
Safeguarded the belongings of the rulers fearlessly
Because of that I was plundered totally

2101. Diya toop yak zarb sarkaar ko
Na tha uzr es hukm-e-bedaar ko
Gave single-barreled cannon to the government
There was no objection to this one vigilant to orders

2102. Teen sad gaadiyan hum se jab keen talab
Mangaa deen ilaaqe se humne woh sab
When three hundred conveyances were demanded from me
I got all of them fetched from the region

2103. Barabar woh hukkaam ke sath theen
Jab hukkaam aaye to humko mileen
They were with the rulers consistently
When the rulers came, I got them back

2104. Piyaadon ko jis dam zaroorat hui
Humari taraf se aanat hui
When the foot-soldiers were in need
Assistance was provided from my side

2105. Magister ko bhi hum ne raazi rakha
Hua jo ke irshaad fauran kiya
I kept the Magistrate also happy
Did at once whatever was commanded

2106. Us balwa mein asbaab Sahib ka hum
Mangaya hai chabre se usko baham
Sahib's belongings; in that rioting; I
Arranged to bring them together with an escort

2107. Diya fauz-e-kohi ke rahne ko ghar
Mudaaraat unki bhi ki beshtar
Provided accommodation for stay of the voluminous army
Also treated them very hospitably

2108. Rasad ka bhi achcha kiya ehtimaam
Rahe khush sab hukkaam aali maqaam
Made good arrangement for provisions also
All the highly placed rulers were pleased

2109. Ali Wardi Khan ne kiya tha ghazab
Sharifon par daala tha ranj-o-taab
Ali Wardi Khan had acted irately
Had hurled sorrow and feebleness at the noble men

2110. Kaha hum ne us se ke aiye badgumaan
Karunga main hukkaam par yeh ayaan
I said to him, 'O distrustful one!'
I shall reveal this to the rulers

2111. Tera jab ke sabit karenge qusoor
Dilaawenge hum tujh ko phaansi zaroor
When your crime will be proven
I shall definitely get you hanged

2112. Jo ashkhaas badkhah-e-hukkaam hain
Har ek tarha duniya mein badnaam hain
Those people who are evil-wishers of the rulers
They are defamed in the world in everyway

2113. Sare dast ab maslahat hai yehi
Ataat mein bandhe kamar har koi
Now at present this is expedient
That everyone should be ready for service

2114. Gharaz meri taqreer maqbool kar
Azam ka rasta liya bezarar
Therefore accepting my discourse
Took the route to the greatest, without detriment

2115. Raees aur raaya rahe shaadmand
Zara bhi kisi par na aaya guzand
Landlords and tenants lived happily
No harm came upon anyone at all.

Kawaaif Raeesaan-e-shahar

Particulars of magnates of the town

2116. Raeeson ki likhta hoon ab daastaan
Khataa se jo hain saaf aiye doostaan
Now I write the tale of magnates
O friends, who are clear from any default

2117. Bade ghaur se hum ne dekha tamaam
Hamesha se jo log the nek naam
I observed everywhere with great care
The people who always had a good name

2118. Woh hukkaam ke jurm se hain bari
Kisi nau ka khatka nahin ek zari
They are free from offences against the rulers
There is no fault of any kind at all

2119. Rahe woh hi balwa mein sabit qadam
Jo English Bahadur ka bharte the dam
They are the ones who remained steadfast during the riots
Who always praised the English Bahadur

2120. Yahaan ek Mufti bade nek the
Buzurgi mein es shahar mein ek the
A Mufti here was very noble
In eminence he was matchless in this town

2121. Gaye es jahan ko woh jab chod kar
Yahaan unse baqi rahe do pisar
When he departed from this world
He was survived here by two sons

2122. Bade bhai Munsif hue dar huzoor
Bafazl-e-Khuda woh to hain beqasoor
The elder brother became a Munsif in the Court
By God's grace he is innocent

2123. Woh choote to ab tak hain Sadr-us-sudur
Rahe unpe afzaal-e-Rabb-e-Ghafur
The younger one is a Sadr-us-Sudur till now
May the grace of the All-Forgiving Lord remain upon him!

2124. Rahe Shah Aali Guhar Sabz Posh
Tha unki mohabbat ka har ek ko josh
There was Shah Ali Guhar Sabz Posh
Everyone had fervour of love for him

2125. Bhateejee bhi unke hain durrey khush aab
Koi aftaab hai koi maahtaab
His nephews also are like pearls with beautiful vesture
One is the sun and the other the moon

2126. Nawaazish Ali mere ghamkhaar hain
Rasees aur khiradmand hoshiyaar hain
Nawaazish Ali is my sympathetic friend
He is noble, intelligent and clever

2127. Tababat ke fun mein woh hain Bu-Ali
Unhi se tababat ko raunaq mili
In practice of indigineous medicine he has unrivalled expertise
like Avicenna
Medical practice has flourished due to him

2128. Raeeson mein the Shaikh Wahid Ali
Alimullah Sahib the kaamil vali
Among the nobles was Shaikh Wahid Ali
Alimullah Sahib was a perfect saint

2129. Hue yahaan se raahi-e-mulk-e-adam
Kare unke ladke pe Khaliq karam
Left from here for the dominion of hereafter
May the Creator be kind towards his son!

2130. Diya Baksh Ilahi ne saail ko zar
Muakhkhar muqaddam muqaddam par kar
Baksh Ilahi gave money to the petitioner
More than posterior, antecedent, superior

2131. Hua naam Hafiz ka roshan jun maah
Khalaaeq ke hain dil se woh khairkhah
Name of Hafiz was enlightened like the moon
He is a true well-wisher of the people

2132. Deewaan Debi Parsad naami rahe
Khiradmandon mein woh giraami rahe
Diwan Debi Prasad was famous
Among wise men he was respectable

2133. Karun khubiyaan unki kya aashkaar
Riyaasat ke kaamon mein the hoshiyaar
Which virtues of his should I disclose?
He was efficient in administrative work

2134. Azeez aqriba unke sab hoshmand
Zamaana ka unpar bhi pahuncha guzand
All his dear ones and relatives are intelligent
He too was affected by the ravages of the times

2135. Hain munshi Shiv Lochan bahut nek naam
Hain daftar mein sarkaar ke shaad-kaam
Munshi Shiv Lochan is very well-reputed
He is successful in government office work

2136. Bade nek hain Shaikh Ahmad Husain
Rahen khush karen khub aaraam-o-chaiyn
Shaikh Ahmad Husain is very noble
May he remain happy, in great comfort and peace

2137. Husain Baksh Sahib hain aaqil bade
Woh ilm-o-amal mein hain qaabil bade
Husain Baksh Sahib is very intelligent
He is very capable in knowledge and action

2138. Hain Ahmad Ali Najaf Ali ke pisar
Saaid azal hafiz khush siyar
Ahmad Ali is the son of Najaf Ali
Fortunate, excellent, a good-charactered hafiz

2139. Hain Yusuf Ali mard har dil azeez
Khiradmand hain aur ahle tameez
Yusuf Ali is a man liked by everyone
Is intelligent and a person of fine etiquette

2140. Kareemdad Khan hain bade hoshmand
Raeeson mein naam unka hai arjmand
Kareemdad Khan is very sensible
Among nobles his name is honourable

2141. Khuda Baksh hain mard ahle-sho'oor
Rakhe shaadmand unko Rabb-e-Ghafur
Khuda Baksh is a competent and wise man
May the All Forgiving Lord keep him happy!

2142. The sarkaari ohde pe Baijnath Singh
Aur bhai unhi ka hai Shivnath Singh
Baijnath Singh was on a government post
And Shivnath Singh is his brother

2143. Hain bete bhi unke bahut nek khu
Hai naamaawari ki unhe justaju
His son also has a very noble disposition
He has a passion for fame

2144. Hain Lala Mohit Narayan wakeel
Nazar mein khalaeq ke hain woh jaleel
Lala Mohit Narayan is an advocate
He is illustrious in the eyes of the people

2145. Jo Gul Lal bhi mard hai khush khisaal
Raha ghadar-e-makruh mein bezawaal
That Gul Lal also is a man with delectable qualities
He remained free of misery in the odious mutiny

2146. Munna Lal Mukhtaar hai zeehimam
Es aafat mein woh bhi tha sabit qadam
Munna Lal Mukhtaar is enterprising
In this calamity he too remained steadfast

2147. Reha har bala se hai ek Ramlal
Use khush rakhe Khaliq-e-Zuljalaal
One Ram Lal is free from all kinds of distress
May the Splendid God keep him happy!

2148. Rahe Jai Kiran Lal bar vaz khesh
Khuda usko bhi shaad rakhe hamesh
Jai Kiran Lal was an individual above style
May God keep him also happy, always!

2149. Riyaasat Husain Baksh ki aam hai
Har ek sahibon mein bada naam hai
Husain Baksh's princely ways are well-known
He is famous amongst each and every sahib

2150. Fasihullah Sahib hain imaandaar
Khush akhlaaq hain woh sadaaqat sheaar
Fasihullah Sahib is honest
He is good-natured and truthful

2151. Amiruddin Sahib jo hain khush navees
Hain woh bhi mere shahar mein ek raees
Amiruddin Sahib who is a calligraphist
He too is a nobleman in my town

2152. Raees-e-kalan Jamna Parshad hain
Ba fazl-e-Khuda shaad-o-aabaad hain
Jamna Prasad is a famous noble
By God's grace he is happy and flourishing

2153. Janak bhi bade mard hain hoshmand
Hai harkat unki bahut dilpasand
Janak also is a very wise man
His activities are very much after one's heart

2154. Khaliq aur masood hain Hansraaj
Firotan bhi hain aur hain khush mizaaj
Hansraaj is courteous and fortunate
Is humble as well as good-tempered

2155. The Qazi Karam Ashraf aali guhar
Zahoor Ashraf unke hain laaiq pisar
Qazi Karam Ashraf was of noble descent
Zahoor Ashraf is his competent son

2156. Hai es shahar mein Gauri Shankar shareef
Khush akhlaaq woh hain lateef-o-zareef
In this town Gauri Shankar is noble
He is good-mannered, soft-spoken and witty

2157. Khonkharpur mein hain Hidayat Ali
Wakalat bhi unki hai chamki bhali
Hidayat Ali is at Khonkharpur
His advocacy is quite successful

2158. Hain bilfael Qazi Saadat Husain
Mite ranj unka tufail-e-Husain
Qazi Saadat Husain is present
May his anxiety be erased by the intervention of Husain

2159. Miyan Minatullah hain nek zaat
Kahan tak likhun unki yaaron sifaat
Miyan Minatullah is a noble person
Friends, how much can I write about his virtues?

2160. Khush iqbaal the Mirza Hasan Ali
Vaz aur tabiyat thi unki bhali
Mirza Hasan Ali was very fortunate
His behaviour and temperament was good

2161. Ba juz ranj-e-Husnain tha kuch na ranj
Ilaaqah bahut aur kasrat se ganj
Except the sorrow over Husnain, there was no other sorrow
Had lot of estates and many markets

2162. Magar betoon ne kar diya ghar tabaah
Nawaazish Ali par thi Haq ki nigaah
But his sons destroyed the house
Nevertheless God was kind towards Nawaazish Ali

2163. Chatradhari Kayasth hain naamwar
Shareef aur masood hain sarbasar
Chatradhari Kayasth is famous
He is entirely noble and fortunate

2164. Rahe nek Hamid Ali Pir mard
Pisar unke rakhte nahin apna fard
Hamid Ali was a noble and spiritual man
There is no individual like his son

2165. Husain Baksh nek aur khiradmand hain
Mohammad Ali ke woh farzand hain
Husain Baksh is gentle and intelligent
He is the son of Mohammad Ali

2166. Alimullah ke bete Barkat Ali
Rahe Nematullah ke woh vaali
Alimullah's son Barkat Ali
Was a friend of Nematullah

2167. Ghulam Chishti ke bete Rahmat Ali
Woh Husnain ke hain mohib dili
Ghulam Chishti's son Rahmat Ali
He is a true lover of Husnain

2168. Rahe Kashi Parshad bhi muntazim
The sarkaari daftar ke woh mohtamim
Kashi Prasad also was a manager
He was superintendent of a government office

2169. Pisar dono unke hue naamwar
Woh hain dono farkhanda aur khush siyar
Both his sons became famous
Both of them are blessed and good-charactered

2170. Hain jo Durga Parsaad Nazir yahaan
Hai akhlaaq unka jahan par ayaan
Durga Prasad, who is a *Nazir* here
His virtues are apparent to the world

2171. Rahe kaam par apne khush woh mudaam
Rakhe khush unhe Khaliq-e-Zulkaraam
He was always happy on his job
May the merciful and kind Lord keep him happy!

2172. Musallas pisr unke hain nek zaat
Woh hain khulq-o-khubi mein aali sifaat
His three sons are noble persons
In civility and virtues they have eminent attributes

2173. Hain Mutawalli masjid ke Qadir Ali
Bahut unki baaten hain meethi bhali
Qadir Ali is the trustee of the mosque
His ways are very sweet and nice

2174. Bechanlal Qanongo khub hain
Khalaaiq hai taalib woh matloob hain
Bechanlal Qanongo is very good
People are his seekers and he is their beloved

2175. Yeh jaano ke hai sahib-e-khandaan
Hamesha rahe fazl-e-Rabb-e-Jahaan
Let it be known that he has an impressive lineage
May the grace of the Lord of the World always be upon him!

2176. Mahabir Parsaad mere wakeel
Nigahbaan rahe unka Rabb-e-Jaleel
Mahabir Prasad is my advocate
May the Glorious God be his protector!

2177. The aali qadar ek Shiv Raj Singh
Woh bhai rahe unke Mehraj Singh
One Shiv Raj Singh was highly respected
That Mehraj Singh was his brother

2178. Pisar Kandhajimal hain unke raees
Tabiyat ke woh bhi hain az bas nafees
His son Kandhajimal is an aristocrat
He also has an elegant nature

2179. Mohammad Ali Khan jo mashhoor hain
Vila munsifi par woh maamur hain
Mohammad Ali Khan who is famous
He is commissioned in the business of justice

2180. Bade munkasir hain Tassadduq Ali
Pidr nek the unke Qurban Ali
Tassadduq Ali is very humble
His father Qurban Ali was very noble

2181. Aur Farzand Ali unke vaali rahe
Riyaasat sharafat mein aali rahe
And Farzand Ali was his guardian
In princely ways and nobility he was grand

2182. Dayaram mohalla jo mashhoor hai
Suno uske maalik ka maskur hai
Dayaram lane, which is well-known
Listen, following is an account of its owner:

2183. Bhujal Singh bada mard naami raha
Raeeson mein woh bhi giraami raha
Bhujal Singh was a very famous man
Among aristocrats he too was venerable

2184. Usi ke gharaane mein hai Ram Ghulam
Hai shahar mein woh bada nek naam
Ram Ghulam is from his family
In this town he is extremely well-reputed

2185. Hain Lala Bihari bhi bas naamwar
Woh Mukhtardin hain bade zee hunar
Lala Bihari is also quite famous
That Mukhtardin is endowed with great talent

2186. Khiradmand bas Ram Parshad hain
Ba fazl-e-Khuda shaad-o-aabaad hain
Ram Prasad is simply intelligent
By God's grace he is happy and well-settled!

2187. Rahe Shah-e-Maaruf mein Ram Dayal
Muazaz woh khush the ba-aulaad-o-aal
Among the chief celebrities was Ram Dayal
Honourable, he was happy with his children and family

2188. Kareem Beg har ek ke hain gham gusaar
Woh Husnain ke dil se hain jaan nisaar
Kareem Beg is everyone's sympathizer
He is heartily devoted to Husnain

2189. Wakeelon mein aalinasab hain Husain
Ali ke tassadduq se karte hain chaiyn
Among advocates Husain has a great lineage
By the graceful charity of Ali, he is in peace

2190. Amanullah Sahib hain vala hasab
Khush unse adna aqasa hain sab
Amanullah Sahib has an eminent pedigree
All and sundry are pleased with him

2191. Hain Ahmad Ali aur Mehboob Ali
Yeh hain dono sahib bhi zinda vali
About Ahmad Ali and Mehboob Ali
Both these persons also are living saints

2192. Ali Baksh Darogha hain bequsoor
Kare shaad kaam unko Rabb-e-Ghafur
Ali Baksh Darogha is faultless
May the All-Forgiving Lord bestow happiness upon him!

2193. Adaalat ke munshi Bhawani Prashad
Khudawand bartar rakhe unko shaad
Clerk of the court, Bhawani Prasad
May the Supreme Lord keep him happy!

2194. Bahut khub hain aur bahut khub hain
Khalaiq hai taalib woh matloob hain
(He) Is very nice, is very nice
People are his seekers and he is their beloved

2195. Aur hain Ganga Parshad aaqil bade
Sarishta mein apne hain kaamil bade
And Ganga Prasad is extremely intelligent
In his department he is very accomplished

2196. Hira Lal ke bete Lala Ganesh
Badanist-e-raavi yeh hai mard-e-besh
Hira Lal's son, Lala Ganesh
In the narrator's opinion, he is an excellent man

2197. Niranjan bada mard naami hua
Gharaane mein apne giraami hua
Niranjan was a very famous man
In his family he was honourable

2198. Buzurgaan uske the aalivaqaar
Aur hukkaam karte the sab iftekhaar
His ancestors were highly dignified
And all the rulers used to honour them

2199. Bahut husn-o-khubi se karta hai kaam
Kachahri mein ab uski hai dhoom dhaam
Works with great elegance and ease
Now he has a splendid reputation in the court

2200. Riyaasat ka sab kaam karta hai woh
Burai se din raat darta hai woh
He does all princely things
Day and night he fears ill deeds

2201. Wakeelon mein ek Oman Parshad hain
Bafazl-e-Khuda khurram-o-shaad hain
Among advocates is one Oman Prasad
By God's grace he is happy and cheerful

2202. Hua Seetal Parshad bhi arjmand
Khudaya na pahunche use kuch guzand
Seetal Prasad was also honourable
O God! May he never receive any harm!

2203. Hain Mukhtaar Debi Charan khush chalan
Woh hai Rai Dampat bhi bas nek tan
Mukhtaar Debi Charan is pleasantly disposed
That Rai Dampat is also a noble man

2204. Hain Qismat Chhaarum ke Tehsildaar
Raiyyat hain wahaan ki sab un par nisaar
Qismat is the Tehsildaar of Chhaarum
All the people of that place are devoted to him

2205. Jamadaar Abdullah the nek zaat
Aur bete bhi sab unke hain ba sifaat
Jamadaar Abdullah was a noble person
And all his sons are also virtuous

2206. Salaar Baksh Dildaar Khan the shareef
Yeh dono the azbas lateef-o-zarif
Salaar Baksh and Dildaar Khan were noble
Both of them were very elegant and wise

2207. Muhalle mein raavi ke hain Brij Lal
Unhe nek-o-bad ka bahut hai khayaal
In the narrator's lane, stays Brij Lal
He is very concerned about good and bad

2208. Es zumrah mein baaqi rahe Maan Khan
Aur hain mard aaqil aur hoshiyaar jaan
In this category remains Maan Khan
And be certain he is an intelligent and astute man

2209. Hain mukhtari ke peshe mein ba kamaal
Bahut khush vaz hain Basheshar Dayal
In the profession of attorneyship he is excellent
Basheshar Dayal has a very elegant style

2210. Hain pisar unke Udit Sahay naamwar
Us balwa mein woh bhi raha nek tar
His son Udit Sahay is well-reputed
In that riot he too remained virtuous

2211. Hai Haider Ali ki jo aulaad sab
Pada unpe Sardar Ali ka ghazab
All the children of Haider Ali
Had to face the wrath of Sardar Ali

2212. Hain Lala Bujhawan jo degree navis
Har ek shaks ke dil se hain woh anis
Lala Bujhawan who writes degrees
He is a hearty friend of everyone

2213. Mohalle mein mere woh sardaar hai
Adaalat Diwani mein hoshiyaar hai
He is a leader in my lane
In civil court he is prudent

2214. Hai Himmat Ali Khan bahut hoshmand
Mohalle mein raavi ke hai arjmand
Himmat Ali Khan is very wise
In the narrator's lane, he is well-reputed

2215. Wakalat ke peshe mein hain Ghaus Ali
Khalaeq par unka hasab hai jali
Ghaus Ali is in the profession of advocacy
His lineage is very evident to people

2216. Bahut husn-o-khubi se karte hain kaam
Kachahri mein munsif ke hain nek naam
Works with great elegance and skill
Has a good reputation in the Munsif's court

2217. Bada mard naami hai Safdar Husain
Hamesha rahe khush ba-aaraam-o-chaiyn
Safdar Husain is a very famous man
May he always remain happy, in comfort and peace

2218. Mahajan-o-Pundit hain sab nek tar
Woh English Bahadur ke the muntazir
All the Mahajans and Pundits are very noble
They were waiting for English Bahadur

2219. Jin ashkhaas se raavi vaaqif nahin
Unhi ki haqiqat ka kaashif nahin
The persons whom the narrator does not know
Their verity he has not revealed

2220. Raeeson mein jo log behtar rahe
Hawakhah-e-English braabar rahe
Those who were better among the noblemen
Continuously remained friends of the English

2221. Unhi ko likha raavi ne aiye azeez
Yeh hai kaifiyat raast kar le tameez
O friend! The narrator has written only about them
Be sure this is the actual condition

2222. Khataa se yeh ashkhaas sab saaf hain
Yeh hi log bas qaabil ausaaf hain
All these persons are free of fault
Only these people deserve praise

2223. Raeesaan-e-shahri rahe basta dust
Madadgaar-e-sarkaar the dar August
Nobles of the town waited with clasped hands
They were helpers of the government since August

2224. Kiya khairkhahon ki tafseel hum
Mufassal kiya hum ne yeh sab raqam
I have given details of supporters
I have narrated all this explicitly

2225. Rahi fikr es ki mujhe daima
Ke kis wajhe se aisa balwa hua
I pondered over this ceaselessly
That why did such a riot happen

2226. Bas az gaur-o-tahqeeq hai yeh kalaam
Mahajan hue baais-e-ghadar-e-aam
This poetical work is worth consideration and research
Mahajans became the cause of the common revolt

2227. Diya jis ko dus us se sau bhar liya
Liya karkara jis ko malta diya
Extracted hundred from the one they had given ten
Took back crisp from the one they had given soggy

2228. Siwa es ke nazrana ki hai raqam
Woh hai saikde panch bekaast-o-kum
Besides this, is the amount of tax
Which is five on hundred, on uncultivated scanty land

2229. Tamassuk khun ko naya karte hain
Vala mul mein sood ko dharte hain
They keep renewing the clink of monetary bonds.
Freely they add interest to the principal amount

2230. Hua asl mein sood jab inzemaam
Laga sood par sood badhne tamaam
When interest became one with the principal sum
Then compound interest over interest multiplied tremendously

2231. Na jab sood se dekha apna panaah
Raha chandi ko peet kar karzkhaah
When did not see appropriate protection from his interest,
The creditor was able to strike wealthy profits

2232. Hai yeh bhi unhu ka nihaayat sitam
Jo karte hain nalish kisi par baham
This also is their extreme oppression
That they ultimately file a legal suit against someone

2233. *Wasooli raqumaat ko zeenahaar*
Nahin dete mujra ve zulmat sheaar
On no account, on recovery of the total amount
Do those dark-mannered ones ever give any rebate

2234. *Mahajan ki illat mein wa hasrata*
Hue mulk neelaam sab barmala
Due to the Mahajans' fault unfortunately
All territories were auctioned publicly

2235. *Hua jis ghadi dakhl neelamdaar*
Raha maalik-e-milk ek aah maar
The moment the auctioneer took possession
The property owner sighed in helpless despair

2236. *Biki jin ki bhi milkiyat daam mein*
Wohi jaa mile balwa-e-aam mein
Those, whose properties were sold for a price
Were the ones who joined in the mass rioting

2237. *The muddat se jo log az bas tabaah*
Liya milk phir cheen go hai gunaah
People who were most ruined since ages
Looted their earlier property back, even though it is a sin

2238. *Wagarna the sarkaar se shaad sab*
Hua muflisi ka yeh sara sabab
Otherwise everyone was happy with the government
The main cause for all this was poverty.

Kaifiyat Raunaq-afroozi Janaab Reid Sahib Sadar Board Bahadur

Situation of the graceful arrival of Janaab Reid Sahib, Chief of Board Bahadur

2239. Hai es daastaan mein khushi ka maqaal
Suno Reid Sahib ki a amad ka haal
In this narration are words of happiness
Listen to the circumstances of Reid Sahib's arrival

2240. Thi taareekh Shabaan ki shanzdah
Hai kya khoob masood yeh saal-o-maah
It was the thirteenth of Shabaan
How very auspicious is this year and month!

2241. Raha baarah sae par chihattar ziyaad
Hai es ja pe Hijri ke sun se murad
It was seventy six over twelve hundred
At this place the context is of the Hijri year

2242. Thi March ki tareekh dusween ayaan
Sun aththaarah sae saath the begumaan
It was the tenth date of March
The year undoubtedly was eighteen hundred and sixty

2243. Tha baaqi sanichar ka din ek ghadi
Ke naakah sada kaan mein yeh padi

Some hours of Saturday still remained
When unexpectedly this call fell upon my ears

2244. Kiya Jaan Ali Khan ne aakar bayaan
Ke Board ke haakim hain aate yahaan
Jaan Ali Khan came up and said
That officers of the Board are coming here

2245. Zabaani Commissioner ke hai yeh khabar
Kaha mujh se ja jald aagaah kar
This news has been conveyed by the Commissioner
He asked me to go quickly and inform

2246. Kaha maine fil-faur saamaan karo
Azakhana mein ja ke haazir raho
I directed to make arrangements immediately
Instructed to be present in the mourning house

2247. Karo roshni ka abhi bandobast
Ke taa ho shab-e-maah dekh us ko past
Make arrangements for lights straight away
Such that a moon-lit night may be dull in its comparison

2248. Sadar Board itne hain aaye yahaan
Hua rashk-e-Firdaus mera makaan
So many officers of the Board came here
That my house became the envy of heaven

2249. Haqiqat mein Sahib hain shurfa nawaaz
Kiya daye-ul-khair ko sarfaraaz
In reality the Sahib is a patron of noblemen
Exalted the one who is inclined towards virtue

2250. Sonneton Sahib Commissioner the saath
Raha hanth mein unke Sahib ka hanth
Sonneton Sahib Commissioner was with him
Sahib's hand was in his hands

2251. Tamanaa ka shaadaab gulshan hua
Qadam se makaan mera roshan hua

The garden of desires became lush green
My house was lighted by his footsteps

2252. Bana burj-e-khursheed maskan mera
Quba mein samaata na tha tan mera
My residence became the bastion of sun
My body could not be contained in quilted coat

2253. Hui roshni aisi har chaar su
Na tha farq din raat mein ek mu
Such was the light in all four directions
There was not a hair's difference between day and night

2254. Qanadeel roshan theen andar ruvaaq
Tuzuk tha bada aur bahut tumturaaq
Chandeliers were lighted in the patio
There was a lot of pomp and show

2255. Hai jaa-e-taajjub ho kyon kar yaqeen
Hai ek burj mein chaand suraj makeen
It is bewildering for one to believe
That the sun and moon reside in a single tower!

2256. Kawal mere dil ke hue sab hare
Haqiqat mein woh hain murabbi mere
All the lotuses of my heart became verdant
They truly are my patrons

2257. Nigahbaan mere hain mere meherbaan
Hain mohsin mere aur mere qadardaan
My custodians are kind towards me
They are my benefactors and my patrons

2258. Unhi se buland apna rutba hua
Yeh qatra tha nacheez dariya hua
My status was exalted due to them
This worthless droplet became the sea

2259. Bahut Reid Sahib ne izzat kiya
Jo puchaa jawaab uska shaafi diya

Reid Sahib gave a lot of respect
Gave convincing replies to whatever was asked

2260. Yehi hai dua meri subh-o-masa
Salamat rahen Reid Sahib sada
This is my prayer day and night
May Reid Sahib always remain secure!

2261. Humare zila ke hain yeh sarparast
Bakhubi kiya yahaan ka sab bandobast
He is the guardian of my town
Has made excellent arrangements here

2262. Razamand-o-khushnood hain khaas-o-aam
Hain Sahib ke haq mein duago mudaam
All the elite and commoners are agreeable and happy
They always say prayers in favour of Sahib

2263. Aaliqadar har ek ko rutba diya
Kare Lord jaldi se unko Khuda
Granted highly respectable ranks to everyone
May the Almighty make him a Lord very soon!

2264. Raaya hai sab parwarishyaafta
Na balwa mein koi tha rutaaftah
All the people receive sustenance and protection
In the riots no one was gloss-faced

2265. Bila jurm jo shaks khaati bana
Khataa afv Sahib ne uski kiya
Whoever became an accused, without committing any crime
Sahib forgave his shortcomings

2266. Hue apne ohde pe jumla bahaal
Hai baaqi ka Sahib ko har dam khayaal
Everyone was reinstated in their former posts
Every moment Sahib is anxious about the rest

2267. Hain laaraib, Sahib bade sarparast
Sifat hai badi hausalah mera past

Undoubtedly Sahib is a great patron
His attributes are grand; my courage is inferior

2268. Raaya to mohtaaj-o-laachaar hain
Magar dil se Sahib madadgaar hain
The subjects are poor and helpless
But Sahib is truly helpful

2269. Collector Session Judge the maujood yaan
Kisi ka nahin haal unse nihaan
The Collector and Session Judge were present here
No one's condition is hidden from him

2270. Hai Sahib ko raiyyat ka har dam khayaal
Na phir haal par unke kyon ho malaal
Every moment Sahib is concerned about the subjects
Why then would he not be grieved over their condition?

2271. Samajh kar ke sarkaar ne maslahat
Zila ko kiya tark ba-manzalat
Government, on understanding the expediency
Relinquished the town with dignity

2272. Hawakhahon se shahar maamur tha
Koi dakhl karta yeh maqdoor tha
The town was being commanded by well-wishers
Did anyone else have the power to interfere?

2273. Har ek jaan nisaari pe taiyyaar the
Namakkhar bilkul madadgaar the
All were ready to lay down their lives
Devoted loyalists were unconditionally supportive

2274. Na jab koi raiyyat ka ho sarparast
To hai hausalah jumla raiyyat ka past
When there is no guardian of people
Then spirits of all the subjects are low

2275. Jab haakim raaya ko kar de mahv
Muhaafiz bhala kaun izzat ka ho

When the ruler effaces the subjects
Who then would be the protector of honour?

2276. Yeh hai amr hukkaam ke dil nasheen
Yehi dil mein mazmoon hai naqsh-o-nageen
In the ruler's heart, this thrust is deeply rooted
This very subject is carved and set in their heart

2277. Raeeson mein khaati na koi raha
Na zalim ka koi mulaazim hua
No one was a wrong-doer among noblemen
Neither did anyone become a servant of the tyrant

2278. Raha hizda sad pe unsath fizoon
Yeh nuskha hua khatm bis said noon
Fifty nine was exceeding eighteen hundred
When this book was completed

2279. Hai Kashful Baghaavat risala ka naam
Hawakhah padh kar ke hon shaad kaam
Kashful Baghaavat is the name of this booklet
Well-wishers may be pleased on reading it.

Khatam Bil Khair

Ended with happiness

Qitah Taarikh
Fashion of Chronicle

Hui jab khatam yeh abiyaat dilkash
When these fascinating couplets were completed

Tabiat ko pasand aayee nihaayat
They were liked exceedingly by mind and spirit

Paye tareekh jab ki fikr maine
When I concentrated in pursuit of the Chronogram

Nida aayi chapti Kashful Baghaavat
A divine voice came: Kashful Baghaavat is being printed

AD 1860

Glossary

Aabaad	rehabilitate, populated, prosperous.
Aabroo	honor, dignity.
Aafaal	acts, actions, deeds, conduct.
Aafreen	well-done, bravo, praise.
Aagaah	aware, informed, acquainted with.
Aajiz	incapable, unable, humble, weak.
Aalaat	implements, tools, weapons.
Aali	high, lofty, elevated.
Aali tabaar	noble descent.
Aali vaqaar	highly dignified, highly prestigious.
Aalim	wise, all-knowing, omniscient.
Aamaadah	ready, prepared.
Aamaal	action, deed, practice, work.
Aan	moment, instant, pride, dignity.
Aaqa	employer, lord, master.
Aariyat	borrow.
Aashkaar	disclose, divulge, evident, obvious.
Abas	uselessly, unavailingly, vain.
Adab	etiquette, decorum, courtesy.
Adam	non-existence, nothingness.
Adl	justice, equity, division.
Adna	ordinary, small, trifling.
Afsaad	quarrels, ruin, riots.
Afwaaj	armed forces, army.

Afzaal	excellence, favours.
Aish	luxury, enjoyment, ease.
Ajab	strange, wonderful, marvelous.
Ajeeb	strange, astonishing, wonderful.
Ajza	parts, constituents.
Akhlaaq	manners, disposition, virtues.
Alam	notification, flag, grief, agony.
Alhazar	God forbid, fear, abstinence, caution.
Altaaf	pleasures, favors.
Amaanat	entrusted stuff, trust, deposit.
Ameer	ruler, rich, governor, prince.
Amin	trustworthy, faithful, revenue official.
Amini	guardianship, custody.
Amr	command, order, business, point.
Amr-o-nahy	commands, prohibitions.
Andesha	anxiety, concern, dread, suspicion.
Anjaam	management, accomplishment.
Aqriba	relatives, kins, allies.
Areeza	request, petition, application.
Arjmand	noble, honorable, worthy, happy.
Asbaab	property, baggage, provisions.
Asfalus	most mean.
Ashad	most violent, vehement, excessive.
Ashkhaas	people.
Asir	prisoner, captive.
Asl	root, source, base.
Ataat	obedience, reverence, worship.
Atfaal	children, progeny.
Atka	entangled, hindered, restrained.
Atraaf	directions, sides, extremes, outpost.
Attaar	chemist, perfumer, name of a poet.
Aud	return.
Auhaam	apprehensions, superstitions.
Auj	zenith, acme, apex, summit.
Ausaaf	attributes, charecteristics, qualities.
Awwal Jamadi	first half of the month of Hijri calendar.

Ayaan	obvious, evident, clear, manifest.
Azaab	punishment, torment, misfortune.
Azakhana	mourning house.
Azbas	quite, more adequately, much.
Azdaad	opposites.
Azeem	great, grand, magnificent.
Azeeyat	oppression, torment, trouble, woe.
Azla	adminstrative district, district, parts.
Azlam	darkest, most cruel.
Baaghi	rebel, insurgent, traitor, mutineer.
Baais	cause, reason, basis, condition.
Baak	fear.
Baaqi	outstanding, arrears.
Baawar	trust.
Badasl	base, born mean.
Badastur	in the usual manner, unchanged.
Badaulat	by the fortune, by the means.
Badkaar	sinful.
Badkhisaal	evil, ill-disposed, ill-natured.
Badnihaad	ill disposed, ill natured.
Badraah	wicked, sinful, evil, debauched.
Badsheaar	bad habit, ill-mannered.
Badsiyar	of bad charactered.
Baeid	distant, far, remote.
Baham	together, jointly, altogether.
Bahar	ocean.
Bajuz	except, save.
Bala	calamity, misfortune, distress, evil.
Balam	spear.
Balwa	riot, tumult, disturbance.
Bamajboori	helplessness, compulsion.
Bamujib	in accordance, consequent upon.
Bandobast	arrangement, revenue settlement.
Baranji	brass, brazen.
Barham	anger, angry, upset, disordered.
Barkhwast	dismissed, adjourned.

Barmahak	touchstone.
Barmahal	opportune, apt.
Barmala	public, publicly, conspicuous, open.
Barpa	create, standing.
Barq	electricity, lightning, firing.
Bartaraf	dismiss, discharge.
Basad	lots of, by a hundred, with much.
Bashar	human being.
Bashinda	citizen, resident, inhabitant.
Batameez	well-mannered, discrect, judicious.
Batin	heart, mind, innermost, inside.
Bavaqaar	dignified.
Bayaan	expressed, expounded.
Bayabaan	desert, wilderness.
Bazaahir	apparently, evidently, visibly.
Bazain	grace, elegance, beauty, adornment.
Bazm	association, meeting, company.
Beadab	impudent, disrespectful, rude.
Beajal	without hour or premature death.
Bedirang	quick, without any delay.
Beem	fear, terror, danger.
Begumaan	doubtless, without suspicion.
Beguzand	unharmed, uninjured.
Behramand	fortunate, lucky.
Behuda	absurd, foolish, obscene.
Bekali	restlessness, uneasiness.
Bekhatar	safe, undaunted.
Bemisaal	matchless, incomparable.
Benazeer	unequalled, unparalleled.
Benishaan	insignificant, issueless, wiped out.
Besh-o-kam	more or less.
Bezaar	disgusted, displaced, annoyed.
Bidat	schism, heresy, violence, tyranny.
Bigad	vitiated.
Bina	foundation, basis, cause, motive.
Bist	twenty.

Boom	land, owl.
Bu-Ali	Persian name for Arabic Ibn Sina and Latinized Avicenna.
Buniyaad	foundation, ground work, basis.
Buzdili	cowardice, dastardliness.
Charkh	sky, heaven.
Chobdaar	mace bearer.
Chohal	merriment, joyful.
Chust	active, agile, smart, alert, smart.
Daad	praise, appreciate, appeal.
Daagh	mark, spot, blemish, stigma, scar.
Daaghi	damaged, soiled, spoiled, tarnished.
Daar	gibbet, cross.
Daastaan	legend, romance, tale, story.
Daawa	claim, demand, law-suit.
Dabeer	secretary, writer.
Dafa	warding off, repulsion.
Daghaa	fraud, deception, treason, betrayal.
Daghal	hypocrisy, deception.
Dain	debt, liability.
Dajjaal	anti-Christ, false, name of religious impostors.
Dakhal	possession.
Daman	rubbish.
Damsaaz	intimate, concordant, harmonious.
Danish	understanding, knowledge.
Dardnaak	sad, touching, pitiable.
Dargaah	shrine, mausoleum, royal court.
Darkaar	wanted, needed.
Darogha	Inspector of Police
Darpesh	confronting, before, in front.
Dastaar	turban.
Dastak	knock, summon, warrant.
Dastur	custom, manner, mode, fashion.
Daulat	wealth, riches, money, state, power.
Dayaanat	faith, honesty, fidelity.
Deegar	other, another, again.

Dilband	son.
Dilbari	loveliness, being a beloved.
Dildaar	captivating, sweetheart, charming.
Dilfigaar	mournful, grief-stricken.
Dilshaad	happy, glad, cheerful.
Doneem	cut into two, slaughtered.
Duago	well-wisher, one who prays.
Durood	to invoke Gods blessings on the Prophet.
Duldul	Prophet Mohammad's mule.
Dushwaar	difficult, hard, troublesome.
Ehtimaam	arrangement, effort, management.
Eijaad	invention, contraption, contrivance.
Faheem	intelligent.
Faiz	favour, bounty, good influence.
Falaah	success, victory, prosperity.
Fana	death, mortality, destruction.
Faqat	just, only, merely.
Faqir	beggar, mendicant, saint.
Fasli	dating system based on land-revenue system.
Faraar	flight, running away.
Faramosh	forgotten, neglected, ignored.
Fareb	fraud, cheat, deceit, deception.
Farhat	pleasure, delight, cheerfulness.
Farkhandagi	luckily, auspiciously, happily.
Farq	difference, distance, change.
Farz	duty, obligation, responsibility.
Fasaad	discordant, seditious.
Fazl	grace, bounty, mercy.
Fida	devoted.
Figaar	wounded, lacerated.
Firdaus	paradise.
Firotan	humble, lowly.
Firoz	victorious, successful, turquoise.
Firqah	sect.
Fitna	sedition, disturbance, devilment.
Fiza	increasing, reinforcing.

Gaam	foot.
Gahan	eclipse.
Gahe	occasionally, once in a blue moon.
Gamakta	echo in musical instrument, shine.
Gardish-e-aasmaan	rotation, vicissitudes of fortune.
Ghaarat	waste, plunder, ravage, raid.
Ghaaratgaraan	raiders, plunderers, destroyers.
Ghaaratgari	plunder, destroy.
Ghadar	perfidy, treachery, mutiny.
Ghafil	negligent, inattentive, unmindful.
Ghaflat	negligence, carelessness.
Ghaib	the hidden, invisible, concealed.
Ghair	outsider, stranger.
Gham	sorrow, grief, sadness, woe.
Ghamgusaar	sympathising friend, comforter.
Ghamkhaar	comforter.
Ghammaazi	backbiting, tale-bearing, winking.
Ghanimat	plunder, prize, boon, blessing.
Gharaz	in short, motive, aim.
Ghazab	irate, rage, anger, extra ordinary.
Ghazabnaak	furious, wrathful, indignant, irate.
Guhar	pearl.
Gulaab	rose, plastering mud.
Gulogeer	kill, put to an end.
Gulshan	rose, flower garden.
Gumnaam	anonymous, unknown, obscure.
Gumraah	be misled, led astray, be seduced.
Gunjaish	ability, capacity.
Guzaarish	request, submission.
Guzand	harm, loss, injury.
Guzar	livelihood, ingress, egress.
Guzasht	passed, ended.
Guzeen	choosing, selection, adoption.
Haajat	need.
Haakim	ruler, officer, commander.
Habshi	African, Abyssinian, Negro.

Hadaf	circle on which aim is taken, target.
Hafiz	protector, one who has memorised the Quran.
Haibat	fear, dread, horror.
Hakeem	physician, doctor, philosopher.
Haq	God, truth, justice, share, claim.
Haqiqat	account, condition, reality.
Harchand	any amount, full possible.
Harut	blackmagic knowing arrested angel.
Hasab	lineage, pedigree, nobility.
Hashmat	dignity, riches, wealth.
Hashr	resurrection, doomsday, tumult.
Hasrata	regret, wistfulness, pining.
Hatim	Arab chief famous for generosity
Hawakhah	well-wisher, sympathizer, friend.
Hazar	prudence, abstinence, caution.
Hazeemat	flight, rout, defeat.
Hazman	watchfulness.
Hijri	Islamic dating system.
Hikayat	story, detracted narrative, report.
Hilaal	cresent, new moon.
Hilah	excuse, trick, prevarication.
Himam	courage, daring, bravery.
Himayat	protection, support, patronage.
Hiraas	terror.
Hisaab	arithmetic, account, reckoning.
Hoshiyaar	watchful, sensible, wise, careful.
Hoshmand	sensible, alert.
Hujjat	argument, reason, proof, objection.
Hukkaam	officers, commanders, rulers.
Hukm	order, command, decree, ordinance.
Humraah	along with.
Humsari	equality, equivalence.
Husnain	Hazrat Hasan & Hazrat Husain.
Huzn	sorrow, grief, affliction.
Huzoor	presence.
Iblees	name of Satan in Islamic tradition, devil.

Idbaar	downfall, fall, ill luck, misfortune.
Iflaak	heavenly spheres.
Ihaanat	affront, insult, slander, contempt.
Ijabat	grant, acceptance, consent.
Ijlaas	sitting, session, bench, meeting.
Ijz	humility.
Ikhtitaam	end, termination, conclusion.
Ikhtiyaar	authority, command, power, choice.
Iltemaas	request, entreaty, prayer, petition.
Ilzaam	accusation, charge, blame.
Imam	leader, chief.
Imtiyaaz	discrimination, distinction.
Inaayat	favour, kindness.
Injeel	Evangel, New Testament.
Injeer	Fig.
Insiraam	management, performance.
Intizaam	arrangement, management.
Inzemaam	to assemble, to meet, to be one.
Iqbaal	prosperity, luck, fortune.
Iqliim	whole world, clime.
Iqraar	promise, assent, admission.
Irshaad	word, behest, command, guidance.
Ishrat	pleasure.
Ishtehaar	advertisement, poster, notification.
Istaadah	standing, straight.
Ittifaaq	agreement, concord, by chance.
Iwaz	recompensation, return,exchange.
Izdehaam	crowd, throng, rabble.
Izhaar	expression, disclosure.
Ja-ba-ja	everywhere, here and there.
Jaali	forged, counterfeit, spurious.
Jabbaar	forceful one.
Jafaa	oppression, violence, retribution.
Jaish	army, troops, enjoyment, pleasure.
Jaleel	great, illustrious, glorious.
Jalwagar	manifest, present, in sight.

Jamadaar	centurion.
Jari	courageous, bold, valiant.
Jaur-o-sitam	oppression, tyranny.
Jawanmardi	gallantry, courage, youth.
Jaza	reward, blessing, compensation.
Jigar	liver, courage, endurance.
Jins	genus, sex, kind, material, category.
Jirah	argument, remonstration.
Jurrat	courage, boldness.
Juz-w-kul	whole, entire.
Kaamiyaab	achieving, successful.
Kaar	action, function, work.
Kaarobaar	business, trade, commerce.
Kaarsaaz	helping, skillful.
Kaash	how I wish!, only if!
Kabeer	dignitaries, high ups, big.
Kad	persistence, effort, endeavour.
Kaifiyat	state, condition, situation.
Kaji	unfair, fraudulent, wrong.
Kajravee	being unprincipled, unholy ways.
Kalapani	banishment for life to the Andamans.
Kalan	large, elder.
Kamaal	perfection, excellent, extreme.
Kamarbasta	in a state of readiness.
Kamayambaghi	as desired, as ought to be.
Kamzarf	mean, narrow-minded, malicious.
Karam	kindness, favour, graciousness.
Kareem	merciful, generous, bountiful.
Karr-o-farr	pomp, splendour, attack and retreat.
Kaseer	multifarious, ample, abundant.
Kashful Baghaavat	unveiling of the Revolt.
Kas-o-naakas	all and sundry.
Kawaif	particulars, details.
Khaak	dust, earth, nothing, ruin.
Khaam	unripe, inexperienced, raw, crude.
Khaamah	pen.

Khaana kharaab	miserable, wretched person.
Khaanumaan	home, household, furniture.
Khaar	thorn, bramble, grudge.
Khabar	news, information, tidings, report.
Khairkhah	approbative, approver, well-wisher.
Khair-o-khubi	goodness, safety.
Khajal	ashamed, penitent.
Khalaiq	people, creation, creatures.
Khalal	disorder, disturbance, derangement.
Khaliq	creator.
Khalish	prick of conscience, worry, anxiety.
Khams	agrarian tax, usually one-fifth of produce.
Khandaan	family, household, dynasty, lineage.
Kharaab	bad, wretched, depraved, corrupt.
Khas	hay, scented grass.
Khasam	enemy.
Khashamanaak	wrathful, angry, raged.
Khasumat	eremite, strife, contention.
Khataawaar	guilty, culprit, miscreant.
Khauf	fear, dread, terror.
Khayaal	thought, notion, idea, imagination.
Khirad	wisdom, intelligence, shrewdness.
Khisaal	qualities, traits of character.
Khiyaanat	embezzlement, defalcation, perfidy.
Khizaan	Autumn, fall.
Khizr	name of supposedly immortalised prophet.
Khoonreez	bloody, sanguinary.
Khudawand	lord, master.
Khur	Sun.
Khurd	small.
Khursheed	Sun.
Khushnood	happy, pleased.
Khush-o-khurram	happy & cheerful.
Kibriya	magnificent, magnificence.
Kinasaaz	malicious.
Kirdaar	characteristic traits.

Kisra	Chosroes/Khusroe a famous king
Kotwal	Police Chief
Koor	blind.
Kufraan-e-nemat	thanklessness, ingratitude.
Kushadah	wide, spacious, expansive, capacious.
Laag	love, connection, relation, grudge.
Laain	accursed, execrable.
Laaiq	worthy of, suitable for.
Laaraib	doubtless, undoubtedly.
Laat	Lord, as in colloquial Hindustani dialect
Lafezan	braggart, boastful.
Laihzah	moment, twinkling of an eye.
Laqab	appellation.
Lashkar	army, armed forces.
Laulaak	raison détre of whole creation.
Lutf	kindness, pleasure, enjoyment, relish.
Maah	moon.
Maahir	skilful, adept, expert, master.
Maajra	incident, occurrence, state, matter.
Maalun	execrated person.
Maamur	appointed, entrusted, commanded.
Maaruf	well known, celebrated.
Maazoor	excusable, helpless, disabled.
Maeeyyat	association, fellowship, company.
Magan	absorbed, engrossed, overjoyed.
Mahbas	prison.
Mahboob	beloved, sweetheart, favourite.
Majaal	power, ability, authority.
Makeen	resident.
Makhfi	secret, hidden, concealed, private.
Makkaar	deceitful.
Manish	temperament, characteristic, like.
Mansoob	attributed, imported.
Maqbool	popular, acceptable.
Maqdoor	authority, power, guts, wealth, means.
Maqsood	aim, object, intent, design.

Maqsoom	fate, destiny.
Mardak	mean fellow.
Mardood	reprobate.
Marghoob	pleasant, desire, desired, agreeable.
Maslehat	logic, expedience, prudence.
Mastoor	written.
Mauza	village.
Mauzoon	well balanced, symmetrical, adjusted.
Mazhab	religion, faith, way of life, creed.
Mazkoor	mention.
Mazmoon	composition, essay, matter, subject.
Meezaan	total, balance, pair of scales.
Mehan	sufferings, trials, tribulation.
Mehtaab	moon.
Midhat	praise, eulogy, encomium.
Milk	property, possession.
Miraas	hereditary estate, ancestral property.
Mirzai	loose-sleeved, quilted waist coat.
Misl	like, resembling.
Mismaar	razed, demolished, destroyed.
Mohayyaa	supply, provide, available.
Mohsin	benefactor, patron.
Mojib	reason.
Moonis	companion, consoler, friend.
Muakkil	deputy, trusted, guardian angel.
Muali	high, best, supreme.
Muawin	assistant, a better tributary.
Mubaddal	change.
Mubtala	involved, fallen into, entangled.
Mudaam	always, perpetually.
Mudabbir	statesman.
Muhaafiz	protector, guardian, keeper, guard.
Mukarrar	encore again, a second time.
Mukhaalif	opponent, adversary, enemy.
Mukhalla	dressed in a robe of honor.
Mukhtaar	attorney, agent, representation.

Mulazim	employee.
Mumaiyyaz	discrimination, differentiate.
Munasib	appropriate, expedient, proper.
Munhadim	demolished, razed.
Munhasar	dependent, limited, confined.
Munsalik	attached, strong, together.
Munsif	judge, fair-minded, just person.
Muntazim	manager, master of ceremonies.
Muqaddam	chief, superior, more important.
Muqeem	residing, stationed.
Mushaba	resembling, analogous.
Mushtamil	including, containing, comprising.
Musibat	trouble, affliction, disaster, calamity.
Mutlaqa	absolute, altogether, not at all.
Muzaffar	victorious, successful.
Naabkaar	notorious, wicked, sinful.
Naamdaar	famous, renowned, celebrated.
Nageen	gem, jewel.
Naghz	exquisite.
Naguzeer	indispensably, indispensable.
Nahang	crocodile, alligator.
Nahusat	bad presage, ominousness, accident.
Naib	deputy, assistant, vice regent.
Namaaz	Persian name of Mohammadan prayer.
Najaabat	nobility, gentility.
Najeeb	of noble birth, noble.
Nakhcheer	prey, game.
Namuraad	disappointed, unlucky, unfortunate.
Nang-o-naamus	honor & prestige.
Narawa	unjustified, unlawful.
Nasab	lineage, genealogy, family.
Nasheb-o-faraaz	declivity-acclivity, ups and downs.
Nasl	race, generation.
Nasq	order, arrangement.
Nazar	look, glance, careful thought.
Nazil	descend, arrive at unexpectedly.

Nazim	administrator, manager.
Nazir	supervisor, an official, spectator.
Neesh	sting, mordent.
Nek	good, virtuous, pious, fortunate.
Nemat	grace, divine blessing.
Nida	divine sound.
Nifaaq	hypocrisy, bearing malice inwardly.
Nigahbaan	watchman, custodian.
Nihaan	hidden, concealed, latent, clandestine.
Niko	good.
Nisaar	sacrificed, devoted, doting.
Niyaam	sheath, a scabbard.
Nosh	eating, honey.
Nutfabad	bad sperm, bastard.
Paihum	regularly, in a series.
Paikaar	war, battle, being pitted against.
Paimaal	ruined, crushed, destroyed.
Panjtan	five holy persons.
Parwardigaar	Providence, God.
Pashemaan	remorseful, disgraced.
Pattidaar	supporter.
Pesha	trade, profession, calling.
Peshwa	leader, guide, chief.
Pukhta	mature, experienced, solid.
Qaaf	caucasus, legendary abode of fairies.
Qaaim	firm, constant, unwavering, standing.
Qaal	theoretical, fact, factual.
Qaasir	failing in, deficient in, in capable of.
Qadar	lot, quantity, divine decree.
Qadardaan	patron, one knowing the worth.
Qadr	respect, honour, worth, value.
Qalam	pen, cutoff.
Qalamrau	dominion, territory.
Qalb	heart, soul, mind.
Qand	sugar, sweet.
Qanoongoh	petty revenue official.

Qaraar	rest, tranquility consistency, stability.
Qasad	resolve, attempt, design, object.
Qaul	saying, utterance.
Qavi	strong, vigorous, mighty, powerful.
Qaza	death, fate, fatality, decree, lapse.
Qeel-o-qaal	controversy, objection, criticism.
Qiyaam	stay, residence, establishment.
Qudrat	nature, universe, omnipotence.
Raahat	comfort, ease, rest, joy.
Raaqim	writer, author.
Rabb	God, preserver, cherisher, sustainer.
Radd-o-badal	change, alteration.
Radd-o-kad	expostulation.
Raees	rich person, landlord, magnate, chief.
Raghbat	keenness, inclination.
Rahzan	highway robbers.
Raiyyat	subjects, people.
Rajab	seventh month of Hijri calender.
Ranj	distress, anguish, agony, toil.
Raqam	written, indited, note, narrate.
Rasad	supplies, provisions.
Rashq	envy.
Rasm	custom, manner.
Raunaq	beauty, color, splendour.
Rawaan	be current, sharp, flowing, running.
Rida	sheet, stole, robe.
Rifaqat	companionship, friendship, loyalty.
Riyaasat	princely state, ways of the rich.
Rooz	day.
Rooza	Persian word for fasting.
Rubkaari	court proceedings, legal code.
Ruposh	absconding, underground.
Rusiyah	criminal.
Rutbah	rank, status, designation, distinction.
Saadat	felicity, auspiciousness, good fortune.
Saariq	thieves, robbers.

Sabat	permanence, endurance, firmness.
Sadaaqat	truth, sincerity.
Sadr-e-Amin	chief custodian, a revenue official.
Sadr-us-sudur	chief of chiefs, a government official
Safa	clean, name of a hill near Mecca.
Safar	second month of Hijri calender.
Safadeed	clear visionary.
Sagheer	small, inferior.
Sahv	omission, oversight.
Sakhaawat	generosity, munificence, liberality.
Salaat	Arabic name of Mohammadan prayer.
Samad	eternal, perpetual, sublime.
Samak	that matter on which earth is resting.
Saman	Jassamine, price.
Sana	praise, eulogy, encomium.
Sanihaa	occurrences, accidents.
Sarbar	honored, respected.
Sareeh	evident, obvious, point blank.
Sarrishta	department.
Sarwat	prosperity, riches.
Saulaak	commanding personality, awe.
Sawaab	rectitude, correctness.
Sazawaar	merit, deserve, deserving.
Seezdah	thirteenth.
Sehan	courtyard.
Shaad	happy, glad, joyful, cheerful.
Shabaan	eighth month of Hijri calendar.
Shab-baraat	a festival that brings fulfilment of wishes.
Shaghaal	Jackal.
Shamiyane	awning, pavillion, canopy.
Shamul	participation, inclusion.
Shareek	join, participate.
Sharminda	ashamed.
Shehnah	police chief.
Sher-e-ziyaan	truculent tiger.
Shimar	Yazid's general.

Shorish	disturbance, commotion, agitation.
Shum	miser, niggardly, unlucky.
Shusham	sixth.
Sidq	truth, veracity, sincerity, honesty.
Sifat	quality, attribute, praise.
Sima	face, countenance, aspect, visage.
Sipar	shield.
Sitam	tyranny, oppression, injustice.
Sufi	mystic.
Sukhan	speech, talk, words, poetry.
Sulah	peace, treaty, truce, patch up.
Taabeh	subordinate, obedient, loyal.
Taalib	summons, demands.
Taareef	praise, admiration, commendation.
Taaseer	effect, efficacy.
Taassuf	regret, remorse, grief, affliction.
Taayyun	fixation, appointment, posting.
Tabaah	squander, ruin, destroy.
Taghaaful	indifference, neglect, negligence.
Tahalka	panic, stir, death.
Tahqiq	research, inquiry, investigation.
Tajviz	suggestion, proposal, notion, plan.
Takhallul	thought, idea, fantasy.
Talaatum	storm, dashing, buffeting.
Talab	demand, summon, want, salary.
Taman	soldiers, army.
Tamandaar	centurion.
Tambu	tent.
Tameez	manners, etiquette, sense, direction.
Tang	tight, distressed, contracted, fed up.
Taqdeer	luck, fate, fortune, destiny.
Taqreer	speech, oration, discourse, address.
Tarab	joy, mirth, merriment.
Tarafdaar	supporter, partisan, partial.
Taraqqi	progress, advancement, promotion.
Tasdeeq	verification, attestation, certification.

Tashrih	explanation, elucidation, exposition.
Tauqeer	veneration, honor.
Tauseef	praise, eulogy, commendation.
Tegh	sword.
Tehsildar	Collector, an official deputed for tax collection.
Tehreer	writing, manuscript, composition.
Tillange	native soldiers.
Tira	dark, gloomy.
Tira-o-taar	depressing, dark & gloomy.
Tonti	spout.
Tufang	gun, musket.
Uboor	crossing, passing, transportation.
Ustuwaar	strong, secure, mighty, firm, bold.
Uzr-e-beja	improper plea, unjustified objection.
Vaali	friend, guardian, protector.
Vadood	friendly, loving.
Vale	but.
Vaqaar	prestige, dignity.
Wafaa	faithfulness, fidelity.
Wala	high, eminent, exalted.
Warid	came, appeared, arrived, befell.
Warris	heir, successor.
Yaar-e-ghaar	intimate friend.
Yaawari	help, support.
Yakta	singular, unique, incomparable.
Yazdaan	God, Zorastrian God of light.
Yazid	opponent of Hazrat Husain.
Youm	day.
Zaadbum	native place.
Zaal	old, father of Rustam; son of Saam.
Zaar-o-nizaar	weak, emaciated.
Zaayid	extra, surplus.
Zahir	obvious, evident, clear, apparent.
Zahoor	manifestation, appearance.
Zaleel	mean, base, contemptible, disgraced.
Zaman	times.

Zameen	earth.
Zameer	conscience.
Zarar	harm, damage, loss.
Zarb	multiplication, hurt, blow, injury.
Zarbulmisl	proverb, saying, aphorism.
Zarghaam	ravenous, tiger, lion.
Zarih	sarcophagus tomb, holy sepulchre.
Zarq	glittery, gaudy.
Zawaal	decay, fall, decline.
Zeba	graceful, adornment, elegance.
Zeenahaar	at all.
Zeeshaan	with dignity, with splendor.
Zee-sho'oor	sensible one.
Zehan	mind, acumen, memory.
Zer-o- zabar	topsy-turvy, upside down.
Zihijja	a term used for Zi-Al Haj; twelfth month of the Hijri Calendar.
Ziqaad	eleventh month of the Islamic calendar.
Zireh	chain, armour.
Zoj-zoj	couples, pairs.
Zudtar	as soon as possible.
Zuljalaal	glorious, splendid.
Zulm	cruelty, oppression, tyranny, harm.
Zulmat	darkness.
Zulminan	bountiful